THE ELEMENTS OF ENGLISH

THE ELEMENTS
OF ENGLISH

AN INTRODUCTION TO THE PRINCIPLES
OF THE STUDY OF LANGUAGE

WILLIAM BRANFORD

Professor of English Language
Rhodes University

LONDON

ROUTLEDGE AND KEGAN PAUL

First published in 1967
by Routledge & Kegan Paul Limited
Broadway House, 68-74 Carter Lane
London, E.C.4

Printed and Bound in Great Britain by
Bookprint Limited, London and Crawley

© *William Branford 1967*

CONTENTS

v

CONTENTS

Chapter Three
SOUNDS AND THE LEARNER

Chapter Four
THE ORGANIZATION OF SPEECH

Chapter Five
GRAMMATICAL PATTERNING

CONTENTS

Chapter Six
THE WORD: FORMS AND FUNCTIONS

Chapter Seven
A SKETCH OF THE SENTENCE

Chapter Eight
A NOTE ON LEXICON

CONTENTS

APPENDICES

PREFACE

I have written this book as a short introduction to the study of the English language: more precisely as an introduction to more advanced descriptions of English. It follows the lines of a first-year university course which, with repeated modifications and afterthoughts, I have been teaching for a number of years. It may, I hope, be of use as an introduction to linguistic studies for the practising teacher or teacher-trainee. I have, however, put English first and teaching second: English is sufficiently interesting to be studied in its own right, and good classroom practice can be built up only on an understanding of the patterns of language and the processes of language learning.

My debt to a number of major studies of English and of general linguistics will be obvious to the professional reader, and my principal sources are generally indicated by references in the text. However, although I have never met Professor C. C. Fries, I should like to mention how much the example of his work has meant to me, ever since I quite accidentally picked up *The Structure of English*.

My colleague at Rhodes University, Mr John Claughton, provided invaluable criticism of the drafts of Chapters II—IV. Mr Kenneth Robinson of the Department of Fine Art very kindly drew the diagrams. Dr Patricia McMagh of the University of Stellenbosch provided helpful comments on Chapter I. All errors, however, are my own. I should welcome suggestions for improvements to the book. Miss Tessa Randell, Mrs Y. Riddin and Miss H. Scott spent a great deal of time and care typing my often illegible drafts. I owe a great deal also to students who have stimulated the effort to be clear, to the publisher for his forbearance, and to the interest, criticism, and patience of my wife.

W.B.

Rhodes University, Grahamstown
September 1965

To
F. W. Branford

Chapter One

SOUND, SHAPE AND SENSE

1.1. The study of language

Although most of us are able to talk without thinking, language is the principal tool of thought and perhaps the most important single factor of the many which distinguish man from the apes. A talkative old lady once asked: 'How can I tell what I think until I see what I say?' We may not all have the same problem as she had. But her question illustrates both the easy unconsidered quality of everyday speech ('The words just flow on; I needn't think at all') and the indispensability of language at other times in bringing our ideas and feelings to a definite form ('I can't think at all without words').

It follows that any balanced study of language must cover both its 'considered' and its 'unconsidered' forms and must deal both with the precisely focused statements of science and poetry and with the easy flow of speech on which human companionship and social life so heavily depend. An ideal study of English would span both the language of *Hamlet* and *Principia Mathematica* at one end of the scale, and the language of shopping and of the family circle at the other. It would begin with the simplest possible material and move on to more complex forms.

I do not of course regard what I have called the language of shopping and the family circle as being particularly simple. On the contrary: to analyse informal English is often very difficult indeed. The 'simple material' with which I shall begin in the next chapter consists of the basic sound-contrasts of English speech: I shall sketch these in some detail before moving on to grammar.

There are several reasons for beginning with simple material. Language itself is by no means simple, and its elements are only partially comparable with the elements of the physical world. The physical world consists of complex combinations of relatively simple substances: carbon, calcium, hydrogen and the rest. Language, similarly, consists of complex combinations of relatively simple sounds, but there the parallel almost ends, for language has human dimensions which matter has not. In a single remark by one man to another, a whole complex of social relations, a complex signalling code, and a thousand years of human history may come to a momentary focus.

Three rather obvious facts are of key importance for a proper

1

understanding of language: we learn a language, we speak it, and we speak it to others. In any discussion of language, it is worth trying to keep all three of these points in sight.

We learn a language: the critical phase in the learning of a first language spans the first five or six years of life, and the transformation of the infant,

Mewling and puking in the nurse's arms,

to the alert and articulate child of six is perhaps the most important of all the metamorphoses of man. Normally we retain for the rest of our lives the skills and perceptions established during these early years: moreover, the child's experience of learning his native language is one which he never repeats. We can never revert to infancy and learn a second language as we learned our first.

Language in infancy is only one component among many in the child's all-important relationship with his mother. Words, then, are not initially learned as abstract symbols, but as means for the expression and satisfaction of our most fundamental desires; it is surely not accidental that the common phrase, 'the mother tongue', still conveys some of the intensity of the mother-child relationship. While we normally learn our first language in the natural setting of family life, our second language is not often begun until the age of six or seven at the earliest; the teacher is not as a rule one of the family and the setting is likely to be that of an organized course of instruction at school.

Further, the habits learned for the first language are likely to interfere in various ways with the learning of the second. In listening for the first time to an unfamiliar language, we are often listening unconsciously for the sounds of our own: as a result, we perceive only a stream of noise, because we are not trained to recognize the sound-elements and sound-divisions of the foreign tongue. Listening even to a language of which one has a reading knowledge only may be even more disconcerting: here we expect to recognize the words, and cannot unless they are spoken slowly. Similarly, in our first efforts at speaking a second language, we continue to use the sounds and patterns of our own. To take a very simple example: an Englishman will say *car* for *qha* (which is Zulu for 'no') and a Zulu *shesh* for *church* because English is without the initial click of *qha* just as Zulu is without the initial consonant of *church*. For the Zulu click the Englishman substitutes one of the sounds of English, just as for the unfamiliar English *ch* in *church* the Zulu substitutes one of the sounds of Zulu.

These 'points of interference', at which elements of the first language are mistakenly taken over into the second, are of key importance to the teacher; they must be tackled systematically if the learner is to progress.

2

We *speak* a language: for this reason I have taken as my first example the problem of making a sound. Sound is the primary material of language: we normally learn speech long before we learn writing, and most writing systems are derivative from speech.

We speak (and listen) *to others*: language is reciprocal: it enables us to act upon others, and others to act upon us. 'A child is born a speaker and born into a world of speakers' (Lewis, 1963); it is language, perhaps more than anything else, that makes him a social being, and it is the 'world of speakers' around him that shapes the language that he learns and speaks.

The study of language has a very long history. The later stages of the development of writing – a slow and complex evolution which probably extended over many generations – must have involved close, if informal, study of the sounds of speech; the earliest alphabetic writing dates probably from more than 3,500 years ago. There are illuminating discussions of language, including some treatment of phonetics, in the works of Plato (428–347 B.C.), and a number of systematic studies have come down to us from Greek and Roman writers. But despite this long history, the study of language, like all the social sciences, is by no means so well advanced or so firmly grounded as are such studies as physics and geology. Many writers are still more concerned with what they think language ought to be than with what it really is. The methods of scientific description – of establishing general principles upon accurate observation of the facts – were first applied to the study of language in Western Europe in the early nineteenth century, though a remarkable description of Sanskrit by the Hindu grammarian Panini dates from the third century B.C. Our map of language, or of some of its most important areas, is consequently much less consistent and complete than is our map of the physical world. Many students, who approach the study of language with a strong desire for certainty, find this rather disappointing.

On the other hand, the study of language over the past two hundred years has established many useful facts and principles. Many of these are not very widely known, and have had little influence on language teaching. There are interesting parallels in medicine. In 1616 William Harvey stated his theory of the circulation of the blood. In 1799, however, George Washington in his last illness was repeatedly bled by his physicians; our practice, in many fields of human endeavour, often lags generations behind our theory.

1.2. The isolated word

I shall begin with a short account of a very simple speech situation, a simple model, as it were, of language in action. I shall avoid, as far as possible, the conventional terms of grammar, not because they are not useful, but because it will be necessary, later in the book, to revise the traditional definitions of some of them. It will be helpful, however, to use in this chapter the terms 'sentence', 'noun' and 'verb', although they are not formally defined until Chapters Six and Seven.

Consider, for a start, an isolated English word:

FIRE

Such a word, entirely on its own, communicates nothing, or nothing with any certainty. It might be a noun or a verb; a statement, a question, a command, or a cry of alarm. If it is a noun, it may signify a large blaze or a small one: a fire on the hearth, or a house or city on fire: it may also designate the shots fired by a body of soldiers, or a vehement passion of hatred or love. There are other possibilities if it is a verb. In complete isolation, therefore, the word exists simply as a sound in the air or a set of marks on the page.

The meaning of FIRE may of course be limited and clarified in various ways. In writing, we may add punctuation:

Fire.   *Fire?*   *Fire!*

– which helps to clarify its status as statement, question or command, though there is still a certain ambiguity about the first and third examples. Consider '*Fire.*' This may still be either statement ('What do you smell?' '*Fire.*') or command ('The troops were given the order: "*Fire.*"') Similarly '*Fire!*' may still be either a cry of alarm or the command to shoot.

In speech, of course, the ambiguity might also be reduced. Indeed, the punctuation marks which have been used for partial clarification of the meaning of FIRE are primarily symbols for particular effects of speech: if I say *Fire*, beginning the word as it were on a middle note and ending it on a lower one, the falling pitch of my voice marks the word as a statement. On the other hand, if my voice shifts on *Fire* from a middle to a higher note, the rising pitch marks it as a question. We may write these alternatives with arrows to indicate the downward or upward change of pitch:

↘ Fire   ↗ Fire

While this change of pitch or tune is a definite clue to a change of meaning, neither ↘ *Fire* (with falling pitch) nor ↗ *Fire* (with rising pitch) is quite unambiguous by itself. ↘ *Fire* (like '*Fire*') is still either statement or command; ↗ *Fire* is still either a question or a warning,

4

though a human voice, actually uttering the word, is likely to communicate its meaning more effectively than can any diagram or written description of the sound.

1.3. Contexts

For a completely unambiguous effect, however, *Fire* requires more than either punctuation or even the speaking voice can convey. Only when we perceive the word in a definite setting will the meaning be clear beyond reasonable doubt. There are two possible kinds of setting. One is an actual experience or event: the other is a setting in the form of speech or writing. It is usual to call either of these two kinds of setting a *context*: we can define a context in formal terms as:
(a) 'The setting in experience of a particular object or statement' (Drever, 1955), or:
(b) 'The parts which immediately precede or follow any particular passage or text, and determine its meaning' (*The Shorter Oxford Dictionary*).

A context of type (a) is a context of experience; a context of type (b) is a linguistic context: since experience includes language, all contexts of type (b) can be regarded as special cases of type (a).

For a context of experience imagine two men out walking. One of them notices a cloud of smoke rising from a valley ahead of them, and utters the word *Fire*. This word is sufficient to draw his companion's attention to the smoke, and the smoke itself may be said to define his meaning.

A context of the second kind consists primarily of words. Suppose that the men who saw the fire arrive at a village from which it cannot be seen. They tell the people: 'There's a big fire over at Pete's place.' Here the context of *fire* is an English sentence *within* the people's general experience of fires; the actual fire is out of sight. It is clear from the sentence, however, that *fire* is a noun and not a verb, and that its meaning is 'blaze' or 'conflagration', not 'shooting' or 'passion'. Most people will have no difficulty in reacting appropriately to the message – provided that they know English and have previous experience of fires.

A *signal* – and it is often useful to think of words as signals – implies above all a sender, a receiver and a code intelligible to both. In the case of language, the sender is the speaker or writer, the receiver is the listener or reader, and the code is the language shared by these two.

This brings us to a basic principle for all language study: that meaning depends on context. The isolated word is usually without definite meaning: we interpret a word or signal by the setting in which we find it. The setting or context which we have now devised for *fire*

5

is the sentence: 'There's a big fire over at Pete's place', spoken in a particular situation. The important elements of this context are:

(i) The utterance: the particular English sentence framing the word *fire*;
(ii) The speaker and the listener;
(iii) The actual fire at Pete's place and any other relevant physical circumstances.

1.4.   Words and things

We have here a linguistic element (the sentence), a psychological element (the experience of speaker and listeners) and what I shall in future call a *referent* (the actual fire to which the word *fire* in this instance refers). It will be seen that the context of a word is by no means simple: in particular, the relationship of word and referent, and the nature of the referents of a good many words, are often difficult to state. I have simplified my example by assuming that the speakers are referring to an actual fire, but in many uses of the word (e.g. 'Fire is dangerous') this will not be the case.

Again, it is quite easy to find contexts in which *fire* has no direct reference to physical combustion:

> Signora, your performance lacks fire,

as a director might say to an actress: or the words of Sir Walter Ralegh:

> But love is a durable fire
> In the mind ever burning.

Taking first the utterance, 'Fire is dangerous', what is the referent of *fire*? We have here no fire at Pete's place, or anywhere else for that matter, and if we say that the word refers simply to the 'notion or idea' of fire, we have still to explain the basis of the 'notion or idea'. This basis is presumably our past experience of the word, which may link it with the fire at Pete's place, fires on the hearth, camp fires, locomotive furnaces, and perhaps with fragments of history and myth such as the Great Fire of London or the burning of Troy. *Fire*, in short, labels or stands for a class or group of events (or of past experiences of listener and speaker) which have certain features in common.

The various events or phenomena for which we use the common label *fire* will, of course, be far from identical with one another. It will be relatively easy to see what the fire at Pete's place has in common with the Great Fire of London; less easy to see what these share with the *fire* of a body of soldiers; less easy still to link these instances with the meaning of *fire* in the director's complaint to the actress or the poet's *durable fire*. Our basic principle must probably be to avoid confusing thoughts with things: 'The linguistic sign unites, not a thing and a name, but a concept and a sound-image' (De Saussure, 1959). Clearly, however, one of the primary functions of a certain type of word is to act as a general label for a class or group of experiences or things. Thus the word *dog* is the label for a population of extremely varied shapes, temperaments and sizes, and the common element of dogginess which a Great Dane shares with a chihuahua could be defined only by a biologist.

Fire and *dog*, accordingly, are examples of words which, as a rule, have referents. The referent will vary with the context, and may be simple, as in the case of 'my dog' or 'The fire at Pete's place', or complex, as in 'Fire is dangerous' or 'Dogs smell'. Referents, of course, need not exist tangibly and in the physical world, as do fires and dogs; the words *justice*, *love* and *nine* have referents too. *Nine* is a particularly instructive case: *nine pigs*, *nine pence* or *nine people* are visible groups; *nine*, however, is invisible: it is a quality which all groups of nine have in common. We can symbolize this quality in a word or a figure, but it will remain an abstraction, quite distinct from the physical world which numbers enable us to analyse and describe.

Words with referents, then, whether the referents are simple or complex, abstract or physical, may be said to act as classifying tools. 'Dogs smell' is a statement about a class of animals. 'This is my dog' identifies a certain animal as a member of the class *dogs*; 'I have nine dogs' assigns my particular group of dogs to the class or category *nine*.

1.5. Full and empty words

Words of another kind, however, can hardly be said to have referents, or to classify experiences and things. In the remark under analysis: 'There's a big fire over at Pete's place', the word-groups *big fire* and *Pete's place* have quite definite referents. (We can postpone for the time being the question of the relationship of *big* to *fire* and of *Pete's* to *place*, which will be examined in § 5.6. It would be difficult, however, to say what are the referents of *there's a* and *over at*. The four words that make up these two groups are relation-words rather than reference-words. *There* is a characteristic word for beginning a statement; *'s* is a reduced form of *is*, one of the most important 'linking' elements in English grammar. *A* has important functions, that will be examined later, in the structure of word-groups and sentences. *Over* and *at* are common in formulae for explaining where something is. All four words help to establish the grammatical shape of the sentence and to state the relationship between *Pete's place* and the *big fire*; all four contrast in function with *Pete, place, big* and *fire*. Incidentally, if we are dividing the elements of this sentence into a 'referring' and a 'non-referring' group, the *'s* of *Pete's*, which simply marks a relationship, seems to belong with the 'non-referring' group (*There, 's, a, over* and *at*) rather than the 'referring' group (*Pete, place, big* and *fire*).

The contrast of function will perhaps be clearer if the sentence is written down with the reference-words left out:

There's a —— —— over at ——'s ——.

We have now only the framework of a sentence, but the gaps, or *slots* as they are sometimes called, can be filled in with a great many different sets of reference-words to convey different meanings:

> There's a *green parrot* over at *Daoud's house*.
> There's a *pretty girl* over at *Shaka's kraal*.
> There's a *strong backwash* over at *Butler's beach*.

Each of these sentences is built on the same frame of structural or non-referring elements, though it is important to realize that the reference-words are also part of the sentence-structure: the framework by itself is not an English sentence and the reference-elements like *pretty girl* and *big fire* play a double role both in filling out the structure and in referring to the external world. They do not, however, establish sentence-framework in the way that the other elements do: if they are written by themselves:

big fire   Pete's place

the sentence-outline is less clear, and it is less simple to find a number of different ways of completing it.

This kind of contrast between two kinds of words with different functions is found in many languages besides English, and various names have been suggested for the words of each kind. Chinese grammarians make the distinction between 'full' words and 'empty' words, the 'full' words being those with obvious referential content, the 'empty' words those that function primarily as units of sentence-structure. Some writers state the contrast as one of 'content words' versus 'structural words'. Others contrast 'lexical elements' (full words) with 'grammatical elements' (empty words), working thus in terms of the *lexicon* or dictionary, which gives the meanings of words, versus the *grammar* which gives their patterning in sentences. It is as well to be familiar with all three ways of stating the distinction.

8

There's a		*big fire*	
Empty = ⎫		Full = ⎫	
Structural = ⎬ element		Content = ⎬ element	
Grammatical ⎭		Lexical ⎭	

It is also important to grasp that there is no final, clear-cut line of division between words of the one kind and words of the other. Any 'content' word used in a sentence (or as a sentence on its own, as is *Fire!*) has inevitably a structural or grammatical function. Many primarily structural words may be said to have a lexical content, as have, for instance, *over* and *at*, which 'refer' to physical relationships in space as well as establishing grammatical relations within a sentence.

1.6. Sound, shape and sense

We may now return to our starting-point to sum up our description of the word *fire*, and to fill in certain points which have had to be passed over. We have noticed the three main aspects of the word:

      (i)   its sound;
      (ii) its function in sentence-structure;
      (iii) its referential function.

SOUND. We did not pause to describe the sound of *fire*. We may observe certain points:

(a) Different people – e.g. speakers of English in Scotland, Boston and Nigeria – may pronounce the word in different ways – but most of their pronunciations are likely to be recognizable to other English-speaking people.

(b) The spelling of the word is rather a poor guide to the sound. Though *f* has much the same sound in *fire* as in *fish* or *flight*, *i*, *r* and *e* form a special combination which has very little to do with the sounds of these letters in other words. (Compare *i* in *fit* or *fill*, *r* in *rat* or *rise*, *e* in *set* or *sell*.) English sounds and their relation to spelling will be examined in some detail in Chapters Two and Three.

(c) For most speakers the sound of *fire* will be in three parts, which we can represent approximately as 'f', 'I' and 'er', giving these spellings their normal English sound-values.

(d) None of the parts has a meaning which has anything to do with the meaning of *fire*. Each of the parts has a possible meaning: 'f' is a sound made by cats; 'I' is a personal pronoun; 'er' a common signal of hesitation. These meanings, however, do not add up to the meaning

9

of *fire*, even though the sounds combine to give something like the sound-sequence *fire*. Many of the sounds of English, as we shall see, are meaningless on their own.

Even the complete word *fire*, pronounced on its own in a flat and toneless voice, is uncertain in meaning. Only in a definite setting or context does it become meaningful.

SENTENCE-FUNCTION. The immediate context of *fire*, as we have seen, is normally an English sentence. In this chapter we have, as it were, 'heard' the word in three one-word sentences:

(1) *Fire.*   (2) *Fire!*   (3) *Fire?*

and in one longer one:

(4) *There's a big fire over at Pete's place.*

We may now note that the one-word sentences are given sentence-form primarily by a rise or fall in the pitch of the voice that speaks them, which gives each sentence its 'shape' as statement, command or question. In writing, these variations of pitch (and of some other sound-features) are symbolized by punctuation marks. With these changes, incidentally, the grammatical status of *fire* is altered from noun (Sentence 1) to verb (Sentence 2) and back again to noun (Sentence 3). Most English words show their grammatical status only when used in sentences: in a one-word sentence the principal clue to this will be the tone of voice: in a longer sentence we can also judge by the relationship of the word in question to other words. This, of course, is the case with the use of *fire* in:

(4) *There's a big fire over at Pete's place*

contrasted with its use in:

(5) *They were given the order to fire.*

(In either of these sentences, incidentally, we notice that there are a good many possible substitutes for the word *fire*; nouns like *pig*, *car* or *gum-tree* could take the place of *fire* in Sentence (4) without altering the basic framework of the sentence; verbs like *stop*, *advance* or *retreat* could similarly take the place of *fire* in Sentence (5). The concept of a sentence as a grammatical 'frame' will be developed in Chapter Five.)

REFERENTIAL FUNCTION. We have seen that *fire*, which in some of its uses, though of course not in all, has an easily identifiable referent, is a word contributing more to 'content' than to structure. Its own 'content', as we have seen, will vary very considerably from one context to another, but it will vary only within certain limits, which we can call the limits of the English usages of the word. Its principal use is to refer either to a class or category of events (fires in general) or to a particular item belonging to this class (for example, the fire at Pete's place).

1.7. System

The varied and complex functions of *fire* do not derive from any mysterious properties in the sound or appearance of the word. They derive from its role as a unit or element of the complex human system which we call the English language. Their meaning depends entirely upon their functioning in the context of this system: the system, one might say, confers the meaning.

This can be illustrated by presenting two alternative settings for the same simple event. The event is that of a man running with a leather bag, and suddenly falling down. If this event takes place as an isolated incident in the street, it may have no particular meaning except for the man concerned. If, on the other hand, it takes place in the setting of a rugby football match, the leather bag being the ball, the run and the fall may be intensely significant: the spectator who knows the rules of rugby will perceive their purpose at once. The fall, indeed, in the context of a rugby game, may constitute a try, and may decide the issue of an international match.

Just as the system of rugby gives the action of touching the ground with a leather ball (under various strictly defined conditions) the significance of a try, so the system of language gives a sound or a mark on paper (again under strictly defined conditions) the significance of a word. The conditions, in both cases, are established beforehand by men. The word's significance and function are not inherent in the sound, but are given by the system and by the human group – the English-speaking community – on which the system depends. In the words of John Locke:

> Sounds have no natural connection with our ideas, but have all their significance from the arbitrary imposition of men.

1.8. Rules and descriptions

Although there is an instructive parallel between the system of a language and the rules of a game, there is also a highly important difference. The rules of rugby have been worked out completely, and formally written down. All players of rugby acknowledge them, and all disputes about rugby are settled in terms of the rules. All decisions about possible alterations to the rules rest with a central governing body.

For the English language, on the other hand, there is no governing body and no single, universally accepted text of the rules. At various times there have been efforts to establish an English Academy or some similar body for the regulation of our language, but these have never succeeded. Even if such an Academy had come into being when it was first proposed (about two hundred and fifty years ago) it would almost certainly have failed to control the development of English. It is difficult, if not impossible, to drill any community out of its established habits of speech and writing. Though education can probably do much to alter the language which we use for better or worse, its influence is inevitably limited. In any conceivable human society there will always be a good deal of activity, including speech and writing, beyond the influence of the educational system. Further, the effects of the educational system itself, in language as in other matters, are not always what the educators intend.

In the absence of rules, the scientific student of language must rely upon description. By a description of a language I do not mean a list of typical utterances drawn up more or less at random like some of the phrasebooks for foreigners. The student must not only observe and record the language: he must discover the principles by which it works, and organize his description so as to reflect in the most accurate and economical way the actual practices of speakers and writers.

The rest of this book aims at an outline description of English, by way of an introduction to more detailed and technical descriptions of which several are listed at the end. Chapters Two, Three and Four sketch the sound-system, Chapters Five, Six and Seven the grammar: Chapter Eight is a short note on the vocabulary or 'lexicon'.

1.9.   Dialect and style

Any description of a language must take into account the variations between different speakers and different occasions.

The word *dog*, for instance, is spoken in different ways by different speakers. If we write the southern English pronunciation as *dog*, we could write a common Suffolk pronunciation as *dorg*, and a fairly common South African pronunciation as *dork*. Judging by sound, there is little to choose between these three renderings of the word. The Suffolk pronunciation might make the speaker conspicuous at a cocktail party in Oxford, just as the southern English pronunciation might make the speaker conspicuous at a farmers' meeting in the eastern Transvaal.

It may or may not be an advantage to be conspicuous in this way:

this will depend partly on the personality of the speaker, partly on the tolerance or intolerance of the group. It will, however, be a great disadvantage to be unintelligible: if there is a danger that what was intended as 'dog' may be interpreted as 'dock', variation in speech has passed the limit of safety. We shall consider the point more fully in Chapter Two; for the moment I need only point out that there are two main types of variation in English: variation between speakers and variation between occasions.

By variation between speakers I mean the sort of variation that one might observe between the kinds of English used by a Scot, a South African and a Virginian. By variation between occasions I mean differences between the kinds of English used by the same person in a lecture, at a party, and in writing the minutes of a meeting.

Variation between speakers gives rise to *dialects*: 'regional' dialects in the case of forms varying between places (e.g. Edinburgh and South African English); 'class' dialects in the case of forms varying between different social groups in the same place (as with the various kinds of English spoken in London). The great importance of dialect is that some forms of the language carry a higher social prestige than do others: whatever our feelings about this, it has an important influence on our lives.

Fortunately, most dialects of 'educated' English have a good deal in common, especially as regards grammar, but it is always advisable to specify the kind of English that one is describing. The dialect on which this book is largely based is that of the educated middle class of Southern England; it is, however, readily intelligible in most parts of Africa and the United States. The dialects of many educated people in Africa and India, however, differ in important ways from English of this kind; some of these differences and some of their implications for the teacher of English are outlined in later chapters.

Most of the available descriptions of English concentrate, as does this book, upon the English of educated people. There are good reasons for doing this, but it is important to realize at the outset that they are social reasons. The language of educated people does not hold a monopoly of accuracy, beauty, tenderness, or expressive force; it is the most important form of the language simply because the positions of power and influence in society tend to be held by educated people. Thus there is no linguistic reason why *isn't* is preferable to *ain't*, but there are excellent social reasons for avoiding the use of *ain't* at certain times and with certain people.

At the same time it is important to realize that many well-educated people, particularly in the United States, use *ain't* informally in speech, though they would avoid it in writing and on formal occasions. The social status of a given item will vary between different speakers

13

and different communities: the word *leg*, for instance, can be used quite freely among most English-speaking people today, though many Victorian ladies are said to have blushed at it.

Variation of speech between different occasions gives rise to contrasts of 'register' or *style*: such contrasts as that of 'We acknowledge with thanks the receipt of your communication' versus 'Thank you for your letter'. The same kind of contrast appears between such forms as *O.K.*, *Certainly*, and *At your Majesty's pleasure*.

Style, of course, is not simply a matter of contrasts between formal and informal English. Problems of style involve rather complicated decisions about fitting language to occasions: the language of a wedding ceremony, for instance, will be very different from that of the speeches after the wedding, and the speeches, again, are likely to be in an English very different from that of the ante-nuptial contract. Some of the severest difficulties for the foreign learner of English are in this complex field of style.

As will be shown later, the principal contrast in this field is between written and spoken English. Here, for instance, is a sentence composed for the eye rather than for the ear, though it does not greatly please either:

'The Rags (Wiping Rags) (Maximum Charges) Order 1943 (as amended) shall have effect as if in Article 2 thereof for the figure "8" where it occurs in the last line there were substituted the figure "11½" '. (Gowers, 1958).

Here, on the other hand, is a sentence that simulates the movement of actual speech, though it is taken from a novel:

'Then they tucked the old man into a beautiful room, which was the spare room, and in the night sometime he got powerful thirsty and clumb out on the porch-roof and slid down a stanchion and traded his new coat for a bottle of forty-rod, and clumb back again and had a good old time, and towards daylight he crawled out again, drunk as a fiddler, and rolled off the porch and broke his left arm in two places and was most froze to death when somebody found him after sun-up.'

Mark Twain: *The Adventures of Huckleberry Finn*, 1884.

Genuine unscripted speech, as will be shown later (Chapter Four), is often much more remote from the norms of the written language.

Here, finally, is a short passage of eighteenth-century English which gives me considerable pleasure, though it is perhaps conceived and organised not so much as audible speech as for the printed page:

'It is not easy to discover from what cause the acrimony of a scholiast can naturally proceed. The subjects to be discussed by him are of very small importance; they involve neither property nor liberty; nor favour the interest of sect or party. The various readings of copies, and different interpretations of a passage, seem to be questions that might exercise the wit, without engaging the passions. But, whether it be, that *small things make mean men proud*, and vanity catches small occasions; or that all contrariety of opinion, even in those that can defend it no longer, makes proud men angry; there is often found in commentaries a spontaneous strain of invective and contempt, more eager and venomous than is vented by the most furious controvertist in politicks against those whom he is hired to defame.'

Dr Samuel Johnson, *Preface to Shakespeare*,
1765.

Chapter Two

THE ENGLISH SOUND-SYSTEM

2.1. Speech and writing

Speech comes first in our study of language, and writing second. Speech is the basic material of language; writing is primarily a record of speech, though a great deal of writing (as often in correspondence and accounting) does not correspond to any actual speech.

The social importance of speech is increasing. Until quite recently, writing was the only means of keeping permanent records or transmitting messages over long distances; with the development of recording apparatus and telecommunications, this is no longer the case, though the skills of writing are still indispensable for most of us.

2.2. The observation of sounds

One of the reasons for beginning this text with a short outline of the English sound-system is that you will be able to check most of the data for yourself if English is your home language. It is most important that your study of pronunciation should be experimental from the very beginning. Use your fingers, a mirror and a flashlight to explore what is happening in your mouth when you utter a particular sound. Check, if possible, by observing a friend. Try out all the examples in this chapter by speaking them – not in a whisper, but aloud. Better still, listen to them, repeated as often as possible, by somebody else whose first language is English. We do not hear our own voices accurately, and it is difficult to make a sound and at the same time to listen to it.

For a practical understanding of the English sound-system, it is necessary to memorize a substantial number of principles and facts. This is relatively easy if the student divides up the material and learns a short section at a time. It may be impossible if he tries to learn it all at once, or does not practise constantly. The skills and insights of phonetics are useful to the teacher and interesting to anyone with an interest in language, but one cannot build them up in oneself unless one is prepared to work at them.

2.3. Speakers of English

Of the millions of people using English today, a very substantial number learned English in infancy as their first language. I shall refer

16

to these people as *native speakers* of English, irrespective of their place of birth. The remainder are those whose first language is not English, but who learned English in later life. There is, of course, a borderline class, consisting of a limited group of speakers who may be almost equally proficient in English and in another language. There are, for instance, a good many homes in Africa in which two languages – Xhosa and English, Afrikaans and English, Gujerati and English – are used on an apparently equal footing. Generally, however, there is a degree of specialization in one's use of a particular language, if one knows two languages or more. Many South African Indians, for instance, speak Gujerati to their parents (particularly to their mothers) and English to their friends.

The dialects of native speakers of English vary very considerably. But there is an important psychological difference between the English of *all* native speakers and the English of *all* speakers who learned it as a second language.

If English is your first language, the English sound-system, in one of its many forms, is already almost a part of you. Your unconscious mastery of the system is apparent in every word you speak, and for the very reason that this mastery is unconscious, you may have difficulty in explaining it to others, or to yourself. Yet the sound-system of our native language is a vital element of our culture, which is well worth understanding for its own sake.

If English is not your first language, you have the advantage of an outsider's perspective. It is significant that some of the best studies of English have been produced by people such as Otto Jespersen, who learned it as a second language. But you must remember that the sounds of a language can be learned accurately only by listening to native speakers or recordings of native speakers, though a text can enable you to see what some of the problems are, warn you of difficulties, and help you to study the formation of sounds by your vocal organs, and to begin the comparison of the sounds of your own language with those of English.

In either case, it is important that you should remember that the English sound-system varies considerably between different dialects of English and that the description which follows has been worked out primarily for speakers of a particular dialect, namely RP. RP stands for 'Received Pronunciation'; there are reasons, however, for using the abbreviation rather than the words in full. 'I should like it to be understood . . . that RP means merely "widely understood pronunciation" and that I do not hold it up as a standard which everyone is recommended to adopt' (Jones, 1963). RP, very roughly speaking, is the language of the educated community of Southern England and of BBC news bulletins; it shares most of its essential features with

educated South African English, and is readily understood by most
speakers of English, wherever they may be.

2.4. Making and hearing contrasts

All signalling systems depend upon contrasts. A traffic robot uses
contrasting lights: red for *stop*, amber for *caution* and green for *go*.
Semaphore signals, of which ordinary railway signals are a simple
form, use contrasts of position between the signalling arms; a raised
arm indicates 'Line clear', a horizontal arm 'Stop'. The Morse code
uses contrasts between arrangements of dots and dashes: speech uses
rather more complex contrasts between sounds or arrangements of
sounds.

There is, for instance, a contrast of quality between the vowels of
top and *tap*, and a contrast of arrangement between the sounds of *top*,
opt and *pot*. The basic sound-units of these three words are similar,
though not quite identical, and the principal difference between the
words arises from the orders of the sounds. Most English words are
distinguished from one another by contrasts of these two kinds.

We shall begin with contrasts of quality. Compare the words *ten*
and *ken*. Except for their initial sounds, the two words, considered as
sound-sequences, are identical; it is only the difference between these
initial sounds that enables us to recognize *ten* and *ken* as two different
words. We shall write these sounds as /t/ and /k/, using the slashes //
as a reminder that we are discussing sound-elements, not letters of the
alphabet. Let us also avoid referring to /k/ and /t/ as 'kay' and 'tee';
kay and *tee* are the names of letters, not of sounds. The first sound of
ken is not *kay* but /k/; if it were *kay*, the pronunciation of the word
would be something like *kay-en*. There is a similar difference between
/t/ and *tee*. The clearest way of naming a sound-unit is to use the sound
itself: when discussing sounds, one avoids all kinds of confusion if one
consistently says /k/ and /t/ instead of *kay* and *tee*.

The formation of /k/ or /t/ involves a set of movements by the vocal
organs which we shall consider presently. As speakers of English, we
have learned both to make these movements and to hear the resultant
contrast of sound between /k/ and /t/. A good many pairs of English
words are kept apart by this difference only: *kin* and *tin*, *came* and
tame, *kill* and *till*, *kick* and *tick*. (Notice that our spelling sometimes
represents the sound /k/ by *k* and sometimes by *c*; /t/ is more consistently represented by *t*.)

All speech and all listening depend primarily upon the habits or
skills involved in contrasts of this kind: upon the speaker's ability to
make the basic sound-contrasts of the language that he is using, and
upon the listener's ability to hear them.

We do not either make or hear these contrasts automatically or instinctively. We *learn*, during early childhood, to make certain contrasts and to hear them; we do not begin life with the English sound-system (or that of any other language) already built into us. The contrast of /t/ and /k/, for instance, is quite often blurred in the speech of small children. Some will say *krain* for *train* and *cry* for *try*; others *tat* for *cat* and *tar* for *car*, and it may take them months or even years before the contrast is clearly established.

Further, the contrasts that we are able to make and hear in later life without special training depend very often upon those of the language which we learned in the early years of life.

Native speakers of English often have considerable difficulty with the sounds of the Bantu languages, such as the bilabial sounds in Zulu which are now written as *bh* and *b*. Both these sounds are made with the lips brought close together, but for one, the initial sound of *bheka* ('look'), the air is released outwards, as in English /b/, and for the other, the initial sound of *beka* ('put'), the air is sucked inwards. English people who cannot manage this contrast may confuse such pairs as *bheka* and *beka*, *bhonga* ('roar') and *bonga* ('praise'), or *bhuza* ('buzz') and *buza* ('ask'). They may have even greater difficulty in making or distinguishing the various 'clicks' used in Zulu or other Bantu languages. The reason for this is that English has no 'sucked-in' (implosive) sounds and no clicks (except the one that is sometimes made to encourage a horse). Native speakers of Bantu languages have parallel difficulties with certain English sounds. They are often, for instance, unable at first to hear or articulate the contrasts between *bird*, *bed* and *bad*, which are not paralleled in the sound-systems of the Bantu languages. Problems of this kind are likely to arise in the learning of any second language.

The right kind of training, however, can overcome these difficulties, though if training is to be really effective the teacher will need, amongst other things, a sound understanding of the vocal organs and of how they produce the sounds of the languages in question. He ought also to be aware of the principal differences between the sound-system of the language that he is teaching and that of the home language of his pupils.

Our survey of the sounds of English must accordingly cover both

(a) the basic units of sound which are contrasted in speech, and

(b) the various actions of the vocal organs upon which these contrasts depend.

2.5. The phoneme

Phoneme is a common and convenient term for a basic sound-unit, such as /t/ or /k/ in English. A phoneme can be described in a preliminary way as:

> (i) 'The smallest contrastive linguistic unit which may bring about a change of meaning' (Gimson, 1962).

We shall later expand this description. What it means is evident if we compare *ten* and *ken*. We can 'bring about a change of meaning' for *ken* by substituting /t/ for /k/, and /t/ and /k/ are the smallest units which we can exchange in order to make this alteration. The keyword of the description is *contrastive*; our ability to 'hear' a language depends entirely on our ability to hear contrasts between phonemes. Note that although the phoneme 'may bring about a change of meaning', it has no inherent meaning of its own.

We could make a rather rough list of the phonemes of English by collecting sets of contrasts like that of *ken* and *ten*. Adding words of the same pattern to our original pair, we arrive at the list:

> *ben, den, fen, gen, hen, ken, men, pen, wren, ten, when*

yielding eleven contrasting sound-units, and by varying the pattern we might collect others. The list ought not, of course, to be limited to sounds at the beginnings of words or syllables. We should consider sounds in any position, such as the middle elements of such pairs as *bid* and *bad*, or the final elements of such pairs as *bid* and *bit*. This would yield such lists as:

> *bid, bit, bin, bill, big,*

(varying the final element) or

> *bid, bead, bed, bad, bud, booed, board, bard, bird*

(varying the middle element). The drawback to such a list, however, is that all the contrasts in it may not be apparent to speakers of dialects other than RP; *bed, bird,* and *bad,* for example, may not be clearly distinguished in certain African dialects of English. Further, we have set up our contrasts solely in terms of *hearing,* and have not taken into account the process of *speaking* and the action of the vocal organs in forming our contrasting sounds.

With this action in mind, compare the words *pin, tin,* and *kin*. They are distinguished or 'kept apart' by the contrasts of the phonemes /p/, /t/ and /k/. For /p/ there is a momentary closure of the lips, followed by an audible release of air. For /t/, there is also a closure and an audible release. This time, however, the closure does not take place

20

at the lips, but (for most English speakers) between the tongue and the ridge behind the teeth. For /k/, the closure is still farther back; the back of the tongue is lifted to touch the soft palate, forming a momentary obstruction before the release of air which is the principal source of the sound.

The contrasts of /p/, /t/ and /k/, accordingly, are based on simple differences between three units of sound. The closure and (sometimes, but not always) the release are common to all three, but they are distinguished by the point of closure: each, in other words, is formed in a particular and distinctive way, but the three form a set with certain elements in common. To this set we shall presently add the related units /b/, /d/, and /g/. The six sounds in this group are termed *plosives*.

Variation. It is important to realize that the exact sound of any phoneme, such as /p/ or /k/, may vary quite considerably, not only between different speakers, but quite often for the same speaker at two different points in the same remark. Sufficiently sensitive recording apparatus would probably show that no two utterances are ever quite identical. These variations in the 'shape' of a particular sound may arise almost at random from the particular circumstances of the speaker, or may depend in a fairly predictable way on the quality of the neighbouring sounds.

There are often, for instance, some differences between the two forms of /p/ in *pit* and *spin*. In *pit* the /p/ is spoken with a sometimes audible puff of air which is not present in the articulation of /p/ for *spin*. If a strip of paper about half an inch wide is held in front of the mouth while the two words are spoken, it is likely to stir for the /p/ of *pit* but not for that of *spin*.

These two variants of /p/ tend to occur in particular and predictable circumstances. For instance:

(a) 'Aspiration' (the puff of air) is usual when /p/ precedes a vowel in a stressed syllable, as in *pin, pill, pet, pat*;

(b) Aspiration is absent or much reduced when /p/ follows /s/, as in *spin* or *spill*, or precedes /l/ or /r/ as in *please* or *pray*.

In English, if we transpose aspirated and unaspirated forms of /p/, suppressing the puff of air, for instance, in saying *pit*, and artificially producing it in saying *please* or *spin* (which thus become something like *p'h'lease* and *sp'h'in*), we may sound rather odd, but the meaning of the words is not changed. Aspirated and unaspirated /p/ are variants (or *allophones*) of the /p/ phoneme; the difference in sound between them is not used (in English) to signal a difference of meaning.

21

We must now extend our definition of the phoneme. A phoneme is evidently not one particular sound so much as

> (ii) 'A family of sounds in a given language which are related in character' (Jones, 1962), and which, in spite of minor differences, 'sound the same to a native speaker of the language' (Roberts, 1956). Such a family is the group of sounds which in English includes aspirated and unaspirated /p/. The English variants of /t/ form a second family, and those of /k/ a third. There are many others.

The words 'in a given language' are an important part of the description of the phoneme. What holds good for one language may not hold good for another. In English, aspirated and unaspirated /p/ are members of the same phoneme, but in several other languages they are not. Swahili, for instance, distinguishes *paa* (roof) from *phaa* (gazelle); the 'h' in this spelling of *phaa* represents the puff involved in aspiration. Sotho, similarly, uses aspiration to distinguish *pela* (quick) from *phela* (live). The non-distinctive sound-features of one language may be distinctive features of another; it follows that a phonemic system can be set up only in relation to a particular language. English uses one set of contrasts, Swahili another set, and so with all the languages of the world. Certain individual sounds may, of course, be very similar in two or more different languages, but the system of sound-contrasts in any language, considered as a whole, will be unique. (See also § 3.6).

2.6. Phonemic systems

Phonemic systems are strictly economical. The vocal organs, as will be shown in § 2.8, are capable of making a very large number of different sounds, and a fairly large number can be distinguished by a moderately well trained ear. English, however, uses (in RP) only about 43 to 45 basic sound-units, and for any language the number is likely to be strictly limited. For certain Polynesian languages, some investigators have put the total at under twenty. For certain languages of the Caucasus, the total is said to be nearer a hundred. It will obviously be easier, on the whole, to work a signalling system if it uses a limited number of basic units. A relatively small number of units will yield a great many different combinations. Imagine a language using only ten different sound-units. If these were combined only in groups of four, they would constitute a vocabulary of ten thousand different words (corresponding to the number-sequences 1000 to 9999, plus the decimal sequences from 0000 to 0999). More combinations would be possible if we allowed groups of one, two and three units.

There is, however, one important difference between a theoretical set of sound-combinations and a living language. We have counted combinations of our ten basic units *in any order*; such combinations, as we shall see (§ 3.3), are not characteristic of living languages. English, for instance, combines /t/ and /l/ as /lt/, but not (except in adjacent words or syllables) as /tl/.

2.7. Sounds

A sound is caused by vibrations at its source, which are transmitted by the molecules of the air (sometimes by other media) and perceived by the ear. The source may be a vibrator, such as the strings of a violin or a guitar, or a resonating column of air, as in a brass wind instrument. The quality of the sound may be modified by a resonance chamber, such as the wooden body of a violin or the interior of a flute: the latter is an example of a variable resonance chamber, since its acoustic properties can be adjusted at will by fingering the holes.

2.8. The vocal organs and the contrasts of speech

The human vocal organs form a fairly complex system of adjustable vibrators and resonance chambers. I emphasize *adjustable*. 'Every utterance is a movement' (Stetson, 1951): our study of utterance begins with an analysis of the system of movements which generates human speech.

Most of the sounds of speech are caused by vibrations set up in a column of air moving upwards from the lungs and out through the throat, mouth and nose. The principal sources of vibration are either the vocal cords or a constriction somewhere in the throat, nose or mouth, which narrows and disturbs the passage of the air. The cavities of the face, throat, nose and mouth act as resonators.

The primary uses of the vocal organs are, of course, for eating and breathing. The vocal cords, with the epiglottis (a kind of tongue just above the larynx), act as a valve to close off the passage to the lungs, and must have functioned in this way long before the development of articulate speech. The adaptation to the purposes of speech of what is now the vocal tract is one of the most remarkable adjustments in the natural history of man.

Phonetics, the general study of the sounds of speech, has three main branches:

Articulatory phonetics, the study of the production of speech by the vocal organs;

c

Acoustic phonetics, the study of the sound-waves of which speech consists;

Auditory phonetics, the study of the reception of sounds by the auditory organs.

Articulatory and auditory phonetics are studies within the general fields of human physiology and neuro-physiology. Acoustic phonetics, on the other hand, is a branch of physics. The main concern of this section is with articulatory phonetics: the study of the mechanisms which produce the sounds of speech.

In terms of these mechanisms, we can divide the action of speaking into four principal phases:

(1) *The lungs*, activated by the diaphragm and the intercostal muscles of the chest, send up the air into the passages above them.

(2) The *vocal cords*, two folds of ligament and elastic tissue opening from the windpipe into the throat, may vibrate as they allow the air to pass.

(3) The *velum*, or soft palate, may open or close off the nasal cavity.

(4) The *mouth*, the most flexible of the resonance chambers of the system, finally determines the quality of the emerging sound.

The four stages thus involve in turn the lungs, the vocal cords, the velum and the mouth. The lungs, in turn, are acted upon by powerful muscles of the thorax and abdomen. This is worth remembering: speech is far from being a local activity of the tongue or mouth, and much closer to being an activity of the whole body, intimately bound up with breathing, upon which life itself depends. Our speech, as many poets have perceived, is in a sense our breath. Speech requires very considerable energy: it has been calculated that 'Reciting for one hour takes the same amount of energy as walking for the same time along a road which climbs to over 300 feet' (Kaiser, 1957).

We may now consider in detail the possibilities at each stage of articulation. Since language depends on sound-contrasts, our main interest will be to discover how the vocal organs establish the contrasts of speech.

(1) Contrasts of *loudness* or *volume* depend largely on the action of the lungs and the muscles of the chest and diaphragm which control them. The two sets of muscles involved in this stage of articulation are:

    (a) The diaphragm and other abdominal muscles which control the upward expansion or downward contraction of the chest cavity.

(b) The intercostal muscles (between the pairs of ribs) which contract or expand the side walls of the cavity.

These muscles provide the original motive power for nearly all the sounds of speech, besides controlling three important speech elements – *breath-groups, syllables and stresses* – which we shall consider when we examine the patterns of connected speech (§ 4.2).

(2) Contrasts of *voiced and unvoiced sounds,* and contrasts of *pitch,* depend largely on the vocal cords. The contrast of voiced and unvoiced sounds distinguishes /p/ and /b/ and a number of other pairs of English consonantal sounds. For /v/, for instance, there is a vibration of the vocal cords, which do not vibrate in the same way for /f/. We thus call /v/ a *voiced* and /f/ an *unvoiced* sound. The distinction between voiced and unvoiced sounds is important in English; you should make a point of learning it. There are various tests for the presence of voice:

(a) You can hear the contrast most clearly by stopping your ears with your fingers and comparing /f/ with /v/ or /s/ with /z/; the extra vibration on /v/ and /z/ is known as *voice.*

(b) Lay a finger on your Adam's apple. You will probably again feel vibration for a voiced sound, but not for an unvoiced one.

(c) Voiced sounds can be sung. Try singing /v/ and /f/; it is impossible to sing a voiceless sound. If you extend the test to other sounds, you will notice that all vowels are voiced.

The vocal cords function primarily as a valve closing off the windpipe during swallowing and muscular exertion. *Cords* is a somewhat misleading word: they are in fact a pair of movable folds of elastic tissue, rather like lips, that are open for breathing or closed to keep foreign bodies out of the windpipe and lungs. The opening between them is known as the *glottis.* They can be moved with great rapidity and, when partly closed, vibrate in the stream of moving air.

The pitch of the voice, often an important clue both to sentence structure and to the feelings of a speaker, depends on the speed of these vibrations. The cords may open and close again with great rapidity: we express the frequency of their opening and closing again as a number of (vibration) *cycles per second* (*cps*). For the ordinary speaking voice of a man, the figure may be 100 to 150 cps.; for a woman's voice, about 200 to 325 cps. The greater the speed of vibration, the higher will be the note.

Three possible positions for the vocal cords are here shown diagrammatically, as if from above:

25

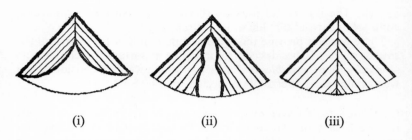

(i)   (ii)   (iii)

The dark areas represent the cords: the white space between them the glottis.

Diagram (i) is the position of the cords when wide open. Air escapes freely through the glottis, as in breathing or for such a sound as /s/, for which the friction or vibrations are caused in the mouth cavity.

Diagram (ii) shows the cords close together, vibrating in the air-stream; the glottis is reduced to a narrow opening. The vibration (*voice*) is heard in all vowel sounds and in a number of English consonants.

Diagram (iii) represents the vocal cords when tightly closed, as for swallowing or muscular effort. Lung air is pent up below them. If it suddenly escapes, the result is the *glottal stop*. An exaggerated form of this stop is the sound heard at the onset of a cough. In speech, this feature has three phases:

    (i)   An abrupt closure of the glottis;
    (ii) Compression of air below it by the lungs;
    (iii) An abrupt escape of air when the glottis re-opens.

The three phases, of course, follow one another with great rapidity. We are thus more likely to 'hear' a glottal stop as the sudden cutting-off and resumption of the adjacent sounds than as a sound on its own account. It is sometimes heard between the words *the end*, and between those of *all our*, and again between those of

India Office
and *over-estimate,*

though here some speakers will insert an /r/ instead. As we do not mark differences of meaning in English by means of the glottal stop, we shall not count it as one of the phonemes of English. In some other languages, such as Arabic, it marks differences of meaning and is, accordingly, a phoneme.

(3) Contrasts of the third type are those of *nasal versus oral sounds*, controlled by the *velum* or soft palate, which can be raised to close off

26

the nasal cavity from the mouth. Diagrams (iv) to (vi) show positions of three different types: the more heavily shaded portion represents the tongue, and the flap marked V at the back of the roof of the mouth is the velum.

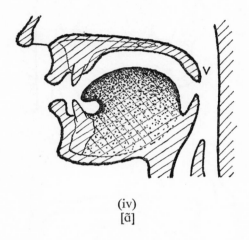

(iv)
[ɑ̃]

Diagram (iv) shows the velum lowered as in normal breathing; there is no closure in the mouth, and the airstream escapes both by the mouth and by the nose. This position does not represent any of the phonemes of RP English – the diagram roughly pictures the vowel of the French word *blanc*; square brackets are used for the symbol below the diagram to show that it represents a phonetic value, not an English phoneme, and the diacritic [˜] marks that the vowel is nasalized. Similar vowels are common in some English dialects, though the actual nasalization of vowels – i.e. the lowering of the velum for air to pass through the nose – is not one of the signalling features of English.

Diagram (v) shows the velum lowered, but this time there is a closure in the mouth, and the airstream escapes by the nose only. This is the general position for the three nasal consonants, /m, n, ŋ/ – the three consonantal sounds of RP *morning*. The consonant shown in the diagram is /m/, for which the closure is at the lips. For /n/, the closure is between the tongue and the ridge behind the teeth, and for /ŋ/ it is between the back of the tongue and the velum. These three are the only normally nasalized sounds of RP English; they are usually voiced.

Closure of the nasal passage, as when one has a cold, transforms the nasal consonants into the related phonemes /b, d, g/, so that /mɔ:nɪŋ/ (*morning*) becomes /bɔ:dɪg/.

27

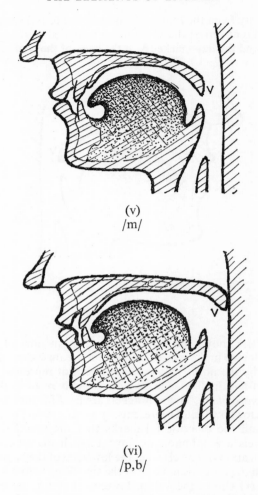

(v)
/m/

(vi)
/p,b/

Diagram (*vi*) shows the velum raised, as it normally is for all RP sounds except the three nasal consonants. The tongue and lips in the diagram are in position for /p/ or /b/, which are distinguished only by the presence of voice for /b/.

As only three English phonemes are marked by nasalization, the nasal-oral contrast is clearly less important in English than is the contrast of voiced and unvoiced sounds.

(4) The sound-contrasts of the fourth and most complex set arise in the *mouth*. These will be outlined in some detail in the sections on

28

vowels and consonants; they cannot at this point be conveniently summarized, because there are so many possible ways of adjusting the shape of the mouth cavity. It may, however, be useful to end this section with a sketch of the tract as a whole.

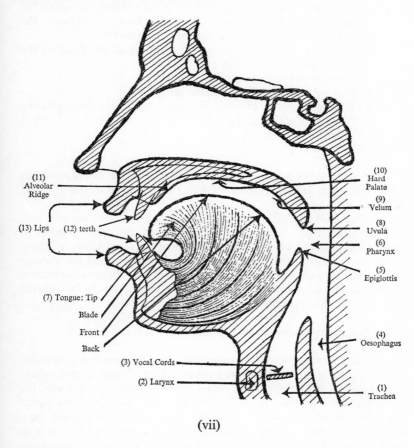

(vii)

Diagram (vii) presents a cross-section of the vocal organs. Working upwards from the bottom, it shows:

(1) The *trachea* or windpipe;
(2) The *larynx*, a casing of cartilage and muscle, protecting the trachea;
(3) The *vocal cords*;
(4) The *oesophagus*, or gullet, the food-passage;

(5) The *epiglottis*, a fold drawn over the windpipe when swallowing;

(6) The *pharynx*, the cavity between the back of the tongue and the back wall of the throat;

(7) The *tongue*, which has no obvious sub-divisions, but which for convenience of discussion is treated as having four parts: the *tip*, the *blade*, the *front* and the *back* (see arrows);

(8) The *uvula*, the small appendage hanging at the back of the throat from the soft palate;

(9) The *velum*, or soft palate;

(10) The *hard palate*, arched over the mouth;

(11) The *alveolar ridge*, between the upper teeth and the beginning of the curve of the hard palate;

(12) The teeth;

(13) The lips.

Exercises. Make notes or rough drawings (or both) of the positions of lips, tongue, velum and vocal cords for each of the sounds listed below:

/f/ as in *flame*; /v/ as in *van*; /n/ as in *never*; /d/ as in *dog*.

Remember that although a knowledge of the vocal organs is essential for the teacher or student of language, it is probably pointless to try to memorize the diagram out of relation to what the various organs *do*. You should accordingly study the vocal organs in position or in movement *for particular sounds*, and particularly for related sequences such as /p, t, k/, or /m, n, ŋ/.

2.9.   Notation: phonemics and phonetics

Speech and writing are related in various ways. For certain languages, spelling gives a fairly consistent representation of sounds. In English, this is not so. There may be a difference of spelling – as there is, for example, between the vowels of *eight*, *late* and *wait* – with no corresponding difference of sound. There may, on the other hand, be a difference of sound – such as that between the vowel-sounds of *dog*, *so* and *to* – which is not reflected in the spelling. We cannot, therefore, rely on conventional spellings in our study of the sounds of English. A number of special notations for the transcription of sounds have accordingly been devised. In this text, we shall follow a scheme based on that of the International Phonetic Association.

In transcribing sounds, it is convenient to use the ordinary letters of the alphabet as far as possible, but we must work to the rule that each sound-unit is consistently represented by the same symbol.

As we have only twenty-six letters for representing over forty units of sound, a few special symbols and some special combinations of ordinary symbols will be needed.

It is important to realize that the sounds of a language can be mapped or described in either of two rather different ways, each with its own conventions for notation.

We may wish to give the fullest possible account of these sounds *as sounds*. We may, on the other hand, wish only to describe those contrasts of sound which function in the language as *signals*. The first approach is termed *phonetic*, the second *phonemic*.

A phonetic description or transcription is necessarily more detailed than a phonemic one, because it aims to show all the distinguishable features of speech, and not simply those that happen to be meaningful. Thus a phonetic transcription of English will use special marks to distinguish the aspirated and unaspirated allophones of /p/ – [pʰ] and [p⁼] – described in § 2.5. Phonetic transcriptions are enclosed in square brackets [ ], to distinguish them from phonemic transcriptions for which slashes // are used.

A phonetic description is a necessary preliminary to a phonemic analysis, since we must know what the sounds of a language are before we can decide which of the contrasts among them are essential to the signalling system of the language. What follows is an outline in largely phonemic terms, but this must assume that the reader can already produce the basic sounds of English, and is only possible because the phonetics of English have already been worked out in detail in a number of major studies.

It is important to grasp the difference between phonetic and phonemic analyses. A complete phonetic analysis is concerned with *all* the measurable qualities of sound and *all* distinguishable actions of the vocal organs. A phonemic analysis, on the other hand, is primarily concerned with sounds as units in a signalling system, and with the specific actions of the vocal organs which produce the contrasts upon which signalling depends. Thus a phonemic study of English would be concerned with such contrasts as that of /b/ and /p/, which are signalling units in English, rather than with that of aspirated and unaspirated forms of /p/, which are not.

2.10. Stress, pitch and length

Listening to English, or to any other language, we perceive subtle contrasts of prominence between different units of sound in the same sequence. Thus, in the word *sonority*, the second vowel stands out as the most prominent sound of the word, and in the sentence *Put the cat down!* the word *down* will often, though not always, be the most conspicuous.

Such an effect of prominence has usually several causes. Among these causes are contrasts of stress, pitch and length between different sound-units.

Stress is usually defined as relative loudness or 'volume' from the listener's point of view, relative energy from the speaker's. A stressed syllable is marked thus: *so¹nority*.

Pitch ('the height or depth of a sound') depends on the relative frequency of the vibrations of which the sound consists.

Length, or the relative duration of sounds, is important for establishing certain contrasts between vowels, for reinforcing our perception of stresses, and for signalling transitions between one segment of speech and the next.

Any particular contrast of sounds is likely to involve more than one of these factors. When I 'raise my voice', the noises I make generally become not only louder, but shriller and more prolonged; in more technical language: 'the prominence of certain words or syllables in an utterance is likely to result from a very intimate combination of qualities of length, stress, pitch and inherent sonority' (Ward, 1962).

Our three features of length, stress and pitch operate in rather different ways. Length is perhaps chiefly important in relation to phonemes, stress in relation to syllables, pitch in relation to complete utterances. We shall explore this more fully later, but a short illustration may help at this point:

(a) In *bead* and *bid* we have a contrast primarily of *length* between the vowels /i:/ in *bead* and /ɪ/ in *bid*, though length is here not the only distinguishing factor.

(b) Between the words *¹permit* (the noun) and *per¹mit* (the verb) there is a contrast of *stress-pattern*. The stress falls on the first syllable of the noun and on the second syllable of the verb, though this, again, is not the only feature on which they differ: there is also a contrast of vowel-quality.

(c) Compare the sentences:

> *You'd like some tea.* (Statement)
> *You'd like some tea?* (Question)

Here there is a difference of pitch-pattern, which involves each sentence as a whole, though the most significant changes of pitch are probably on the word *tea* in each case.

Effects of prominence, in short, are by no means simple, and will have to be discussed in some detail later. For the moment, we need only note that contrasts of stress and length are of some importance for distinguishing vowels – stress for such a pair as the first and second vowels of *supper*, length for such a pair as the vowels of *heed* and *hid*. These points will be taken up in later sections; see also §2.14 and 4.4.

2.11. Syllables

Our perception of syllables depends largely on effects of prominence. Vowels tend to be more prominent than consonants: their carrying power is generally, though not invariably, greater. If /uː/ and /p/ are pronounced with the same force, /uː/ will be heard at a considerably greater distance. We perceive the syllables of such a word as *development* as 'peaks of prominence' of sound, and since vowels are generally more prominent or 'sonorous' than are consonants, these 'peaks of prominence' tend to coincide with the vowels (Jones, 1962). A syllable generally consists of a vowel preceded or followed by a consonant or consonants in patterns like CV (*be*), VC (*on*), CVC (*bad*).

Every syllable, however, does not contain a vowel, despite some dictionary definitions to the contrary. The word *little*, for instance, contains only one vowel sound, but is clearly a two-syllable word. Compare *button* and *battle* (/bʌtn̩, bætl̩/). Where a consonant functions as a syllable peak, as does the last consonant of *little*, it is marked in transcription as *syllabic* by the subscript /ˌ/.

'In theory a syllable consists of a sequence of sounds containing one peak of prominence' (Jones, 1962). In practice it is often difficult to determine syllable boundaries objectively. Does *penny*, for instance, divide as /pen-ɪ/ or as /pe-nɪ/? Syllable peaks, however, could be determined objectively by suitable recording apparatus, and their role in establishing rhythms makes them important units of speech. The physical basis of the syllable is in the action of the intercostal muscles of the chest: these, during speech, produce a rapid sequence of chest pulses which provides the energy for the syllabic 'peaks' of sound. This process is described in more detail in § 4.3.

Some writing systems are based on the syllable rather than the phoneme: these include the scripts of ancient Akkadian (the language of Babylon and Sumeria) and modern Japanese and Cherokee.

Syllable patterns vary between languages, and an unfamiliar syllable pattern may be a point of difficulty for the foreign learner. Thus the pattern of such an English syllable as *spread* is unfamiliar to native speakers of Spanish or Mandarin Chinese, who will accordingly have difficulty in pronouncing it. In discussing difficulties of this kind (see § 3.3) and indeed in our general analysis of English sounds, it will be convenient to have labels for the positions of phonemes in the syllable:

Initial: at the beginning;
Medial: in the middle;

Final: at the end.

/p/, for instance, is initial in *pot*, medial in *opt* and final in *up* and *top*.

2.12. Vowels and consonants

Two broadly different classes of sounds, traditionally known as *vowels* and *consonants*, have been distinguished from very early times. We are now in a position to improve upon the notion that the vowels are the *letters* a, e, i, o, u, and to state the contrast in terms of the actions of the vocal organs in forming sounds. This may, of course, yield groupings rather different from those to which we are accustomed.

If we compare the three sound-segments of a word like *pool*, for which the phonemic transcription is /pu:l/, they appear to belong to two different classes, or possibly to three.

/p/, as we have seen (§ 2.5), involves a complete interruption of the airstream by closing the lips, which are then opened for a sudden ('plosive') release.

/u:/ involves no interruption of the airstream, is voiced, and can be sung.

/l/ involves interruption of the airstream (by the tip of the tongue against the alveolar ridge). The air escapes at the sides of the tongue. The resultant sound, normally voiced in English, is easily prolonged and can be sung.

Parallel differences emerge when we compare the three segments according to their typical positions in the syllable:

/p/ is typically the first or last element in a syllable (*pool, scoop, cap, part*);

/u:/ is typically central (*scoop, food, fool*);

/l/, like /p/, is often a first or last element (*loot, fool, lunatic*), but is also very common in medial positions between a consonant and a vowel (as in *glad, splice, fly, help, self, health*), and as a syllabic peak as at the ends of *little, table, capable* (See § 2.11).

/u:/ and /p/ typify the contrast between vowels and consonants. /l/ is evidently an intermediate type.

Vowel: 'In ordinary speech a vowel is a voiced sound for which the air passes through the mouth in a continuous stream, without closure or such narrowing as to produce audible friction' (adapted from Ward, 1962). Vowels are typically, but of course not always, central or 'nuclear' in the syllable.

Consonant: A sound voiced or unvoiced, with closure or narrowing in the upper resonance chambers. Consonants are typically, but again not always, marginal in the syllable.

All the sounds of English, however, do not fit neatly into one of these two categories. For this reason, our example included /l/, traditionally a consonant, but with some vowel-like qualities – a relatively unobstructed airstream, voice, sonority, and a capacity for being indefinitely prolonged. We have seen that /l/ – for example, in the second syllable of *little* – can function as a syllabic peak.

The borderline cases, in some ways intermediate between vowel and consonant, are the phonemes:

$$/m, n, ŋ, l, r, j, w/.$$

On the grounds of their characteristic positions at syllable margins, we shall class these among consonants, though /r, j, w/ will be assigned to a special class of semivowels.

It is important, however, to see that 'vowel' and 'consonant' are not rigid opposites, but rather groupings which gradually shade off into one another through the intermediate cases listed above.

This does not make the basic distinction between vowels and consonants any less useful. The existence of a number of borderline cases does not alter the difference between the central members of the two classes – between an undoubted consonant such as /p/ and an undoubted vowel such as /u:/. This gradation between central and borderline cases is extremely common. It arises in biology in the case of such groups as sea-anemones and duckbilled platypuses, though it may irritate those who feel that all facts must fit ready-made pigeon-holes exactly.

2.13. The English consonants

The English consonants can be arranged in a number of groups, each group having in common a certain mechanism of articulation. You may find it convenient to study one group at a time, perhaps after reading over the whole of this section (i.e. to § 2.13.7) for a preliminary view of the whole range of consonantal sounds. As soon as you understand the formation of particular sounds, such as /p/, and of particular groups, such as the plosives, you will be in a position to begin exploring the system as a whole, tracing the relationships between such a pair as /m/ and /b/ or such a trio as /l/, /n/, and /r/.

2.13.1. *Plosives* /p, b; t, d; k, g/

A typical plosive is the phoneme /p/, which was briefly described in § 2.5. To form /p/, the velum is raised to close off the nasal cavity, and the lips are momentarily closed; air pressure builds up behind them and is fairly abruptly released. The vocal cords are not vibrating; if they were, the resultant sound would be /b/, which differs from /p/ only in its being voiced whereas /p/ is not.

The complete articulation of an English plosive sound follows the same three stages as that of /p/:

> (i) *Closure*, interrupting the airstream;
> (ii) *Hold*, during which the air behind the closure is compressed;
> (iii) *Release*, the abrupt escape of air.

In certain positions, however, there may be no audible release. This is the case in RP when /p/ precedes another plosive, as in *hopped* or *lopped* (/hɒpt, lɒpt/), or a nasal as in *topmost* or *topknot*.

Since the compression of air behind an oral closure is a feature of all English plosives, the velum is raised for all sounds in this group to prevent the escape of air through the nasal cavity. The oral closure is made by the lips for /p, b/, between the alveolar ridge and the tip and blade of the tongue for /t, d/, and between the back of the tongue and the velum (soft palate) for /k, g/.

The six English plosives form a sequence of three pairs, according to the point of closure:

> At the lips for /p, b,/ (*bilabial plosives*);
> At the alveolar ridge for /t, d/ (*alveolar plosives*);
> At the velum for /k, g/ (*velar plosives*).

They are distinguished from one another in a number of different ways:

(a) By the *point of closure*, as shown above;

(b) By *voice*: /b, d, g/ are normally voiced, /p,t,k/ are not;

(c) By *energy*: /p, t, k/ are normally spoken with greater muscular effort and force of breath than are /b, d, g/. We can accordingly use the label *fortis* (strong) for /p, t, k/ and *lenis* (weak) for /b, d, g/. This is a subsidiary contrast, since it is correlated with the presence or absence of voice: you will notice that the lenis group /b, d, g/ are voiced and the fortis group /p, t, k/ unvoiced. Accordingly, in stating the principal contrasts between plosives, it is usual to mention only the point of closure and the presence or absence of voice. In whisper, however, it is possibly the fortis-lenis contrast that distinguishes consonants normally kept apart by the presence or absence of voice, since this contrast persists after the 'switching-off' of voice when we whisper.

Aspiration. Aspiration was explained in § 2.5 as the audible puff of air on the release of a plosive sound. The phonetic symbol for aspiration is a raised 'h' as in [pʰ]. The unvoiced plosives, /p, t, k/, are relatively strongly aspirated in certain environments and relatively unaspirated in others. The voiced plosives, /b, d, g/, are normally unaspirated.

A full account of aspiration is beyond the scope of an introductory text. You should note, however, that aspiration in /p, t, k/ can be predicted from their environment: as previously noted for /p/:

(a) Aspiration is normally present when /p, t/ or /k/ precedes a vowel in a stressed syllable, as in *pin, tin, kin*;

(b) Aspiration is absent or much reduced when /p, t/ or /k/ follow /s/ as in *spin, skin, stint*, or precede /l/ or /r/ as in *play, slay*, or *tray*.

Aspiration in English is a non-distinctive feature: we do not use it to signal contrasts of meaning as do speakers of Urdu who, for instance, contrast *kana* (one-eyed) with *khana* (to eat) by means of aspirated and unaspirated /k/. On the other hand, unaspirated /p, t, k/ tend to sound un-English, and part of the contrast between these plosives and /b, d, g/ may depend on our hearing the aspiration. In Singapore, many Chinese speakers of English do not aspirate these plosives: this reduces the contrast between /p, t, k/ and /b, d, g/, so that in this kind of Singapore English, *peas* and *bees, town* and *down, curl* and *girl*, sound very nearly alike (Saunders, 1962).

Spellings. Normal spelling represents the plosives, perhaps, rather more consistently than it does some other sounds. Note, however, that there is no /p/ in *philosophy* or *psychology*, no /b/ in *debt* or *doubt*, that the first phoneme of *can* is /k/, and that RP *stopped* and *dropped* end in a /t/.

/p/: pen, spend, drop.
/b/: ben, about, drab.
/t/: ten, attend, trend, act, stopped.
/d/: den, Adam, and, add.
/k/: ken, can, act, tack.
/g/: gun, eager, dog.

Minimal pairs. Two words that differ by a single phoneme are known as a 'minimal pair'. For /k/ and /g/ such pairs are *curl* and *girl*, *pick* and *pig*. Contrasting pairs for the remaining plosives can be drawn from the sequence *pin, bin, tin, din, kin*.

2.13.2. *Fricatives* /f, v; θ, ð; s, z; ʃ, ʒ; h/

A typical fricative is /f/, the first phoneme of *five*, which can be compared with /p/ in order to contrast plosive and fricative articulations. For both, the nasal cavity is closed off, both are unvoiced, and both are formed at very nearly the same point. For /p/, however, there is a complete closure between the two lips, and for /f/ a narrow opening between the lower lip and the upper teeth. This narrow

37

opening causes 'audible friction' in the escaping air, just as a narrow passage causes turbulence in a stream of water: hence the term *fricative* for this class of sounds.

Just as /p/ is matched by the corresponding *voiced* bilabial plosive /b/, so /f/ is matched by a voiced labiodental fricative /v/, formed in the same manner as /f/ but with the addition of voice. Like the plosives, the fricatives form a series of pairs, each pair with a voiced and an unvoiced member. But /h/, normally unvoiced, is not opposed in English to any corresponding voiced phoneme (see below):

Spelling. The nine English fricatives are:

/f/	as in *f*ast, a*ff*air, lea*f*, *Ph*ilip.
/v/	as in *v*an, e*v*er, lea*v*e, ne*ph*ew.
/θ/	as in *th*in, *th*igh, e*th*er, brea*th*.
/ð/	as in *th*en, *th*y, lea*th*er, brea*th*e.
/s/	as in *s*it, *c*ease, e*s*cape, lo*ss*.
/z/	as in *z*eal, ro*s*e, ro*s*es, bu*zz*.
/ʃ/	as in *sh*eet, A*s*ia, dou*ch*e.
/ʒ/	as in plea*s*ure, confu*s*ion, rou*g*e, vi*s*ion.
/h/	as in *h*eat, a*h*ead, per*h*aps.

Point of articulation. For all these fricative sounds, the velum closes off the nasal cavity, and the airstream through the larynx and the mouth is narrowed at some point but not stopped. The 'audible friction' characteristic of the group is set up by this narrowing of the airstream, which takes place at five different points:

For /f/ and /v/ (*labiodental fricatives*), the narrowing is between the lower lip and upper teeth, which are pressed together so that the air has to force its way between them. /f/ is unvoiced, /v/ voiced.

For /θ/ and /ð/ (*dental fricatives*), the tip and front of the tongue lightly touch the inner surfaces of the upper teeth; the escaping air is forced between the tongue and the teeth. /θ/ is unvoiced, /ð/ voiced.

For /s/ and /z/ (*alveolar fricatives*) the contact is between the tongue and the alveolar ridge; the tongue is hollowed to form a groove down the middle, in which air friction takes place. /s/ is unvoiced, /z/ is voiced.

/ʃ/ and /ʒ/ (*palato-alveolar fricatives*) are formed in rather the same way as are /s/ and /z/, but the contact between the tongue and the roof of the mouth extends farther back, and friction is set up over a wider area. /ʃ/ is unvoiced, /ʒ/ voiced.

For /h/ (the *glottal fricative*) there may be a *slight* narrowing of the passage between the vocal cords, though this narrowing is as a rule too slight to result in voice. Friction is set up throughout the vocal tract.

In modern English, /h/ occurs only before a vowel, and the quality of a particular /h/ depends very considerably on the vowel that happens to follow it. Indeed, /h/ may be regarded as the onset *normally unvoiced*, of the vowel that is to follow. Though /h/ is occasionally voiced, in English the contrast of voiced and unvoiced /h/ sounds is non-phonemic – we do not use it for signalling differences of meaning.

The unvoiced fricatives /f, θ, s, ʃ,/ are normally articulated with greater muscular energy and force of breath than are the corresponding voiced fricatives /v, ð, z, ʒ/. Like/ p, t, k/, /f, θ, s, ʃ,/ are accordingly *fortis* consonants in opposition to the *lenis* series /v, ð, z, ʒ/.

The fricatives are a somewhat complex group, distinguished from one another on a number of variables:

(a) By the point or area of narrowing, as shown above;
(b) By voice, which contrasts /v, ð, z, ʒ/ with unvoiced /f, θ, s, ʃ, /;
(c) By force of breath, which *may* contrast the *fortis* /f, θ, s, ʃ/ with the *lenis* /v, ð, z, ʒ).

As with the plosives, the fortis–lenis contrast is subsidiary to the contrast on voice versus absence of voice, and it will be sufficient for the moment to distinguish between fricatives (i) according to where the narrowing takes place (in technical language, the point of articulation) and (ii) according to whether they are voiced or not.

It is helpful, however, to bear in mind the contrast between three shapes of the tongue for the three pairs /θ, ð/, /s, z/ and /ʃ, ʒ/. For /θ, ð/ the surface of the tongue that is lifted to the teeth is relatively flat, and the airstream passes through a narrow slit between tongue and teeth; for the other two pairs the tongue is somewhat grooved down the middle, with a narrow groove for /s, z/ and a wider one for /ʃ, ʒ/. These four, /s, z, ʃ, ʒ/, are sometimes called *groove fricatives* for this reason. For fricative /r/ see § 2.13.6.

Minimal pairs:

/v, f/: fan, van; calf, carve;
/θ, ð/: thigh, thy; loath, loathe;
/s, z/: seal, zeal; hiss, his;
/ʃ, ʒ/: (no English words are contrasted on this opposition only: but compare /ʃ/ in *fission* with /ʒ/ in *vision*).

2.13.3. *Affricates* /tʃ, dʒ/

The unvoiced affricate /tʃ/ is heard initially and finally in *church*; the voiced affricate /dʒ/ initially and finally in *judge*. For both, the velum blocks off the nasal cavity and the tongue is raised to make a closure (rather than a narrowing) at about the same position as it makes the narrowing for /ʃ/ and /ʒ/. The release is slower than it would be for a plosive, resulting in a 'fricative' sound: an affricate may be regarded as a combination of a plosive and a fricative. The two phases in the formation of an affricate, the closure and the fricative release, make it uncertain whether it should be regarded as one phoneme or two.

Spellings

/tʃ/: *ch*eese, fea*t*ure, na*t*ure, wre*tch*.

/dʒ/: *g*in, fra*g*ile, a*dj*acent, ma*j*or.

Note that *wretch* is transcribed /retʃ/ and *adjacent* /ədʒeɪsn̩t/.

The affricates are normally classed with the plosives under the general heading of *Stops*.

Minimal pairs:

/ʃ, tʃ/: chic, chick; shop, chop; wash, watch;

/ʒ, dʒ/: leisure, ledger.

2.13.4. *Nasals* /m, n, ŋ/

Consonantal sounds in English other than fricatives or stops are *resonants*. A resonant is a voiced sound for which 'the only function of the mouth and nose is to modify the sound already produced in the larynx' (Gleason, 1961). Among the resonants, it will be convenient to begin with the nasals.

The nasals /m, n, ŋ/, the three consonantal sounds of RP *morning*, have already been introduced in § 2.8. and run parallel in certain ways to the series of plosives.

Compare /m/ and /b/. For both, the lips are closed and the vocal cords normally vibrating, but for /b/ the velum is raised to close off the nasal cavity and build up pressure in the mouth for the plosive release which is normal for this sound. For /m/, however, the velum is lowered and the air escapes steadily through the nose: the nasal cavity acts as a resonator for the sound established by the vibration of the vocal cords, and there is no abrupt release or plosion. We have already seen that when the nasal cavity is blocked, /m/ is converted to something very like /b/ (§ 2.8).

All three nasals are normally voiced, and for all three the velum is lowered to allow the free escape of air through the nasal cavity. They differ on the point of closure in the mouth:

For /m/, as for /p/ and /b/, the closure is *bilabial*, i.e. between the two lips.

For /n/, as for /t/ and /d/, the closure is *alveolar*, i.e. between the tongue and the alveolar ridge.

For /ŋ/, as for /k/ and /g/, the closure is *velar*, i.e. between the tongue and the velum.

Spellings:

40

/m/: *may*, re*m*ain, s*m*ite, see*m*.
/n/: *n*o, a*n*d, s*n*eeze, *kn*ife, moo*n*.
/ŋ/: si*ng*, si*ng*er, fi*n*ger.

Note the difference between the middle consonant of *singer*, /ŋ/, and the middle consonants of *finger*, /ŋg/.

No 'native' English word begins with /ŋ/; the very few words in our vocabulary which do, such as *ngoma* in *ngoma dancing* (from Zulu) are borrowings from Bantu languages, in some of which /ŋ/ is quite common as the initial sound of a word.

/n/ is quite often *syllabic*, as in *cotton*, *button* (see § 2.11); in such positions it functions as a syllabic peak without a supporting vowel: we transcribe these words /kɒtn̩, bʌtn̩/, marking the syllabic status of /n/ with the subscript /ˌ/.

2.13.5. *Lateral* /l/

/l/ is the initial phoneme in *love*, the second in *old* and the last in *call*. Its relationship to /n/ makes it convenient to introduce it at this point.

Compare /n/ and /l/. Both are voiced, and can readily be prolonged or sung: for both the lips are slightly open, and for both the tongue-tip is raised to the alveolar ridge. For /l/, however,

(a) the velum is raised to close off the nasal cavity;

(b) the airstream escapes past the sides of the tongue, or past one side only: hence the term *lateral*.

There are two principal variants or *allophones* of /l/ in English, exemplified in the first and second /l/'s of *little*. For both the tongue-tip meets the alveolar ridge, but:

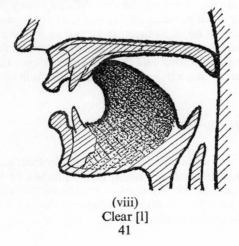

(viii)
Clear [l]
41

For *clear* [l], e.g. the first /l/ of *little*, the main part of the tongue slopes steeply away from the tip; this allophone is found before vowels as in *love, blow* or *glad* and before /j/ – /j/ is the initial sound of *yard* – as in *million* or *failure*;

For *dark* [ł] (note the phonetic symbol), the back of the tongue is somewhat raised towards the soft palate: this allophone is found before consonants, as in *help, salt* and *cold*, and finally, i.e. at the ends of words, as in *feel, fill*, and as in the second /l/ of *little*.

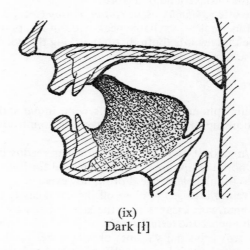

(ix)
Dark [ł]

/l/, like /n/, is frequently syllabic, as in *able, little*: /eɪbl̩, lɪtl̩/.

Japanese learners have considerable difficulty with /l/, for which there is no equivalent phoneme in Japanese. Many Japanese speakers have no [l] sound at all; for others, an [l] and an [r] are allophones of the same phoneme, so that they have alternative forms such as 'loku' and 'roku' for *six*, or 'kore' and 'kole' for *this*. Hence their difficulty in English is not so much in the formation of /l/, as in confusion of /l/ with /r/.

2.13.6. *Post-alveolar frictionless continuant* /r/

The phoneme /r/, as in *rat, very* and some Scottish and American pronunciations of *far*, has a number of allophones. In RP the commonest allophone is the *'frictionless continuant'* /r/ for which the position of the vocal organs is rather similar to their position for /l/, as is clear from the diagram below:

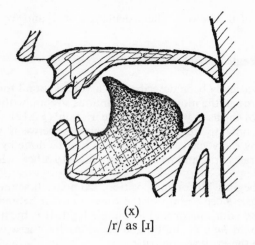

(x)

/r/ as [ɹ]

(a) Frictionless continuant /r/. (Phonetic symbol [ɹ]). This allophone is voiced; the velum is raised to close off the nasal cavity and the tongue-tip is raised but does not quite touch the alveolar ridge. The lips are open; their exact position will depend upon the vowel that is to follow.

(b) Fricative /r/, (phonetic symbol [ɹ]), is likely to follow /d/ or one of the fortis plosives, /p, t, k/. Here the /r/ merges with the release of the plosive, and the result is a 'fricative' rather than a resonating sound. This fricative /r/ may be formed relatively far forward as an alveolar fricative, or as far back as the uvula; a uvular /r/, [ʁ], is sometimes used by Scottish speakers.

(c) *Alveolar tap* /r/, or 'one-tap' [ɾ]. For this, the tip of the tongue taps the alveolar ridge once. One-tap [ɾ] is common between vowels: *very, sorry, Mary, bury, for ever.*

(d) Rolled /r/ (Phonetic symbol [r]), is a rapid succession of taps by the tongue-tip on the alveolar ridge. This is usually heard only in highly stylized speech, e.g. in formal recitation of verse, though it is sometimes thought to be typical of some Scottish dialects.

For a detailed account of allophones of /r/, consult Gimson (1962).

As is well known, there is no /r/ phoneme in some dialects of Chinese: so that speakers of the Hokkien dialect of South China tend in English to produce *loyal* for *royal*, *play* for *pray*, and so on. If you compare the formation of /l/ and /r/, you will see one of the reasons for this substitution (Saunders, 1962).

2.13.7. *Semivowels*

The phonemes /j/ and /w/ are sometimes grouped with /r/ in a special class of *semivowels*. The articulation of /j/ and /w/ is outlined in § 2.16.5.

2.14. The English simple vowels

A vowel has already been described as 'a voiced sound for which the air passes through the mouth in a continuous stream, without closure or such narrowing as to produce audible friction' (§ 2.12).

We have now to consider how contrasts between vowels are established by the vocal organs. This can best be done by taking the clearest contrasts first, and working from these to others which are less obvious.

We shall begin with tongue-position. Compare first the vowels of *heat* and *heart*. Keep the tip of the tongue at rest behind the lower teeth, and use your mirror and a suitable light. It is most important that you should *look* at the tongue-positions for these two vowels, and not take the evidence on trust.

You will see that for the vowel of *heat*, /i:/, the front of the tongue is considerably raised; for that of *heart*, /ɑ:/, the whole of the tongue is kept relatively low: this is why the doctor makes patients say /ɑ:/ when he wants to look into their throats.

Now try the vowel of *hoot*, /u:/. For this you will have some difficulty in seeing the tongue, since your lips will be fairly closely rounded, but if you manœuvre carefully with your light you will be able to see that for /u:/ the back of the tongue is raised rather high, towards the roof of the mouth. If we compare the positions of the highest part of the tongue for these three vowels, we get something like the triangle

/i:/ /u:/
/ɑ:/

There are reasons for taking these three vowels first. One is that they represent fairly extreme positions of the tongue. Another is that *something like* this group of three vowels occurs in a number of languages other than English: Zulu and Xhosa, for instance, have a fairly similar trio and so has Afrikaans. The phonetic values will differ from one language to another: Xhosa and English [i] sounds are not identical, and the vowels of any particular language function in a unique system of phonemic contrasts.

Compare now with our three original vowels the vowel of *hat*, /æ/, using again the mirror and the light. For this vowel, the tongue is not raised as far as it is for /i:/ and the raising takes place farther forward than it does for /ɑ:/. Thus /æ/ is lower than /i:/ and in front of /ɑ:/: our vowel triangle becomes the quadrilateral:

44

/i:/   /u:/
    /æ/   /ɑ:/

though this, of course, is only a very approximate and schematic
representation of the actual positions of the tongue. Tongue-position,
however, is the principal means of contrasting English vowels, though
it is not the only one.

If you add to our set the vowel of *hurt*, /ɜ:/, you will notice that in
the sequence /i:, ɜ:, ɑ:/ – the vowels of *heat, hurt, heart* – the tongue
moves progressively farther back and lower down in the mouth. You
will notice again that the formation of these vowels depends more on
the positions of the front and back of the tongue than on that of the tip.

You will notice also that with a little practice the sequence /i:, ɜ:, ɑ:/
or the sequence /u:, ɜ:, æ/ can be spoken as one continuous vowel
sound; vowels, unlike consonants, shade gradually off into one
another without a clear-cut change of mechanism between one item
and the next.

A slight movement of the tongue, incidentally, is made in articulating a number of vowels which it is convenient to treat as single
phonemes. Compare the vowels of *jaw* and *joy*, prolonging both, and
using your mirror and light. For /ɔ:/, the vowel of *jaw*, the tongue is
held stationary: for /ɔɪ/, the vowel of *joy*, you will see that it moves
upwards and forwards. We shall call such a movement a glide; the
contrast of /ɔ:/ and /ɔɪ/ is a contrast of a gliding with a non-gliding
vowel. 'Gliding' vowels are known as diphthongs and will be discussed
in § 2.16; for the time being we shall compare only simple vowels, i.e.
those for which the tongue is kept still. (We shall ignore for the
moment the very slight movement of the tongue that a number of RP
speakers make for vowels such as /i:/. This feature is non-phonemic:
i.e. not essential to the contrast between one vowel and another, and
need not detain us.)

Our tentative vowel-quadrilateral has two dimensions of contrast:
      (a) Front, centre, back: from /i:/ across to /u:/;
      (b) High, mid, low: from /i:/ down to /æ/.
Vowels contrast on one or both of these. Thus the highest position of
the tongue for /ɜ:/ is farther back than it is for /i:/, farther forward
than for /u:/, lower than for either of these, and a little higher than it is
for /æ/.

The position of the highest part of the tongue for each of the remaining simple vowels can now be compared with the positions for
the vowels which we have taken as points of reference. The vowel of
RP *bet*, for instance, /e/, is lower than /i:/, higher than /æ/ and farther
forward than /ɜ:/. You will have realized by now that vowels are
highly variable, but the following diagram is a reasonably accurate

guide to the *relative* tongue-positions for simple vowels for substantial numbers of RP speakers:

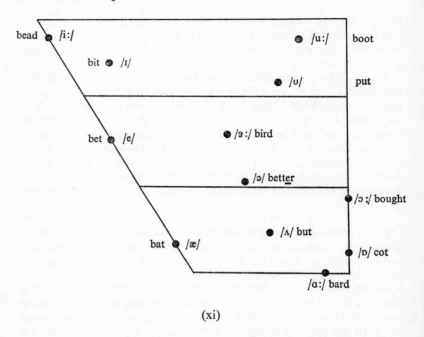

(xi)

Lines between different areas of articulation can be drawn only roughly, but, as the diagram shows, the simple vowels of RP fall into three series:

(i) Front vowels: /iː, ɪ, e, æ/;
(ii) Central vowels: /ɜː, ə, ʌ/;
(iii) Back vowels: /uː, ʊ, ɔː, ɒ, ɑː/.

The members of each series differ on tongue-height, so that by referring to the two dimensions of the quadrilateral we can give a rough description of any simple vowel. Thus RP /iː/ can be called a high front vowel and RP /ɑː/ a low back one.

Schwa /ə/. The commonest RP vowel is /ə/, which is the second vowel in *butter* and the first vowel in *about*. This is the only vowel with a name (in our terminology) other than its own sound: it is commonly called *schwa* after a sign called 'shewa' which is used in writing Hebrew. We name other vowels by their sounds: /iː/, for instance, is known as '/iː/' and /uː/ as '/uː/'; *schwa*, however, requires a special

46

name because it is difficult to say it by itself. If you try to produce the second vowel of RP *butter* on its own, you are likely to produce /ɜ:/, the vowel of *bird*, whereas the sound of *butter* is /bʌtə/, not /bʌtɜ:/, the last element being *schwa*. This mid-central vowel is normally *unstressed* (for stress, see § 2.10); speaking it in isolation, however, we tend to stress it. Stress, as will be shown later, is a matter of contrast; the unstressed quality of *schwa* shows up only by contrast with a stressed vowel in its neighbourhood, such as the first vowel of *butter*. The other mid-central vowel, /ɜ:/ (as in *bird*), contrasts with /ə/ in being longer and as a rule stressed; both are articulated in the same area, and both are rather variable.

Schwa is reflected in many different spellings: **a**lone, **cup**board, **wom**an, doc**tor**, ob**lige**. In ordinary conversation the word *a* is frequently spoken as /ə/: /ðaets ə kæt; hi et ə bʌn/.

The meaning of the vowel diagram. We can now consider the vowel diagram as a whole. One or two precautions will be in order: it is important to remember that:
(a) It is conventionalized. Each dot (●) represents the highest point of the tongue for the vowel in question. The actual distance in the mouth between two such points may be a matter only of millimetres. For the sake of clarity, the diagram is not drawn to scale, and accordingly opens out these distances very considerably. The boundary line follows that of the cardinal vowel chart, which is presented in the next section.
(b) The diagram is set up for a particular dialect, namely RP. A different dialect would require a different diagram. This point will be expanded in a later section.
(c) Positions on the diagram show only one type of vowel-contrast, namely contrast on tongue-position. English vowels are in fact contrasted on several other variables.

Vowel-contrast. It is important to realize that simple English vowels may contrast with one another in several different ways. The most important contrastive factors are tongue-position, length and lip-rounding, but there are a number of others.

(i) *Tongue-position.* This is the primary mechanism for contrasting vowels, and has accordingly been presented first (see diagram). Vowels such as /i:/, for which the tongue is high, are often called *close* in contrast to *open* vowels such as /ɑ:/, for which the tongue is relatively low.
(ii) *Length.* Certain pairs, e.g. RP /i:/ and /ɪ/, as in *heel* and *hill*, are perhaps more clearly contrasted on length than on tongue-position. Five of the twelve simple vowels are normally long:

47

/iː, uː, ɑː, ɔː, ɜː/.

The colon after the symbol is a reminder that the vowel is long. The remaining simple vowels are normally short.

The actual length of the vowels here classed as 'long' varies considerably with their environment. Compare the /iː/'s of *bead* and *beat*, *peas* and *peace*. A 'long' vowel is longer in a syllable ending with a voiced consonant, such as /d/ or /z/, shorter in a syllable ending with an unvoiced consonant, such as /t/ or /s/. (Moving to the unvoiced consonant involves an earlier 'switching off' of voice for the vowel.)

(iii) *Lip-rounding*. Compare /iː/ and /uː/ again. For /iː/ the lips are spread, for /uː/ they are 'fairly closely rounded' (Jones, 1962). Four of the five back vowels – those of RP *food, put, port, pot*:

/uː , ʊ , ɔː ɒ, /

– are spoken with somewhat rounded lips. This rounding is most evident for /uː/, slighter for /ʊ/ and /ɔː/. /ɒ/ may have no rounding at all. You will notice that the degree of lip-rounding decreases as we move down the series of back vowels: for the high back vowel /uː/ it is quite pronounced: for the low back vowel /ɑː/ the lips are 'neutrally open'.

Other factors in the formation of vowels are the positions of the jaws, tension and (in many languages but not in English) nasalization. For the 'high' or 'close' vowels such as /iː/ and /uː/, the jaws are relatively close together; for 'low' or 'open' vowels such as /æ/ and /ɑː/, they are relatively far apart.

For tension, compare /iː/ and /e/. You may feel a somewhat greater muscular tension, particularly in the tongue, for /iː/; for /e/ the tongue is relatively relaxed. Some writers regard high and low vowels as 'tense', and mid vowels as lax, but this distinction is not very well established and many people have difficulty in feeling it.

Nasalization of a vowel takes place when the velum is lowered to allow the escape of air through the nose as well as through the mouth. The phonetic sign of nasalization is [˜] placed over the vowel, as in [stæ̃nd], representing an American rendering of *stand*. RP speakers do not nasalize their vowels; American speakers of English very frequently nasalize a vowel that precedes a nasal consonant. Afrikaans nasalizes several vowels, and uses this feature, for instance, for distinguishing *kans* from *kaas*: [kɑ̃ːs] : [kaːs]. Nasalization of vowels is also a phonemic feature of many African languages: thus Yoruba distinguishes [hɑ̃] (*itch*) from [ha] (*scrape*) by nasalization of the vowel.

For English vowels, however, tongue-position is the key variable, and if you are a native speaker of English you should probably learn tongue-positions first, though length and lip-rounding are also important.

Spelling. A short list of spellings for RP simple vowels may be useful. Remember, however, that it is drawn up for RP and not, for instance, for American English. Variation among vowels will be discussed in a later section.

/i:/: fr*ee*, b*e*, dr*ea*m, k*ey*, mach*i*ne
/ɪ/: b*i*t, s*y*mbol, vill*a*ge, bu*i*ld
/e/: b*e*d, d*ea*d, *a*ny
/æ/: c*a*t, gl*a*d, m*a*rry, pl*a*it
/ʌ/: c*u*t, s*o*n, y*ou*ng, bl*oo*d
/ɑ:/: p*a*ss, p*a*rt, h*ea*rt, s*e*rgeant, c*a*lm
/ɒ/: d*o*g, w*a*s, c*ou*gh
/ɔ:/: f*o*r, s*a*w, *ou*ght, *a*ll, d*oo*r
/ʊ/: p*u*t, w*o*man, g*oo*d, c*ou*ld
/u:/: f*oo*d, d*o*, s*ou*p, r*u*de, ch*ew*
/ɜ:/: b*i*rd, h*e*r, t*u*rn, w*o*rd
/ə/: *a*bout, moth*e*r, doct*o*r, col*ou*r

2.15.   Cardinal vowels

The vowels presented so far have each a number of variant forms.

/ɪ/, for instance, was described in the previous section as short, fairly high and fairly fronted (see diagram). For many South African speakers, however, it tends in some phonetic contexts to move lower, towards /ə/ or /ɜ:/, so that *pin* in their speech becomes [pən] and *wicked* [wɪkəd]. Contrast RP [pɪn, wɪkɪd]. For many speakers, however, /ɪ/ at the end of a word, as in *duty*, becomes a vowel higher and sometimes longer than is normal /ɪ/. Thus, as Ward (1962) points out, for some South African speakers *busy* becomes [bɪzi:] or [bi:zi:]. Variants of this sound can be heard from children shouting 'Mummy!' Sometimes, however, the final sound of *Mummy!* is lengthened to something like [i:] or [əɪ].

Situations like this will be considered later. The immediate point is that the /ɪ/ phoneme – in terms of item (ii) of our definition (§ 2.5) – is not one particular sound but 'a family of sounds' which are phonetically similar and which function phonemically in contrast with members of other families such as the variants of /e/, keeping apart such pairs as *pin-pen*, *din-den*, or *kin-ken*.

For certain purposes, however, we need a scale of exact sound-values rather than a system of rough contrasts. If a given vowel has to be described *precisely*, it will not be enough to say that it is like the first vowel of *father*, which varies very considerably beween dialects and individual speakers.

The eight cardinal vowels, devised by Professor Daniel Jones, and recognized by the International Phonetic Association, provide a standard scale for judging vowel quality. They form 'a set of fixed vowel sounds having known acoustic qualities and known tongue and lip positions' (Jones, 1962). All other vowels can be described in terms of their relationship to these eight, which are familiar to phoneticians and available in various recordings.

Cardinal no. 1, [i], is defined by Professor Jones as 'the sound in which the raising of the tongue is as far forward as possible and as high as possible consistently with its being a vowel, the lips being spread' (Jones, 1962). Do not confuse cardinal [i], an exact sound-value, with the English phoneme /iː/, a 'family of sounds' in a particular language. 'Consistently with its being a vowel' in the definition is a reminder that if the tongue were raised farther than the limit for cardinal [i], friction would be set up in the narrow passage for the airstream, and the result would be a consonantal sound, probably a fricative [j].

Cardinal no. 5, [ɑ] is similarly defined as 'a sound in which the back of the tongue is lowered as far as possible and retracted as far as possible consistently with the sound being a vowel, and in which the lips are not rounded'. Do not confuse this cardinal with the English phoneme /ɑː/. 'Consistently with its being a vowel' in the definition is a reminder that if the tongue were lowered farther than the limit for cardinal [ɑ], the result would be a consonantal sound, possibly a uvular fricative /r/, [ʁ], for which see 2.13.6 (b).

The eight cardinals form a sequence of points as nearly as possible acoustically equidistant for the four 'front' vowels, measuring downwards, as it were, from [i], and a similar sequence for the four 'back' vowels, measuring upwards, as it were, from [ɑ].

The cardinal vowels are useful in the same way as are survey beacons. The expert can locate a particular vowel, for instance, as 'slightly lower and farther back than cardinal [i]'. Cardinal vowels are written with square brackets, which here, as elsewhere, denote phonetic as opposed to phonemic values (§ 2.9).

The following are *rough indications* of the values of the cardinals:
1. [i]   French *i* in *si*; German *ie* in *Biene*;
2. [e]   French *é* in *thé*; Scottish *ay* in *day*;
3. [ɛ]   French *ê* in *même*;
4. [a]   French *a* in *la*;
5. [ɑ]   French *a* in *pas*;
6. [ɔ]   German *o* in *Sonne*;
7. [o]   French *o* in *rose*; Scottish *o* in *rose*;
8. [u]   German *u* in *gut*.
Sounds roughly equivalent to cardinals 2, 3, 4, and 7 are used in the formation of certain English diphthongs (§ 2.16).

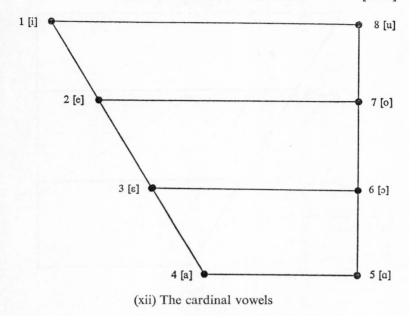

(xii) The cardinal vowels

Cardinal vowels, however, should not be confused with vowels in any particular language. An English vowel such as /i:/ is a phoneme, i.e. a family of sounds including several allophonic variants. Cardinal vowels are invariable sound-values, or rather, they vary as little as is humanly possible. They can be learned *only* from an expert or a good recording, such as the records ENG 252–3 and 254–5 of the Linguaphone Institute, 207 Regent Street, London, W.1.

2.16. Diphthongs and semivowels

Being highly variable, the diphthongs provide some instructive contrasts between dialects, and in particular between RP and non-RP speakers (see § 2.3). It is important to realize that many of these do not involve 'British' versus 'non-British' English; within South African English, for instance, there are now both RP and non-RP dialects, roughly corresponding to differences in education and occupation between different sections of the English-speaking community. I shall occasionally abbreviate South African English as SAE.

2.16.1. *Glides to* /ɪ/ (*Diagram xiii*)

For /aɪ/, the vowel of *time*, probably the commonest diphthong in colloquial RP, the glide is from a low front position to a higher front one, i.e. from the neighbourhood of cardinal [a] in the direction of /ɪ/,

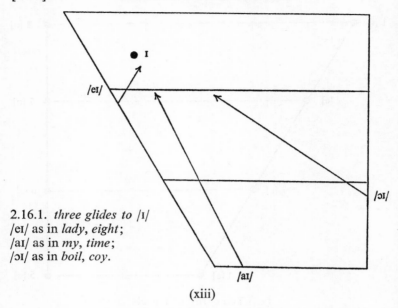

2.16.1. *three glides to /ɪ/*
/eɪ/ as in *lady, eight*;
/aɪ/ as in *my, time*;
/ɔɪ/ as in *boil, coy*.

(xiii)

though the movement generally stops short of the /ɪ/ position. You can easily see this glide if you use your mirror and light.

In some kinds of non-RP SAE, the /aɪ/ glide begins farther back than in the diagram above, i.e. closer to /ɑ:/, and stops sooner. Thus *while* becomes something like [wɑ:l] and *light* very nearly [lɑ:t].

/eɪ/, the vowel of *weight* or *lady*, is a much shorter glide, upwards towards /ɪ/ from a mid-front position. Cockney speakers sometimes substitute [aɪ], as in [laɪdɪ, traɪn]; a song from *My Fair Lady* ('The rain in Spain stays mainly in the plain') is a reminder of this.

/ɔɪ/, the vowel of *boy* or *coin*, is a glide forwards and somewhat upwards from a low back position. It is less variable than the previous two, though Suffolk speakers sometimes substitute a non-gliding vowel, so that *boy* becomes [bɔ:].

2.16.2. *Glides to /ʊ/ (Diagram xiv)*

/aʊ/, the vowel of *cow* and *mouse*, is an upward glide in the direction of /ʊ/, starting from a point about midway between the positions for cardinals 4 and 5, [a] and [ɑ]. In a phonemic transcription the diphthong can thus be written /aʊ/ or /ɑʊ/, though /aʊ/ is now the more usual form of the sound. The lips become slightly rounded during the course of this glide.

52

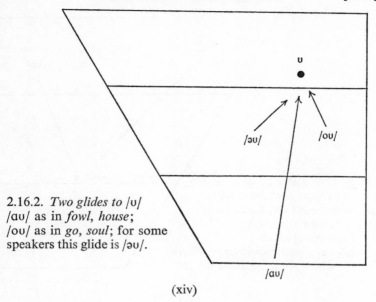

2.16.2. *Two glides to* /ʊ/
/aʊ/ as in *fowl, house*;
/oʊ/ as in *go, soul*; for some
speakers this glide is /əʊ/.

(xiv)

/oʊ/ or /əʊ/, the vowel of *go home*, has a variable starting-point:
near *schwa* for some speakers, or farther back at about the level of
cardinal [o] (though still considerably centred) for others. The lips are
slightly rounded during the latter part of the glide.

[oʊ] and [əʊ] are variants of the same phoneme: no two English
words are contrasted on the difference between them. [oʊ] is the more
conservative of the two forms.

2.16.3. *Glides to* /ə/ (*Diagram xv*)

/ɪə/, the vowel of *here* and *idea*, is a glide to a mid-central position
from a higher front one: approximately from /ɪ/ to /ə/. The lips are not
rounded. In non-RP SAE this glide sometimes starts from a higher
position than that of /ɪ/ so that *here* becomes approximately [hiə].

/ɛə/, the vowel of *fair* and *bare*, is also a glide towards a mid-central
position, but this time from a starting-point near cardinal [ɛ]. In non-
RP SAE it is often reduced to [ɛ:] so that Mary becomes [mɛrɪ] and
fair hair becomes [fɛ: hɛ:].

/ʊə/, the vowel (for some RP speakers) of *pure* and *manure* (/pjʊə
mənjʊə/) is a glide towards a mid-central position from a fairly high
back one. It is probably the rarest RP vowel; both in British and
South African speech it is frequently levelled to [ɔ:].

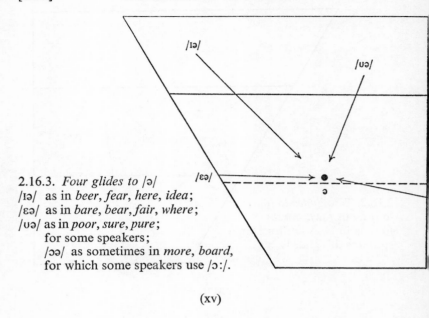

2.16.3. *Four glides to* /ə/
/ɪə/ as in *beer, fear, here, idea*;
/ɛə/ as in *bare, bear, fair, where*;
/ʊə/ as in *poor, sure, pure*;
   for some speakers;
      /ɔə/ as sometimes in *more, board*,
   for which some speakers use /ɔ:/.

(xv)

/ɔə/, the vowel (for some speakers) of *more* and *board* is also rare: *more* and *board* tend to be spoken as /mɔ:, bɔ:d/. Gimson (1962) points out that some RP speakers still differentiate *Shaw, sure* and *shore* (/ʃɔ:, ʃʊə, ʃɔə/), while others level all three to /ʃɔ:/.

2.16.4. *Triphthongs*

Diphthongs are either 'centring' or 'non-centring', the centring diphthongs being the glides towards *schwa*, the non-centring diphthongs the glides in other directions.

All the non-centring diphthongs – glides to /ɪ/ and /ʊ/ – may be followed within the word by the neutral vowel /ə/ as in *player* and *fire* – /pleɪə, faɪə/ – to form complex vowel units sometimes known as *triphthongs*. The five units of this type are

   /eɪə/: *player, greyer, stayer*;
   /aɪə/: *fire, desire, higher*;
   /ɔɪə/: *employer, lawyer* (sometimes /lɔ:jə/);
   /oʊə/: *Sower, Noah, lower* (sometimes /əʊə/);
   /aʊə/: *bower, our, flower*.

54

2.16.5. *Semivowels*

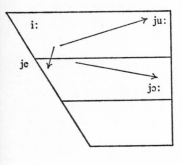 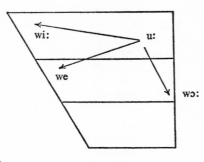

(xvi)

Two additional glides, normally reckoned among consonantal rather than vowel sounds, are the semivowels /j/ and /w/.

/j/, the initial sound of *year*, the 'unrounded palatal semivowel', is a glide for which the tongue begins in the approximate position of the vowel /i:/ and moves quickly to another vowel position which it holds for longer. The direction of the glide will vary according to the vowel following /j/; some common /j/ glides are shown in the diagram. The lips are unrounded and the vocal cords vibrate.

At the beginning of a word, /j/ is commonly spelled *y*, but it is often not at all clearly represented in English spelling, as in *union* and *beauty* (/ju:njən, bju:tɪ/). Compare:

(a) *Year, yacht,* /jɪə, jɒt/;
(b) *Puny, tune, cube:* /pju:nɪ, tju:n, kju:b/;
(c) *Spume, stew, skewer:* /spju:m, stju:, skjʊə/.

/w/, the initial sound of *will*, is known as the 'labio-velar semivowel'. The glide begins from the approximate position of /u:/, and the tongue moves towards another vowel position. (Three characteristic /w/ glides are shown in the diagram.) The lips are closely rounded, and the vocal cords vibrate, though some speakers use an unvoiced /w/ (phonetic symbol [ʍ]) for some words spelled with *wh*: *which, white, whale*. Note that /w/ is the initial sound of *one*.

The principal contrast between these two sets of glides is that the /j/ glides begin farther forward, and the /w/ glides begin farther back. This can be felt by setting a finger on the tongue and articulating /ju:, jɔ:, wi:, we/. Notice the retreat of the tongue for /ju:/; contrast the initial retreat (to the /w/ position) for /wi:/ and the forward thrust that follows it.

/r/, frequently classed as a semivowel, was described in § 2.13.6

55   E

2.17. The phonemes of RP: reference lists

A two-page list of RP phonemes may be useful for reference at this stage. Remember, though, that a different dialect would in all probability require different lists of vowels and diphthongs; the consonants are less variable.

Capital letters may not be used in phonetic transcription unless the rules of transcription require them. Thus a capital [R] would signify a voiced uvular roll which is seldom heard in English. In phonemic transcriptions of English, use all symbols in the forms given below. Two which are commonly confused are the signs for the central vowel /ɜ:/ and the voiced palato-alveolar fricative consonant /ʒ/: note that the consonant symbol has a flat top and a tail extending 'below the line' in script. This symbol, again, should not be used for /z/.

2.17.1. *Consonants*

In the following chart, the unvoiced member of a pair is given on the left. The resonants are normally voiced. Consonants other than /w/ and /j/ (§ 2.16.5 are discussed in § 2.13.

Point of Articulation	Classes according to mode of articulation						
	STOPS		FRICATIVES		RESONANTS		
	Plosives	Affricates			Nasals	Lateral	Semi-vowels
Bilabial	p b				m		w
Labiodental			f	v			
Dental			θ	ð			
Alveolar	t d		s	z	n	l	r
Palato-alveolar		tʃ dʒ	ʃ	ʒ			
Palatal							j
Velar	k g				ŋ		
Glottal			h				

2.17.2. *Simple vowels*

Simple vowels are discussed in § 2.14.

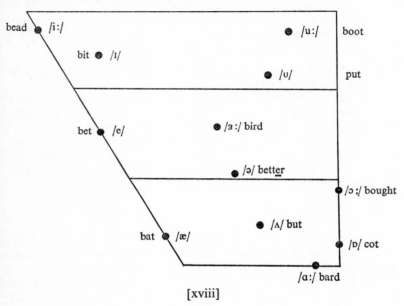

[xviii]

2.17.3. *Diphthongs*

Diphthongs are discussed in § 2.16.
Glides to /ɪ/: /eɪ, aɪ, ɔɪ/: *bay, buy, boy*.
Glides to /ʊ/: /aʊ/; /oʊ/ or /əʊ/: *bough, go*.
Glides to /ə/: /ɪə, ɛə, ɔə, ʊə/: *here, hair, poor, pure*.

2.17.4. *Short descriptions*

It is useful to remember that short 'phonemic' descriptions of consonants and simple vowels can be written in terms of the principal
points of contrast within the vowel and consonant systems.

For such a 'shorthand' description it is sufficient to label a simple
vowel as:

  (i) High, mid or low;
  (ii) Front, centre or back;
  (iii) Short or long.

Thus /æ/ is (i) relatively low, (ii) front, and (iii) short; /u:/ is high,
back, and long. Note that /ɜ:/ and /ə/ contrast also on stress: /ɜ:/ is

mid-central, long, and stressed, /ə/ mid-central, short, and unstressed. Consonants can in the same way be identified according to:

(i) Presence or absence of voice;
(ii) Nasal or oral quality;
(iii) Mode of articulation;
(iv) Point of articulation.

Thus /p/ is (i) unvoiced, (ii) oral, (iii) plosive, and (iv) bilabial; /n/ is (i) voiced, (ii) nasal, (iii) resonant, and (iv) alveolar.

Diphthongs and semivowels can be described, as in § 2.16, in terms of the direction of the glides of which they consist: thus /aɪ/ is a glide upwards from near the position of cardinal [a] in the direction of /ɪ/.

A short description of this kind will, of course, reflect only the broad contrastive features of a sound-unit: it must not be confused with detailed phonetic description of particular sounds, which lies beyond the scope of this text.

2.18.   The stream of speech

Our diagrams of vowels and consonants are useful, and indeed indispensable, for reference and as an aid to memory, but it is important to remember that all maps and diagrams have their limitations.

The first of these is that speech is movement, while diagrams cannot move: diagrams and descriptions *separate* units of sound as speech does not. Take the word *fish*: this consists of three sound-units, but we do not break it up when we say it: the pattern is not: (1) /f/; (2) /ɪ/; (3) /ʃ/; the sequence is /fɪʃ/, one smooth continuous operation. In analysis or description, we separate the phonemes:

/f/:   unvoiced oral labiodental fricative consonant;
/ɪ/:   high front short vowel;
/ʃ/:   unvoiced oral palato-alveolar fricative consonant;

and we can identify each of these three units primarily because it occurs again in thousands of other sequences of English sound. But it is important to remember that our descriptions are of movements that flow into one another: we are in effect using three stills to represent a moving picture. If we speak of 'position' for a phoneme we really mean a moment in a sequence of movement: the notion of position is misleading if it leads us to forget the continuous flow of movement that generates our speech (see also § 4.3).

Speech is a stream of continuous activity: the phoneme, so to speak, is only a recurring pattern in the stream. For any phoneme, of course, there will be a recurrent set of movements, not identical for all occasions, but broadly similar. Thus for /f/ sounds we shall have certain common features: the glottis wide open, the vocal cords not vibrating; the velum raised to close off the nasal cavity, a narrow passage between lower lip and upper teeth, and the air escaping with audible friction.

This combination, however, is an episode of movement rather than a stationary 'pose'. It may be helpful to regard the 'pose' or 'position' as a kind of 'target' for the actual movements of speech: a target which may or may not be 'hit'. In articulating 'fish', the vocal organs need not wait to hold the /f/ position before moving on to /ɪ/, and in a detailed analysis of their movements we might distinguish the three stages of 'onset', 'hold' and 'release':

(i) during the *onset*, the vocal organs are moving up to the target position;
(ii) during the *hold*, they are on it, and
(iii) during the *release* they are moving towards the target of the following sound.

Such an analysis, however, would involve a more detailed description than is possible or necessary in the present text. What is important for the moment is simply that speech is movement and that in rapid speech we often cut the movements short: many sounds occur in reduced or syncopated forms, and many others are often left out altogether.

Thank you, for instance, has several manifestations, ranging from full and formal articulation to a mere gesture at the word:

/θænkjʊ : hæŋkjʊ : ŋkjʊ : kjʊ/.

A given form will be appropriate to certain social occasions and not to others: /kjʊ/, for instance, will be generally inappropriate in bidding farewell to one's hostess after dinner, though it may be natural and appropriate in rapid conversation at a family meal, in which a very careful /θæŋkjʊ/ might possibly carry ironic or mocking overtones: children teasing each other often use very formal pronunciation.

And, in the same way, has variants ranging down the scale from formal to casual:

And further witnesseth . . .	/ænd/
William and Mary	/æn/
Chops and tomato sauce	/ən/
Dagwood and Blondie	/n̩/

The items that are most often reduced in this way are grammatical and connective words like *and*, *in* and *of*, and familiar formulae like *Thank you* and *How do you do?*

Two phonetic features of connected speech are worth noting:
(a) A short vowel is often reduced to *schwa*. Thus *can* will often be heard as [kən] rather than [kæn], *could* as [kəd] rather than [kʊd].

(b) /t/ (in South Africa, at any rate) is often reduced to one-tap [ɾ], as in [beɾə] for *better* or [gɒɾə] for *got to.*

(c) /r/ is commonly inserted as a link when a vowel at the end of one word would otherwise be followed by a vowel at the beginning of the next. This *linking* /r/ can often be heard whether it is reflected in the spelling or not: i.e. both in such sequences as *tear it, poor Alice,* and in such sequences as *India and China,* or *banana and pineapple.* In the latter case the inserted /r/ is termed *intrusive.*

A change of stress will often affect the form of a vowel. Thus /ˈkɒnvɪkt/ (noun) becomes /kənˈvɪkt/ (verb), with reduction of the first vowel from /ɒ/ to /ə/: compare /ˈɒbdʒɪkt – əbˈdʒekt; ˈpens – ˈsɪkspəns/.

Reduced forms are likely to be used in informal contexts and for familiar material: fuller forms for formal contexts and unfamiliar material. In an informal setting, such a sentence as 'I've got to go to the Petersons' ' might be spoken in some such form as

[aɪgɒɾəgə t ðə ˈpiːtəsənz].

Here the familiar sequence *I've got to go* is much reduced, but the word *Petersons'*, the part of the signal that might be missed, is brought out quite clearly. We can often reduce familiar items without risk of un-intelligibility, but certain other items must, quite irrespective of questions of courtesy or formal style, be spoken as clearly as possible. There is an important difference in speech between items that carry a heavy load of information and items that carry relatively little. To signal *Petersons'* we need a clear initial /p/; on the other hand we can reduce the /t/ of *got* in *I've got to go* without much risk of not being understood: this phoneme is part of a familiar sequence which we can 'pick up' even if part of it is left out. Speech, in other words, has the very important quality of *redundancy*: certain items can be slurred or omitted without destroying the signal, just as we are able to grasp the sense of a handwritten letter even if certain words are blotted or illegible.

For a more detailed discussion of reduced forms see Gimson (1962), Chapter II, or Ward (1962), Chapter 16.

Chapter Three

SOUNDS AND THE LEARNER

3.1. Learning the system: the native speaker

The phonemic system of a language is something that we learn: it is
worth pausing at this point for a note on the learning process.

The newborn child is capable of producing sounds, and is likely to
make one not unlike cardinal [ɛ] very shortly after birth. But he speaks
no particular language, and the noises that he makes are often not at
all clearly related to the categories of the International Phonetic
Alphabet: hence it is often not easy to describe them. During the first
two months of life, front vowels (in the general region of [i] and [ɛ]) and
back consonants (resembling [h] and the glottal stop) are reported to
predominate. As the child develops, the number of different sounds
which he is able to make will gradually increase; at the age of two
months the average American infant is said to have a repertoire of
about seven distinguishable sounds, and at the age of a year, this
number will have risen to about fifteen (Irwin, 1957).

We cannot, of course, assign these early sounds to 'phonemes' since
at this stage they are elements of babbling rather than of language;
further, it is unlikely that the child acquires speech by mastering
separate sounds corresponding to particular phonemes: he is perhaps
more likely to learn 'patterns of movement which are quite large in
time' at first in rough outline, later with more precision of detail
(Abercrombie, 1965).

Plato notes that our earliest perceptions are those of pleasure and
pain. It seems probable that these perceptions, from a very early age
indeed, are correlated with different types of sound; we have on the
one hand:

(a) Sounds apparently associated with states of discomfort, particularly hunger; this group consists initially of vowels, frequently
nasalized, in the range from [e] to [a];
(b) Sounds apparently associated with states of comfort: these include
a wider range of vowels, not very clearly distinguished, but later
including back or central vowels like /u/ and /ʌ/, and back consonants
resembling /k, g, x/ (Lewis, 1936; for /x/ see 3.2 (i)).

These early sounds are not, of course, 'linguistic'. They are, in all
probability, part of larger patterns of expressive movement: the

61

tensions of hunger or distress, the wriggles of satisfaction. The 'discomfort' sounds tend perhaps on the whole to be 'fronted', probably as a result of the contraction of the facial muscles during crying. The sounds of comfort, on the other hand, tend to be made farther back, perhaps because a child after feeding is likely to lie on his back with his tongue lolling against his soft palate. Thus, one of the typical sounds of comfort may be [gʌ], while the front vowel [ɛ] is often a cry of distress.

While early sounds like these are *meaningful* in the sense that they are signs, for instance, of whether the child is hungry or not, they are also *non-symbolic*; the sound is a direct response to an experience, not a symbol that can be separated from its referent. The sound will cease when the experience comes to an end: a word, on the other hand, is readily separable from the condition that it stands for: we can say 'hungry' when we are not hungry, or 'warm' when we are cold. Adult speech, in short, is *displaceable* as the earliest noises made by children are not.

Further, the sounds of infancy do not fit the patterns of any particular linguistic system: in infancy, indeed, we are likely to produce a good many sounds that have no place in the phonemic system of what is later to become our native tongue.

Although it is quite possible that infants of all races draw initially on approximately the same repertoire of sounds, the child's babbling begins at quite an early stage to 'drift' in the general direction of the speech that he hears around him (Brown, 1958). It appears that the average American child can produce about 27 of the forty-odd basic sounds of American speech by the time he reaches the age of two-and-a-half, though some units, such as /b/ and /d/, are more common in infant speech than in adult English, and some items, such as /ə/, which are very common in adult English, are rare or unrepresented in the early speech of the child. Our figures, of course, are based simply on the number of sound-units that are produced; they do not reflect the child's control of the placing and arrangements of sounds, which will develop much more slowly.

The development of the child's control of sounds is inevitably complex. It involves two distinct processes: the perception of sounds in adult speech and the production of sounds by the child, and it is inevitably bound up with the gradual development of the perception and control of linguistic meaning. If, however, we set meanings aside for the moment, the general development is that of progressively finer discriminations within given ranges of sound. An early step might be to distinguish a stop from a fricative: later, the English-speaking child will begin to acquire the English system of stops. In its adult form, this system is:

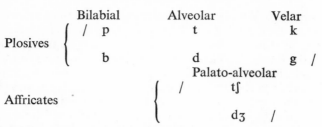

At an early age, the child may be distinguishing stops of only two kinds, labial and oral; i.e. one stop of the general character of /p/ or /b/ against another made farther back. Later, he may discriminate voiced and unvoiced stops, and later still the alveolars and velars. The /t/–/k/ distinction often emerges rather late: many quite large English children are inclined to say /tɑ:/ or /kɑ:/ for *car*, and /kreɪn/ or /treɪn/ for *train*.

It is important to realize that such a development is a matter of growing into the habits and discriminations of one particular phonemic system: in the case of an English-speaking child, that of a particular dialect of English. A child born into a different language community will, of course, acquire a different set of phonemic habits and skills. A Menomini Indian, for instance, will not contrast voiced and voiceless stops, so that he may hear English /p/ and /b/ as the same sound. On the other hand a speaker of Swahili or Urdu will learn to contrast aspirated and unaspirated stops (§ 2.13.1), since this contrast is phonemic in his own language though not in English.

3.2. Learning the system: the foreigner

The foreign learner, unlike the infant learning a first language, has already mastered a complete phonemic system. His progress in learning the sounds of English will be considerably influenced by the differences and similarities between the phonemic system of English and that of his native language. Even to people who are not concerned with the teaching of English as a second language, his difficulties are of considerable interest; one of the best ways of gaining an understanding of the working of the English sound-system, is to try to explore it from the viewpoint of the learner whose home language uses sound-patterns radically different from ours.

Languages, considered as sound, may differ from one another in a number of ways. Among these, four are of special interest at this point:

(i) Languages may differ by the presence or absence of particular items of sound. English, for instance, lacks a velar fricative; thus /x/, the initial sound of Afrikaans *gaan* and *geld* ('go', 'money') is difficult for many English-speaking people. Afrikaans and the southern Bantu languages, on the other hand, are without dental fricatives, so that speakers of these languages have difficulty with English /θ/ and /ð/. Again, the Bantu pupil learning English is likely to have trouble with the vowels, because most Bantu languages, as we shall see, distinguish five to seven vowel units, and South African English, counting vowels and diphthongs together, distinguishes about twenty-two.

The lack of /l/ in the principal dialects of Japanese shows up very pleasantly in Japanese words borrowed from English. Thus Japanese *nairon* is recognizable as an adaptation of 'nylon', *hoteru* as 'hotel', *haihiiru* as 'high heel' and *herikoputaa* as 'helicopter'. In all these cases, and in many others, English /l/ takes the form of an /r/ phoneme in Japanese.

(ii) Even if two languages have similar items of sound, the mechanisms of articulation and the precise phonetic values of these items may differ. Thus Japanese has a sound resembling English /f/, but whereas /f/ is a labiodental fricative, articulated between the lower lip and the upper teeth, the 'similar' Japanese sound is a bilabial fricative, formed between the two lips rather in the way in which one blows out a candle. Again, English *bet* and Afrikaans *elf* and *ses* ('eleven', 'six') contain 'similar' front vowels, but the Afrikaans vowel is usually somewhat lower.

(iii) The *phonemic status* of similar elements of sound may also vary between languages. This has already been shown in § 2.5 and § 2.13. The contrast of aspirated and unaspirated /p/ does not signal a change of meaning in English: a similar contrast, however, is phonemic in Swahili and Urdu. Urdu, for instance, contrasts *pir* (Monday) and *phyr* (then), largely by this means. What is an 'incidental' feature in one language may be a 'signalling' feature in another.

(iv) Similar sound-elements in different languages may also differ in *distribution*. The distribution of an item is the set of contexts or environments in which it can occur. This set or 'territory' is usually limited in certain ways: /h/, for instance, cannot occur finally in English; i.e. we have no word ending in this phoneme. The rules of distribution, however, vary between languages. French has a number of words, such as *jolie* (pretty) and *jeune* (young) with initial [ʒ]. English has a very similar sound, but never in initial position except in such foreign pronunciations as *Jean* in the French manner.

A difference involving both distribution and phonemic status arises between English [w] as in *win* and the Afrikaans sound [w] as in the usual pronunciation of *dwars* or *twee* ('athwart', 'two'). Phonetically the two sounds are quite similar, but they differ in distribution, or 'behaviour in the language'. English [w] is common both initially, as in *win* and *one*, and medially as in *twist* and *quick*. In Afrikaans, however, [w] is never an initial sound: it occurs only medially and then only after /k, t, d, s/ or, in one case, *ghwarrie* (quarry), after /g/. Further, as it is never contrasted with [v], it may be treated as an allophone of the Afrikaans phoneme /v/ (De Villiers, 1962).

Speakers of Bantu languages are likely to have special difficulties with English vowels. Many of these difficulties can be traced to differences between Bantu and English vowel-systems. For instance, one of the most noticeable features of the English of many Bantu speakers is in their treatment of /i:/ and /ɪ/: a native speaker of Xhosa is generally able to make both of these sounds but to have difficulty in placing them: in the same utterance he may produce *six* incorrectly as /si:ks/, *in* correctly as /ɪn/ and *give* incorrectly as /gi:v/. He may at the same time shorten an English /i:/ in certain positions, producing *ship* for *sheep* and *still* for *steal*.

The reason for his difficulty is that English /i:/ and /ɪ/ are contrasted principally on length, and that although he has a similar contrast in his own language, he does not use it in the same way. In English, the contrast is phonemic: it separates such pairs as *kin* and *keen*; in Xhosa, meanings are not contrasted in this way. Xhosa has a vowel, /i/, which is 'long' in some positions and short in others; it will be long, for instance, if it is the penultimate vowel in an utterance and short, as a rule, if it is the last one. Thus of the two /i/'s of *impi* (army), spoken in isolation, the first will normally be long and the second short.

If the Xhosa learner transfers Xhosa habits to English speech, he will correctly produce the penultimate vowels of *unseemly* and *believer* as /i:/ (because in Xhosa the vowel of a penultimate syllable is long), but the same habit may result in his substituting an /i:/ for the penultimate vowel of *community*, which of course is /ɪ/ or for some South African speakers /ə/. Again, a native speaker of English has no difficulty in lengthening the final sound of *lemon-tree*; a Xhosa speaker, on the other hand, is likely to say something rather like [lemɔ:ntrɪ] following the usual practice of Nguni languages in lengthening the penultimate vowel. Notice that this is *not* because Xhosa lacks a short [i] sound – you can hear plenty of short [i] sounds in Xhosa speech – but because the contrasts of short and long [i] are distributed in one way in Xhosa and in quite another way in English.

A more detailed picture of the difficulties of the Xhosa student will emerge if we consider the vowel systems of Xhosa and English side by side. Omitting the English diphthongs for the sake of clarity, and remembering that there are two or more allophones for each of the Xhosa vowels, including 'long' and short variants, we have:

XHOSA   ENGLISH

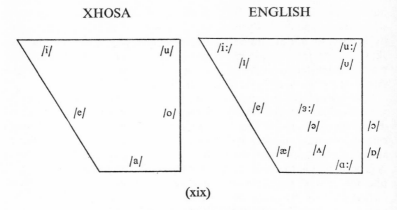

(xix)

(After Hundleby, 1965)

It will be worth taking one more example of the clash of these systems. A native speaker of Xhosa who kindly allowed me to make some recordings of his English tended to interchange [ʌ] and [ɑ:]. He consistently (and correctly) used [ʌ] as the initial vowel of *Upington*, but he also sometimes used it as the initial vowel of *after*. He used [ɑ:] as the first vowel of *Lovedale* and of *studies*. We can perhaps explain the confusion as follows:

In English, /ʌ/ and /ɑ:/ are distinguished in two ways:

(i) by tongue-position: /ɑ:/ is a low back vowel; /ʌ/ by comparison farther forward and slightly raised;

(ii) by length: /ɑ:/ is long and /ʌ/ is short.

Both of these are points of difficulty for the native speaker of Xhosa. In the first place, he has a low central vowel [a] (see below) but the [ʌ] position is new to him; in the second place, the vowels of Xhosa are not contrasted in length as are those of English: the length of a Xhosa vowel depends roughly on its position in the word or statement (Lanham, 1963). It is not surprising, then, that [ʌ] and [ɑ:] were apparently in free variation (i.e. interchangeable) in the English of this Xhosa student, since they are kept apart in English by two distinctive features which are quite unfamiliar to him. A native speaker of English would, of course, have parallel difficulties in distinguishing Xhosa clicks: many Europeans speaking a Bantu language represent all its various clicks by one all-purpose click or cluck: it is worth remembering that the Xhosas who speak respectable English probably far outnumber the Englishmen who speak respectable Xhosa.

This illustrates two highly important principles:

66

(i) The foreign learner of English tends to take over into English the basic habits of his mother tongue;
(ii) The teacher of English as a second language to pupils of a particular language group must learn to compare the phonemic systems of English and the home language of the pupils.

This will involve comparing not only phonemes in isolation, such as English and Xhosa /i/'s but also their behaviour in the language: i.e. the allophones and the rules for their distribution. The teacher, in other words, must know not only which sounds can and cannot be made, but also *where* a particular sound is permissible and where it is not. If we know this we can predict what the difficulties of the learner will be, and prepare drills to enable him to get over them. *Pronounce English Correctly*, by L. W. Lanham and A. Traill (Longmans, 1965), is an excellent handbook of drills for the African learner.

3.3. Sounds in combination

It is probably true that in no case can the phonemes of a language be combined at random. For any given phoneme, certain positions are possible and certain others are not: the total range of contexts in which a given phoneme can occur is said to constitute its *distribution*. A simple case of a restricted distribution in English (already mentioned in § 2.13.4) is that of /ŋ/, which occurs only after a vowel and hence never as the initial sound of a word (except in borrowings from other languages, which are mostly proper names, such as those of Lake *Ngami:* and of the authoress *Ngaio* Marsh:/ŋgɑːmɪ; ŋaɪou/). It is rare, incidentally, to find English /ŋ/ after a long vowel: [siːŋ] is un-English not only because the vowel is wrong but because the use of a long vowel before /ŋ/ breaks an established phonemic pattern.

Other simple instances of restricted distributions in RP are those of the short vowels /e, æ, ʌ, ɒ/, which do not occur finally: another short vowel, /ʊ/, occurs finally only in 'reduced' forms, as in /dɪdjʊ?/. I have already indicated that /ʒ/ in English is never initial and /h/ never final: /h/ must precede a vowel or /j/ as in /hjuː/; /ʒ/ occurs normally only between vowels, as in *pleasure*, or finally, as it does (for some speakers) in *garage*. RP /r/ 'occurs only before a vowel' (Gimson, 1962), though in Scottish and American dialects /r/ is quite common as a final phoneme: *far* and *car*, for many American speakers, are [far] and [kar] (with a low central vowel).

The semivowels /j/ and /w/ do not occur finally in British analyses of RP, though some American writers, such as Bloomfield (1933) interpret such diphthongs as /eɪ/ and /oʊ/ as /ej/ and /ow/, thus making /j/ the final element of *say* and /w/ the final element of *go*. The difference of notation does not greatly alter our picture of the articulations: you will recall that the /j/ glide begins in the neighbourhood of /ɪ/ and the /w/ glide in that of /ʊ/. We need not here explore the reasons for the difference of interpretation, and shall not, in our present analysis, count /j/ and /w/ among possible final elements, but it is worth remembering that many linguists follow a different convention, based on a different interpretation of the facts.

/j/, incidentally, as in *fille* and *coquille*, is quite commonly found at the ends of words and syllables in French.

Consonant clusters. Only a limited number of consonant clusters occur in English, and combinations that occur at the beginning of a syllable cannot always occur at the end. The cluster /sp/, for instance, occurs both at the beginnings and at the ends of syllables ('speed', 'hasp'), but the cluster /spr/ occurs only initially: we have *spread* and *sprawl* but not */espr/ or any similar formation. A complete outline of the consonant clusters possible in English need not be given here, but it is useful to remember that they follow definite patterns, for which the rules can be stated quite briefly. For instance:
Initially in English words:

  (i) /ʒ,ŋ/ do not occur (see above).
 (ii) /tʃ, dʒ, ð, z, v/ occur only alone: the initial clusters of Russian *Vladimir* and Polish *zloty* are 'un-English'.

Other consonants may begin a word either alone or as members of clusters. Of these:

(iii) /b, d, g, θ, s, f/ occur before but not after other consonants: we have *blow*, *drown* and *stow*, but not (except in borrowed words) initial /zb, nd, ts/. *Tsetse*-fly and *tsotsi* (ruffian), for instance, with initial /ts/, have passed into English from Bantu languages.
(iv) /r, l, m, n, j, w/ occur in initial clusters only after other consonants: we have *true, flutter, smooth*, etc. but not, for instance, /rt, lf, ms/ as initial clusters.
 (v) /p, t, k, f/ may occur in initial clusters either before or after other consonants: thus, we have *spend* and *pray, train* and *strain, clean* and *screen, frigid* and *sphere*.

Trademarks and the invented names of products – *Vim, Jik, Esso, Kleen* – conform rather closely to the general rules of English for sound-combination. This matter appears to have been carefully studied by advertising men: for obvious reasons, we are unlikely to get a new shoe-polish for an English-speaking market called *zbe* or *dli*. A touch of unfamiliarity, however, may be a useful point: *Schweppes*, for instance, is a product name that capitalizes upon a

just-sufficiently unfamiliar consonant cluster, /ʃw/, which has the
added advantages of suggesting the opening fizz of a bottle of mineral
water. In rather the same way, 'exotic' names like Gina Lollobrigida
or Claudia Cardinale may have stronger box-office appeal than names
like Mary Brown, provided, of course, that they are not too remote
from English patterns of sounds and association.

In one pattern of English consonant clusters there is an interesting
gap:

/kr/	: *cream*	/kl/	: *clean*
/tr/	: *train*		
/pr/	: *pray*	/pl/	: *play*

The missing cluster, /tl/, is common in South American languages,
though neither /tl/ nor /dl/ occurs in English, so that English-speaking
people are liable to hear /tliːn dlʌvz/ as *clean gloves*, substituting for
the non-English clusters the familiar /kl/ and /gl/.

There are, of course, a good many further restrictions on consonants in initial positions and a quite different set of patterns for
consonant clusters at the ends of English words. Other languages may
follow radically different patterns. Some have clusters that look impossible for speakers of English. Gleason (1961) reports the form
/skˡlxlxc/, 'I'm getting cold' from the Bella Coola language of British
Columbia (here /x/ represents an unvoiced velar fricative, and /c/ an
unvoiced alveolar affricate).

The English cluster /sp/ is often an obstacle to the foreign learner.
Spanish students find it difficult, although a similar pattern appears in
Spanish in such words as *espada* (sword) and *España* (Spain). In
Spanish, however, this combination cannot occur initially and always
follows a vowel: moreover the syllables divide between the /s/ and the
/p/: *Es-paña*, not *Esp-aña* (Lado, 1957). The native speaker of Spanish
accordingly tends to produce *Spain* and *spade* as *espain* and *espade*,
following the syllable patterns of his native language.

Some languages have no consonant clusters at all: others, like
Mandarin Chinese and Egyptian Arabic, are without initial clusters.
Mandarin speakers produce English *flea* and *train* as /feliː/ and
/tereɪn/, inserting a vowel between the consonants as is the custom of
their native language (Yao Shen, 1961). They do this in spite of the
fact that Mandarin has individual phonemes very like English /f, l, r/:
the difficulty is not with the individual sounds, but with the patterns of
combination. (You may recall from § 2.13.6 that Hokkien Chinese,
unlike Mandarin, lacks /r/: Hokkien speakers will thus have a further
difficulty with such clusters.) Speakers of Arabic can often handle
clusters of two English consonants but not clusters of three: they

accordingly produce *splash* as /sɪplaʃ/ and *square* as /sɪkwɛər/ (Maliek, 1956).

In general terms we can state this contrast of distribution as follows. The possibilities for consonants in initial position are:

English	C : *sit*	CC : *slit*	CCC : *split*
Arabic	C		
Mandarin:	C		

i.e. clusters of two and three consonants in initial position are possible in English but not in Egyptian Arabic or Mandarin. By 'consonant' (C) I mean, of course, a consonantal *phoneme*: our description has no reference to spelling.

These examples suffice to show the practical importance of the *distribution* of a given unit in any language, i.e. the set of patterns into which it is able to enter as opposed to the patterns to which it is not admitted. This applies equally to the phoneme and to larger units such as a syllable or word. One will get no practical control of a language by learning units in isolation: together with the units, one must learn their 'behaviour' in speech.

3.4. Complementary distribution

There is one pattern for the distribution of sounds that is of great practical importance both for describing a language and for learning it.

We can illustrate this pattern with three of the allophones of /k/. The closure for the plosive /k/ is formed between the velum (soft palate) and the back of the tongue. Compare the points of closure for /k/ in the sequence:

key ; *cur* ; *car*.

If you have difficulty in feeling this, begin by contrasting *key* and *car*. For the /k/ of *key*, the closure is relatively far forward: for that of *car* it is relatively far back: for the /k/ of *cur* it will be in between the other two positions. (You will get an idea of the difference if you use your mirror and light.) *Car* has the back vowel /ɑ:/; *cur* the central /ɜ:/ *key* the front vowel /i:/. Evidently the point of closure for /k/ is correlated (in English) with the tongue-position of the vowel that follows it. The exact positions, of course, will vary for different speakers and different occasions; on the average, however, taking the point of closure for the /k/ of *cur* as our point of reference, the closure for /k/ preceding a front vowel will be in front of this reference point, and the closure for /k/ before a back vowel will be behind it.

We have now, in effect, established three classes of allophones or non-distinctive variants of /k/: class I before front vowels, class II before central vowels, class III before back vowels. The three types of /k/ can be said to be in *complementary distribution*; which means that each 'occurs in a fixed set of contexts in which none of the others occur' (Gleason, 1961). In other words, the 'fronted' allophone of /k/ does not occur before central or back vowels, nor the 'central' allophone before front or back vowels: their distributions are mutually exclusive.

Each of our three classes may be said to constitute an *allophone* of the phoneme /k/ in English. Within each class there will be a certain amount of random variation; for instance, people asking 'Where's the car?' will differ in their individual renderings of /k/, though they will all produce a /k/ appropriate to the back vowel of *car*, i.e. of the kind that we are here calling a 'Class III' allophone. Each of our three allophones is a member of the 'family of sounds' of which the phoneme /k/, in terms of Jones's definition (§ 2.5) consists. Our picture of the family is not complete, and for a full account of /k/, which we do not need at this stage, we should have to take into account certain features other than the point of closure: e.g. degree of aspiration.

Other variants that illustrate the principle of complementary distribution are aspirated and unaspirated /p/ (§ 2.13.1) and clear and dark /l/ (§ 2.13.5). Another simple case is that of the words *a* and *an*; *a* invariably precedes a sequence beginning with a consonantal sound (*a large cat*), *an* a sequence beginning with a vowel sound (*an enormous cat*); their 'territories' or distributions in the language are thus complementary or mutually exclusive. This illustrates a point that will be elaborated later: that sequences as well as individual phonemes may be in complementary distribution.

It is important to realize that the complementary distribution of allophones ensures that they are non-distinctive. A distinctive feature is one for which we have a choice. Given the framework:

'Where's the /k–/?'

we have a limited choice of units for completing it: /iː/ if our meaning is *key*, /ɜː/ for *cur* and /ɑː/ for *car*. But once we have selected one of these three, the corresponding allophone of /k/ is selected automatically: only by conscious effort can a native speaker of English precede a front vowel with a 'back' allophone of /k/. We may thus be said to choose the word *key*, but not the allophone of /k/ which it contains, and a change of signal – the change from *key* to *cur* to *car* – is brought about by the choice of the word as a whole, the distinctive features being the vowels /iː, ɜː, ɑː/ and not the allophones of /k/ which happen to precede them.

A parallel situation arises with aspirated and unaspirated /p/

(§§ 2.5. and 2.13.1). If we are native speakers of English, we automatically choose aspirated /p/ when we decide to say *pin*, and unaspirated /p/ when we decide to say *spin* or *please*. In Swahili and Urdu, as we have seen, the choice between aspirated and unaspirated /p/ is an entirely different matter. Similarly, in Arabic, the contrast of what in English are simply front and back allophones of /k/ is phonemic: Arabic has, for instance, /kalb/, (*dog*) with a fronted velar plosive, and /qalb/ (*heart*), with a back one (Gleason, 1961). Hence the native speaker of Arabic may be disposed to hear the /k/ of *key* and the /k/ of *car* as two distinctive units of sound: here again we have a feature which is non-distinctive in one language and distinctive in another; the sounds that in English function as two of the allophones of /k/ are in Arabic the separate phonemes /k/ and /q/.

3.5. Variations

In § 2.5 I described an allophone, in a preliminary way, as a non-distinctive variant of a phoneme in a given language. We can now describe non-distinctive variation more precisely. It may help if we focus on a single phoneme, /k/.

Complementary distribution. We have found in the sequence *key, cur, car*, three distinguishable types or allophones of /k/ which are non-distinctive in English and in complementary distribution, each being limited to a particular type of environment.

Free variation. Within each of our three types there may be a further range of non-distinctive variations. Imagine, for instance, the phoneme /k/ in a thousand pronunciations of the word *car*. If we assume that no two utterances are ever completely identical, every /k/ that you hear will be different from every other, though the differences may be too small for any but the most sensitive recording instruments to detect. For this particular set of variants of /k/, the linguistic context was held constant; since they all occur in the same word, they are by definition non-distinctive.

Allophones, generally speaking, are manifestations of a phoneme which are either in free variation or complementary distribution.

It is important to realize that non-distinctive variation has definite limits. If we vary our renderings of a given phoneme indefinitely we shall always reach a point at which the phoneme 'disappears' or turns into something else.

This has been neatly illustrated by experiments with a speech synthesizer described by D. B. Fry (1964). The synthesizer is a device for simulating the sounds of speech: for the experiment in question it was set to produce a continuous range of sounds 'which for English listeners passes from [b] to [d] to [g] in a way which cannot be imitated in human speech because of the articulatory discontinuities in the series'. The sounds were presented in random order to a number of listeners, who recorded whether they heard each item as /b/, /d/, or /g/. For certain sounds the listeners were in complete agreement; certain other sounds, however, were heard both as /b/ and /d/, and still others both as /d/ and /g/. At certain points in the range of sounds the votes of the listeners were evenly divided between /b/ and /d/, or between /d/ and /g/: these 'areas of uncertainty' may be taken to represent the 'boundaries' of the phonemes in question.

A cruder but sometimes helpful approach to the notion of a phoneme is to consider it as a bundle of distinctive features. We have, for instance, defined /d/ as an oral voiced alveolar plosive. This means that its basic or distinctive features are:

(i)   Voice;
(ii) Raising of the velum to close off the nasal cavity;
(iii) Closure in the mouth between the tongue and the alveolar ridge;
(iv) Plosive articulation.

Corresponding to these features of articulation are certain qualities of sound. A sufficiently drastic alteration of any distinctive feature will turn /d/ into something else. If, for instance, we unvoice the sound, it will become /t/; if we could shift the point of articulation far enough back, we might arrive at a sound that was more like /g/ than /d/. If we shifted from a plosive to a fricative mode of articulation we should produce /ð/. Less drastic alteration may not entirely destroy the distinctive quality of /d/ but may give it an 'un-English' quality or hinder the recognition of neighbouring features.

3.6. The phoneme reconsidered

Our preliminary description of the phoneme in § 2.5 has now been considerably expanded. To understand the role of the phoneme in English requires some exploration of the entire sound-system in which English phonemes operate. It may now be helpful to summarize a number of points that have arisen in the discussion. While a basic concept like that of the phoneme can probably never be *completely* defined, it is always advisable to set up one's provisional definition in formal terms; it is generally difficult or impossible to test the validity of a descriptive concept that cannot be formally defined.

(i)   A phoneme is *distinctive*; in other words a phonemic contrast in a given language, such as that of /p/ and /b/ in English, signals (in the given language) a contrast of meaning, e.g. that of *pin* and *bin* or *pile* and *bile*. Words contrasted in this way, i.e. by the difference of a single phoneme, are sometimes known as *minimal pairs*.

(ii) A phoneme, as such, is *without meaning*, though it is a unit for constructing meaningful sequences of sound. A few meaningful units, of course, happen each to consist of one phoneme only; the word *a* for instance, happens to take the form, in connected speech (in many pronunciations but not in all), of the vowel phoneme /ə/, and the word *I* (again in many pronunciations but not all) that of the diphthong /aɪ/. For a minimum meaningful unit, however, we shall reserve the term *morpheme*, which will be explained later (§ 6.3).

(iii) The sounds which are the manifestations of a phoneme are *variable*; the phoneme is thus a 'class' or 'family' of sounds (clear and dark /l/, aspirated and unaspirated /p/) rather than a single invariable sound-unit.

(iv) A phoneme is a feature of a *given language*: there is no such thing as a phoneme common to two or more languages, though two different languages may have phonemes which are relatively similar in articulation, sound, or distribution.

(v) The variant forms or allophones of the same phoneme in a given language are *non-distinctive*: no changes of meaning in English are signalled by the contrast of clear and dark /l/ or by that of aspirated and unaspirated /p/. In other languages the same variants may be distinctive: thus aspirated and unaspirated /p/ are *phonemes* in Swahili and Urdu (see also § 2.5 and § 2.13.1); /k/ and /q/, corresponding to front and back variants of English /k/, are separate phonemes in Arabic. Non-distinctive forms are either in free variation or complementary distribution.

(vi) Allophones of the same phoneme are *phonetically similar*. This is fundamental: if we left it out of our description it would be possible to argue that /h/ and /ŋ/ are members of the same phoneme in English; English has no initial /ŋ/ and no final /h/, so that no two words are kept apart in English solely by the difference of /h/: /ŋ/. But if we examine /h/ and /ŋ/ phonetically, informally by listening to them, or formally by measuring their constituent vibrations by means of a sound spectrograph, or comparing the actions of the vocal organs by which they are formed, it will be clear that they differ quite considerably.

This description of the phoneme might be considerably extended. The word *phoneme* is perhaps the most useful term that has ever been devised for the analysis and description of speech. For this reason, it is particularly important not to abuse or overwork it and to remember that there are many contexts in which the more familiar and less technical word *sound* will do better or just as well.

3.7. Sound and spelling

The scripts of nearly all the languages of the modern world consist of visual symbols for the sounds of speech. The earliest writing, however, did not apparently depend on any correlation of symbol with sound.

'Writing is an outgrowth of drawing' (Bloomfield, 1933). The people of certain prehistoric societies appear to have kept records and transmitted messages by means of drawings which had, perhaps, an origin in ritual or magic. Drawings and tallies can be used for messages and records which have no direct equivalents in speech: a Bushman picture, for instance, of hunters attacking a giraffe conveys a 'meaning' without necessarily corresponding to any particular arrangement of words. In a few early societies, however, there was a gradual development from purely pictorial messages to a *script* in which each symbol corresponds to an item – word, syllable or phoneme – in the language of the writer.

In one type of script, of which Chinese is today the principal surviving example, the symbols represent lexical and grammatical units, without direct reference to sounds. In scripts of the other principal type, the symbols represent units of sound: either syllables, as in the case of Japanese and Cherokee, or smaller sound-units, as in the case of alphabetic scripts like our own. (The sound-units represented may or may not correspond to the phonemes of the language that is being written: in the case of English, this correspondence is far from perfect.)

A simple case of a visual symbol that does not represent any particular unit of sound is a numeral such as the figure 5. This can be rendered *five* in English, *vyf* in Afrikaans, *cinq* in French, *-hlanu* in Xhosa: it is intelligible to anyone who knows the 'Arabic' system of numerals, irrespective of the language he speaks. The characters of Chinese script do not function in quite the same way, since they represent items (but not sound-units) of a particular language. The items that they represent are *morphemes* (§ 6.3), i.e. minimum grammatical units. (Note that Chinese has phonemes but not *letters*, if by 'letter' we understand a visible symbol for a phoneme.)

A script of the Chinese type has the advantage that it can be understood by speakers of mutually unintelligible dialects, since the symbols do not represent units of sound. On the other hand, the existence of a standard written Chinese that does not refer to any particular sound-system is an obstacle to the development of a standard form of spoken Chinese. Further, a script of the Chinese type requires a very large number of symbols: modern Chinese requires about 3,500, and the Chinese classics two or three thousand more. Such a script is obviously difficult to learn, and the Chinese are accordingly gradually introducing alphabetic writing instead.

A syllabic script may be more economical, though the number of distinct syllables varies considerably from one language to another. A phonemic script, in which each symbol represents a phoneme, will need fewer symbols still, since the number of phonemes in a language hardly ever exceeds a hundred and is often under fifty.

A consistently phonemic script, i.e. one with a one-to-one correspondence between written symbol and distinctive unit of sound, probably does not exist. For a number of languages, however, such as Spanish, the relationship between phonemes and letters is fairly consistent. This is not the case with English, though the sounds of English vary so considerably between dialects that this is not altogether a disadvantage. It has been calculated, however, that the forty to forty-five basic sounds of English are rendered in about 2,000 different spellings; we find, for instance, nine different spellings of the /aɪ/ diphthong:

write, cry, high, height, die, either, aisle, eye, buy,

– and four or five different spellings are quite common for each of several other phonemes in modern English: for /ou/, for instance, we have the spellings of *go, low, toe,* and *moan.*

Our alphabet is essentially that of ancient Rome, which over the centuries has been adapted for the scripts of many languages whose sound-systems differ very considerably from that of Latin. The spelling of Old English, the form of our language up to about A.D. 1150, is not particularly consistent. Since the Old English period, many of the sounds of English have changed very considerably: for instance, Old English *stan* [stɑːn] has become modern English *stone; riht* [rɪçt] has become *right, cene* [keːnə] has become *keen.* Some spellings have altered to reflect sound-changes, others have remained unaltered, and change has not always been consistent. After the Norman conquest in A.D. 1066, English came to be written by Norman scribes who did not know the language well and carried into it some of the spelling conventions of Norman-French. Later, a number of spellings were altered to bring the spelling of English words into line with Latin: for instance *debt* and *doubt,* originally spelled *dette* and *doute,* acquired *b*'s to match those of Latin *debitum* and *dubitare.* Up to the time of the invention of printing, spelling was variable: most of our present standard spellings were established by printers during the eighteenth century, long before the discovery of the principle of the phoneme.

A standard spelling, i.e. a fixed spelling for every word in the language, is by no means indispensable for communication. Until

about the time of Shakespeare, a great many writers of English spelled
entirely as they pleased: Shakespeare's contemporary Robert Greene,
for instance, has the five spellings *fellow, felow, felowe, fallow* and
fallowe for the same word in the same pamphlet. A standard spelling,
however, is a great convenience to printers; correct spelling, moreover, is of great social importance because people have strong feelings
about unorthodox spelling. Spelling mistakes are among the most
easily recognizable kinds of error in writing, and are therefore among
the likeliest to attract the displeasure of a client or employer.

Over the long history of English spelling, the consonants have
changed considerably less than have the vowels. There is, incidentally,
more similarity today between the consonants of different English
dialects than there is between the vowels. The reason for this lies
probably in the difference between vowel and consonant articulations.

Compare the sequences /p, t, k/ and /iː ɜː ɑː/. The consonant
sequence /p, t, k/ involves three quite distinct positions of the vocal
organs, and a clear-cut shift from one position to the next. On the
other hand (as shown in § 2.14) the vowel sequence /iː ɜː ɑː/, with a
little practice, can be spoken as one continuous sound with no clear-
cut divisions between its components. Although some consonant
sounds merge into one another in a rather similar way, the 'boundaries'
between consonants are on the whole much better defined than are the
'boundaries' between vowels, and the shifts between modes and points
of articulation, like gear changes in driving a car, can usually be clearly
felt. For vowel changes, however, the feeling is rather that of a fluid
drive: the shift from /e/ to /æ/, for instance, is a matter of a very slight
change of tongue position, instead of a definite shift from one point of
closure or narrowing to another, as for /p/ and /t/. Hence the consonants are in general more distinctive to the ear than are the vowels,
and more stable in the language over long periods of time. For
instance, in modern English *summer, long* and *house*, we have the
same consonant skeletons as in Old English *sumor, lang* and *hus*,
though all the vowels of these words have changed over the past
thousand years.

The greater distinctiveness of consonants can be shown in a very
simple way:

c·ns·n·nts ·nd v·w·ls

can be read off quite easily, although the vowels are not shown; this is
not the case with

·o··o·a··· a·· ·o·e··

which is the same sequence without its consonants. The consonants
form, as it were, the skeleton of the word, the vowels the flesh to which

77

the skeleton gives form. In some early scripts, particularly those of
Semitic languages, only the consonants were written, the vowels being
left for the reader to work out for himself. In modern Arabic and
Hebrew scripts, the vowels are marked by dots above the consonant
symbols (ṅglṡh wṙttṅ ṅ thṡ wẏ ṡ ṅt d'ffċlt t˙ ṙd).

3.8.   The initial teaching alphabet

There are certain advantages in a non-phonemic spelling for an international language of which the dialects differ as much as do those of
English today. Some of these dialects are already to a large extent
mutually unintelligible: recordings of Liberian English, for example,
could be understood only in snatches by Bantu speakers of English in
the Republic of South Africa (Lanham, 1963). If the script were
phonemic, different dialects might well require different scripts, and a
text, say, of Nigerian English might quite possibly be unintelligible
to readers in India.

To the experienced reader, moreover, it may matter very little
whether spelling is phonemic or not. Practised readers do not have to
'spell out' a word, letter by letter. They read, instead, by means of a
swift series of movements of the eye; between each movement and the
next comes a 'fixation' of the eyes upon a short section of the text. 'The
eyes pause, as a rule, from 4 to 10 times along a line of ordinary
length' (Gray, 1956), so that the experienced reader proceeds by jumps
that may involve several words at a time. This kind of skill develops
only with considerable practice, but once it is established, a great many
of the difficulties set up by variant spellings simply fall away. Indeed,
some of the clues by which traditional spelling differentiates words of
identical sound but different meanings – *deer* and *dear*, *wait* and
weight – may at this stage be positively helpful.

To the beginner, on the other hand, traditional English spelling
presents great difficulties: this is true both for the foreign learner and
for children who are native speakers of English. The names of the
letters – /eɪ/ and /dʒiː/ for instance – are often out of keeping with
their most usual phonetic values; on the other hand, to teach the
letters as if each represented a certain sound – to teach *o*, for instance,
as '/ɒ/', – may result in recurrent difficulty with such common pairs as
to and *go*, *on* and *do*.

Some of the problems of the early stages can be by-passed by the
procedure known as 'look and say', in which children are taught to
recognize a written word as a whole instead of spelling it out letter by
letter. This has the advantage of introducing an adult technique of
reading from the very beginning: on the other hand, children trained
by this method only, often have great difficulty later in learning to spell.

A major development in language teaching has been the design and testing of the *Initial Teaching Alphabet* (i.t.a.). This was in large measure the work of Sir James Pitman, grandson of the inventor of the Pitman shorthand system. Since 1961, i.t.a. has been used in a large number of schools for introducing children to reading and writing by means of a system of symbols fairly similar to those of conventional print, but a great deal more consistent in their rendering of sounds. Once the basic skills are well established, the child transfers to the use of conventional spelling.

The Initial Teaching Alphabet has thus to serve two purposes:

(i)   to provide a set of symbols capable of representing the basic sounds of English consistently;

(ii) to provide a bridge for the beginner into traditional English spelling.

For the second of these purposes the unfamiliar symbols of the International Phonetic Association – for instance θ, ʌ, ð, and some of the diphthong symbols – would clearly be unsuitable, and the Initial Teaching Alphabet is in fact not quite consistently phonemic.

It consists of 44 characters, of which 24 are lower-case ('small letter') items of our traditional alphabet, while twenty are new characters, most of which, such as þ for the initial sound of *three*, closely resemble pairs of letters in traditional English spelling. As a general rule, each character in i.t.a. corresponds to one of the segmental phonemes of RP; there are some exceptions to this principle, but these appear to have been made for the sake of a smooth transition to traditional spelling at the end of the i.t.a. course. There is, for instance, a special symbol for the sequence /ju:/ in *due*, and /k/ is rendered in i.t.a. both by c and k. The whole of i.t.a. deserves study as an ingenious compromise between the facts of the English sound-system and those of traditional spelling.

Extensive experiments since 1961 indicate that i.t.a. in the hands of suitably trained teachers is an extremely valuable teaching device for children who are native speakers of English, and work is now in progress at several centres on its application in the teaching of English as a second language.

Chapter Four

THE ORGANIZATION OF SPEECH

4.1. Speech and writing

Up to this point, the focus of our analysis of speech has been upon *phonemic structure*: i.e. upon the formation of basic sound-units by the vocal organs and the combination of these units in the stream of speech. We have been concerned as a rule with very small segments of sound: generally with segments corresponding to individual phonemes such as /k/ or /i:/, though we have also considered some of the rules governing the combinations of these segments to form larger units: the rules, for instance, which permit the sequence /bendz/ in English but not the sequence /sbend/.

Speech, of course, consists normally of much longer sequences than these. The range is from utterances of a single word, such as *tea*, to continuous stretches of three or four hours as in speeches by certain Heads of State. The organization of these longer stretches of speech involves many principles that we have not as yet considered. Indeed, we know at present all too little about the organization of spoken English; despite appearances to the contrary, most of our theories about English are very heavily influenced by alphabetic writing and by the grammatical forms of the written language. It is important to remember at the outset how very different speech and writing really are.

Here is a transcript from a recording of about fifty seconds of consecutive speech by a single speaker:

I think in doing   any language like Afrikaans or or any other language you've got to do the basic work yourself you know get your moment where   where you can   from then it's easy if you're if you hear people speaking it you're picking it up all the time but you have to get over   I know erm in   in Sesuto erm for instance when you could get to the stage of saying hona keng ka Sesut what is this in Sesuto this was a tremendous advance   you know hona keng ka Sesut   then then you're away   you know how do you say or is this good French or you know c'est bon Français   you're away   isn't it or or you know   c'est idiomatique   and then   but this is this is this is the real the real difficulty to get that far   the grind

Parts of this, in its written form, are distinctly difficult to follow. This is simply because ordinary writing cannot show the *organization*

80

of speech: the emphases, sequences and transitions established by the speaking voice. I have presented it without punctuation, except for the spaces, which mark pauses in the original speech; normal punctuation is not designed for speech. It would take a rather complex system of special notation to represent on the printed page the sound-signals which 'shaped' this utterance as speech, and of which normal punctuation is at best a very sketchy and conventional rendering.

No one listening to this utterance as it was originally spoken had the slightest difficulty in understanding it, and, as a sample of informal educated English speech, it is probably not particularly complex or involved. It was spoken informally, to four other people sitting round a fire. On a formal occasion – for instance, in giving a lecture – the speaker would no doubt have used a more formal style. In writing he would probably conform rather carefully to the established conventions of the written language, which differ radically from those of unscripted speech.

The differences in structure between spoken and written English are not, after all, surprising. Speech is for the ear, writing for the eye: it is remarkable that they run parallel to the extent that they do.

Writing, of course, frequently imitates speech. But there is a great difference between conversation in ordinary life and the dialogue of a novel, play or film. Scripted speech – a radio news bulletin, for example – is never organized in the same way as is ordinary conversation.

Abercrombie (1965) suggests a useful distinction between *conversation* – ordinary talking – and *spoken prose*: 'what we normally hear on stage or screen', pointing out that whereas spoken prose is a familiar experience to most of us, written conversation (such as the sample given above) is not. A play or novel in the language of ordinary conversation would be almost as intolerable as an ordinary conversation in the language of a novel or play. Speech is often directly 'lifted' from writing; it is much less common to find writing which is a direct unedited transcription of speech.

Letters, of course, are often dictated, but in this situation we have a speaker who is thinking in terms of writing, and 'correcting' himself as he dictates, and a stenographer trained to shape what she hears for visual presentation – by leaving out, for instance, the *um*s, *ah*s, and asides not intended for the final text. Dictation, in short, (unless, of course, one is dictating from a prepared text) is not a simple matter of writing down equivalents for sounds. Very often it involves radical changes, both in grammar and vocabulary, between the initial sequences of speech and the final paragraphs on the written page.

It is difficult at present to offer any useful account of the organization of speech over stretches longer than a single word. The structure of conversation – of unscripted spontaneous speech – is complex. It cannot be studied in much detail without recordings. Technical accounts of it are difficult, sometimes in disagreement with one another, and beyond the scope of an introductory text like this. For this reason, I propose to discuss it only in rather general terms, without attempting to outline procedures for analysis and transcription.

4.2. The organization of speech

Even the most informal speech is highly organized. Consider again a fragment of our first example:

> I know er in   in Sesuto   erm for instance when you could
> get to the stage of saying   hona keng ka Sesut what is this in
> Sesuto this was a tremendous   advance   you know hona
> keng ka Sesut   then then you're away

In its spoken form, a number of sound-features helped to make this a good deal more coherent than it looks in print.

(i) *Grouping.* In the first place, as the spaces in the printed text suggest, the original utterance was grouped into units of varying length. Unless we can perceive the grouping, we cannot follow the meaning of even quite short sequences of English; for instance, in the newspaper headline:

COLONELS MAN PUMPS

we are at a loss until we have established the grouping either as *colonels* /*man pumps* (the colonels are pumping) or as *colonel's man* / *pumps* (the pumping is being done by the colonel's man). Grouping, then, is of fundamental importance: we shall consider in the next section how groupings are established in speech.

(ii) *Prominence.* Secondly, certain items in almost any stretch of speech are likely to be more prominent than others. Among such items in our example as it was originally spoken were *hona keng ka Sesut, advance* and *away.* Their importance in speech is established by special effects of loudness and pitch, and by grammatical signals which we shall consider later.

(iii) *Rhythm.* Thirdly, apart from the special effects of prominence, one can hear, in most if not all sequences of speech, a fairly regular rise and fall. This is established by contrasts of stressed and unstressed syllables, as in ˈ*What is* ˈ*this in Ses*ˈ*uto,* in which I have marked each of the stressed syllables with the diacritic /ˈ/ – which in this notation *precedes* the syllables that carry stress.

The rhythms and pitches of speech appear quite often to carry significances of their own. Thus, without catching the actual words of a remark, one can sometimes gauge the feelings of the speaker. Small children very probably recognize patterns of pitch and rhythm before they begin to recognize the phonemic structure of words. In the same way the words, *Push off!* or *Voetsak!* or *Hamba!* may all produce the same response in an intelligent dog. It is unlikely that dogs can recognize the phonemic structure of the same command in English, Afrikaans or Xhosa; they are much more likely to recognize intonations. In particular cases like this there may, of course, be a contextual clue such as a lifted hand or stick, though there is abundant experimental evidence that animals respond very readily to tones and even to combinations of tones (Brown, 1958). *Good dog!* spoken with the angry intonation of *Push off!* is more likely to make a dog cringe than to wag his tail. The pitch and rhythm of an utterance are thus to a certain extent independent of the words, and 'meaningful', up to a point, on their own. This is not to suggest that stress and intonation are 'culture-free' in a way that the phoneme is not. A given language is likely to have characteristic patterns of stress and pitch which differ from those of other languages; and a 'foreign accent' is usually a phenomenon of intonation as well as of the features of articulation described earlier.

Some writers on English treat the units of pitch and stress as phonemes of a special type, generally called 'suprasegmental'. The 'segmental' phonemes are those of the kind described in Chapters Two and Three, each corresponding to a particular 'segment' or 'slice' of sound. The suprasegmentals are those operating above the level of the segment: in the two forms of *discount*, for instance, the 'suprasegmental' stress is on the first syllable of the noun and the second syllable of the verb: it is thus at a level different from that of the segmental phonemes which are the same for both words. I doubt, however, whether our description of the phoneme (§ 3.6) really fits the phenomena of pitch and stress with which we are now concerned.

Like the segmental phonemes, however, effects of pitch and stress have a physical basis. 'Every utterance is a movement. . . . Speech is rather a set of movements made audible than a set of sounds produced by movements' (Stetson, 1951). In order to follow these movements, we must now briefly reconsider the mechanism of speech.

4.3. The physical mechanisms

Our speech is formed in our breath: we normally speak on an expiration, a breathing out, and in order to understand the groupings and rhythms of speech we must consider first the mechanism of breathing.

Normal breathing is more rapid, as a rule, than the breathing to which we consciously attend, as in breathing exercises. The frequency of respiration, i.e. of the cycle of breathing *in* plus breathing *out*, varies from 16 to 24 per minute for adults when the body is completely at rest. Children breathe faster, old people more slowly. Any kind of activity, such as speech, will of course increase the speed of respiration.

Respiration (as was explained in § 2.8) is controlled by two sets of muscles:

(i) The intercostal muscles that expand and contract the side walls of the chest cavity;

(ii) The diaphragm and abdominal muscles that act upon the cavity from below.

These muscles act upon the lungs to produce the stream of air in which the sounds of speech are formed. When we speak, however, their action does not resemble a smooth unbroken piston-stroke: for a given breath-group – such a unit as 'then then you're away' – there will be two basic movements: a relatively slow and controlled push of the abdominal muscles, and, imposed on this, a faster pulsating movement of the intercostals.

The 'push' from the abdominal muscles establishes the *breath-group*: this may consist of one or more syllables, up to a maximum of about fifteen (Stetson, 1951). In a multi-syllable breath-group, each pulse of the intercostals constitutes a syllable: thus the five syllables of 'then then you're away' were established by five pulses of the inter-costal muscles of the speaker.

The *chest-pulses*, however, each of which 'carries' or 'forms' a syllable, are not the only elements in the rhythm of speech. The pattern of 'then then you're away' was not:

then   then   you're   a   way

but was more like:

then   **then**   you're   a   **way**

– *then*, *then* and -*way*, in other words, were marked by heavier pulses than were the other two syllables. These stronger pulses are set up by stronger and less frequent contractions of the breathing muscles which from time to time reinforce one of the chest-pulses to produce a *stressed* syllable; the basic elements in the rhythm of English speech are thus:

(i) chest-pulses, forming syllables;

(ii) stress-pulses, contrasting syllables as stronger or weaker.

84

Over the breath-group as a whole there may, in addition, be significant changes of pitch, established by variations in the speed with which the vocal cords vibrate. These vibrations are faster for a higher pitch, slower for a lower one. While an upward or downward change of pitch may extend over several syllables, the most noticeable changes of pitch are often quite rapid, and tend to be made on stressed syllables, so that a chest pulse forming the syllable, a stress pulse accenting it and a change of pitch to give it special prominence may all happen simultaneously. Pitch, however, as will be shown in more detail later, is a feature of the group rather than of the syllable.

4.4. The perception of prominence

The perception of what we loosely term 'stress', which I should here prefer to call 'prominence', reserving *stress* for a narrower and more definite meaning, may involve a number of different factors. Let us consider an actual contrast involving 'prominence', that of ˈobject (noun) with obˈject (verb). It is usual to say that the noun is stressed on the first syllable and the verb on the second, and we may accept this view of the contrast provided that we realize that 'stress' is here a blanket term for several distinguishable features of sound.

These are as follows – the first syllable of the noun is likely to be (1) louder and (2) longer than the first syllable of the verb; (3) correlated with this there is likely to be a contrast of vowel-quality: /əbˈdʒekt/ (verb) against /ˈɒbdʒɪkt/ (noun). (4) Finally the change of pitch between the first syllable and the second is likely to be *upwards* for the verb and *downwards* for the noun.

Our sound-contrast, then, may involve up to four different features: loudness, length, direction of pitch, and vowel-quality. In ordinary speech these operate simultaneously: they combine to give prominence to the first syllable of the noun ˈobject and to the second syllable of the verb obˈject but it is difficult to say which of the four is the most important element in the signal.

In a grammatical context, incidentally, such as the sentence:

I object to that object

the contrast is also established by the positions of the words in relation to others and by such combinations as that of *I* with the first *object* and of *to that* with the second. Thus even if the sounds of the first and the second *object* were identical, the grammar would still establish the difference between them, as it does between the words of identical sound in *Fish up that fish* or *Pick up that pick*.

We can, however, abstract the contrasting sound-features of ˈobject and obˈject and, using a speech synthesizer, test our perception of one feature at a time. The two syllables of *object*, for instance, can be contrasted solely on length, with all other features held constant, or solely on loudness, or solely on the difference of pitch between the two. D. B. Fry (1960) described a series of experiments of this kind, in which groups of listeners reported whether they heard various forms of *object* as noun or verb. Thus when the first vowel was extremely short compared with the second, 82 per cent of the listeners judged the word to be a verb; as the length of the second vowel increased, so did the percentage of listeners hearing a noun, till eventually only one listener in ten was hearing a verb.

It was found, however, that the contrast could be established in several different ways – by differences of vowel length, by differences of volume and by differences of pitch, though pitch appeared to be the factor to which listeners responded most readily. Thus prominence, which in popular accounts of speech is often termed 'stress', is acoustically rather complex: it is not as if a prominent syllable were one for which we simply turned up the volume, or raised the pitch.

In the brief description which follows, I shall as far as possible separate the rhythms established by stress-pulses from the special effects of prominence and grouping established by variations of pitch. Stress, then, will be treated simply as an element of rhythm, a feature contrasting 'strong' and 'weak' syllables in a rhythmic sequence, its basis, as the experimental work of Stetson has shown, being the syllable-forming pulses of the intercostals. Pitch will be regarded as a feature of the breath-group or tone-group: it has a different physical basis in the vibration of the vocal cords. The rather complex question of the combination of effects of stress and pitch in our actual perceptions of speech can be left to a more advanced analysis.

4.5.   Speech rhythms

Postponing for a moment the discussion of special effects of prominence, let us consider first the basic rhythms of speech.

Rhythm is usefully defined in *The Shorter Oxford Dictionary* as 'Movement marked by the regulated succession of strong and weak elements, or of opposite or different conditions'.

The strong and weak elements in the movement of speech are the stressed and unstressed syllables. Stress-pulses (in English) tend to rise at regular intervals of time: one can test this roughly by counting aloud. Contrast the sequences:

(i)   One, two, three, four, five;
(ii) Twenty-one, twenty-two, twenty-three, twenty-four, twenty-five.

The first of these contains five syllables, the second fifteen, but either, rather surprisingly, can be spoken comfortably in about four seconds: the reason for this is that English speech-rhythm is timed by stresses, and that the numbers of stresses in our two sequences are the same. In another counting sequence:

fifty EIGHT fifty NINE SIXty sixty ONE sixty TWO

the intervals between strong syllables are roughly the same, though the numbers of intervening weak syllables vary considerably: between NINE and SIX- there are none, while between SIX- and ONE there are three.

In speech and music, rhythm is essentially a matter of timing. In English, the timing is by stresses; in certain other languages, such as French and Japanese, the rhythm is timed by syllables: each syllable, in other words, tends to occupy roughly the same interval of time.

The basic unit of English speech-rhythm is sometimes taken to be the *foot*. This is defined as a strong syllable either alone or, more frequently, followed by one or more weak syllables (usually not more than six) and corresponding to the interval between the onset of one stress pulse and the onset of the next. The beginning of a foot is marked in transcription with the symbol ᛁ; this automatically marks the position of stresses. We would thus mark the feet of *then then you're away* as ᛁthen ᛁthen you're a ᛁway.

A stress-pulse may at times be silent, in cases where a movement of the breathing muscles does not issue in sound. This will register as a slight pause or interval of silence: such a pause occurred at the point marked ʌ in the sequence: ᛁany ᛁlanguage like Afri ᛁkaans ʌ or ᛁany ᛁother ᛁlanguage; the best-known silent stress is that which precedes a slurred pronunciation of *thank you*: [ˈkkjʊ] (Jones, 1962): the first syllable does not issue in sound, though it is still registered in the movements of the speaker.

In formal speech, the stresses stand out very clearly, as they might in a measured rendering of the opening words of the Declaration of Independence:

ʌ We   ᛁhold these   ᛁtruths to be   ᛁself-   ᛁevident: ʌ that
ᛁall   ᛁmen are cre   ᛁated   ᛁequal: ʌ that they are en
ᛁdowed by their Cre   ᛁator ʌ with   ᛁcertain un   ᛁalienable
ᛁrights: ʌ that a   ᛁmong   ᛁthese are   ᛁlife,   ᛁliberty
and the pur   ᛁsuit of   ᛁhappiness

or in:

ʌ To   ᛁbe or   ᛁnot to   ᛁbe: ᛁthat is the   ᛁquestion

Writers on poetry define a foot as 'a combination of one accented and one or more unaccented syllables' (Brooks and Warren, 1946). In this combination, a number of orders are possible, e.g. weak-strong or strong-weak. According to our present definition, the strong syllable invariably begins the foot: this makes it considerably easier to decide where the feet begin and end.

4.6. Stress-contrasts

Within the word in English, the stress is normally fixed. Thus in *economy*, the stress falls invariably on the second syllable, in ˈ*object* (noun) on the first and in *obˈject* (verb) on the second. Usages may vary in relatively new words such as *television*, in which some people stress the first syllable and others the third, but nearly all 'established' English words of more than one syllable have a fixed internal stress-pattern, which the foreign student must learn.

This stress-pattern within the word, however, is subordinate in connected speech to the overall pitch of the sentence. In the sentence *Ladies enjoy conversation* the principal word-stresses will fall on the first syllable of *ladies*, the second of *enjoy* and the third of *conversation*, but these three stresses will be related in a larger pattern which will depend largely upon the pitch of the voice over the sentence as a whole. Pitch-patterns will be considered in § 4.7.

Stress-signals have several uses in English.

Noun-verb contrasts. Stress, as we have seen with ˈ*object* and *obˈject*, contrasts a number of two-syllable nouns with the corresponding verbs, though in addition to the contrast of stresses in pairs of this kind there is usually a contrast of vowel-quality, as in:

Nouns	*Verbs*
/ˈkɒnflɪkt	kənˈflɪkt
ˈkɒnvɪkt	kənˈvɪkt
ˈprɒdʒekt	prəˈdʒekt
ˈrebəl	rɪˈbel
ˈrebl̩	rəˈbel/

The stressed vowel in the first syllable of the noun tends to change to /ə/, the unstressed neutral vowel, in the corresponding syllable of the verb, though (as appears from ˈ*discount* and *disˈcount*) this change does not invariably take place.

Word-groups and compound words. The position of the stresses also helps to distinguish certain word-groups from compound words. Consider how the meaning of the following is affected by their organization into feet:

(1) ˈThis ˈblack ˈbird ˈisn't a ˈblackbird
(2) ˈIs that ˈgreen ˈhouse a ˈgreenhouse?
(3) ˄The ˈlightship was a ˈvery ˈlight ˈship.

One of the tests for items of this kind, where the initial combination is that of adjective and noun, is whether a qualifier, such as *rather* or *extremely*, can stand in front of it: *a rather green house* is English, but *a rather greenhouse* is not. This test, however, cannot be used for groupings of noun and noun, such as *steamᴵboat* and *ᴵsteamboat*.

A combination that operates as a compound unit in speech is often still written as two separate words. Thus South Africans normally write *phone box*, *cool drinks* and *week-end*, but are apt to stress these items as *ᴵphone box* (not *phone ᴵbox*), *ᴵcooldrinks* and *ᴵweekend*, though these renderings cannot perhaps be termed RP. Note how the improbability of * *rather ᴵcooldrinks* establishes the status of *cooldrinks* as a single grammatical unit: the referent of *cool ᴵdrinks*, incidentally, varies to an extent that the referent of *ᴵcooldrinks* does not; *cooldrinks*, in my experience of South African English, are invariably non-alcoholic, *cool drinks* may be either alcoholic or soft.

Separable verbs. A similar contrast partly marked by the position of stresses is that between the two roles of *blew up* in:

(1) ᴧThe   ᴵwind   ᴵblew   ᴵup the   ᴵtunnel.
(2) ᴧThe   ᴵspy   ᴵblew up the   ᴵtunnel.

Blew up in sentence (2) is an example of a separable verb: without substantial change of meaning the sentence could be re-written *The spy blew the tunnel up*. **The wind blew the tunnel up*, however, is un-English; if it has a meaning, the meaning is very different from that of sentence (2). *Blew up* in sentence (1) is also an independent lexical item with a specialized meaning quite different from that of the combination *blew up* in sentence (2). The placing of the stresses in the two sentences and their organization into feet helps to mark these differences of grammatical status and lexical meaning.

4.7. Pitch

Stress in English is a feature of the syllable. Its primary function is to establish the contrasts of strong and weak syllables which are the basis of English speech rhythms. Pitch, on the other hand, is a feature of the breath-group or tone-group and its functions are more complex than are those of stress. In general, the significant feature of pitch in English is its direction – e.g. rising, falling or level, as in

It's a ↘ pig.   (Statement, with a fall on *pig*.)
It's a ↗ pig?   (Question, with a rise on *pig*.)
It's a pig.   (Monotone: improbable without either rise or fall.)

The direction of change, upwards or downwards, can be marked with a curving arrow as shown.

Pitch varies from speaker to speaker and, for the same speaker, from one utterance to another. However, the important contrasts of pitch, like those of stress, are the contrasts *within* a given utterance. What matters is thus relative rather than absolute pitch. A speaker who twice repeats the request *Eat up your fishcake* may give *fishcake* a pitch of 400 vibrations per second on both occasions, but if *eat* has 200 vibrations per second on the first occasion and 800 on the second, the relative pitch-prominence of the words will be reversed.

In a number of languages, pitch is an inherent feature of the word, and two words otherwise identical may be distinguished solely on pitch. Thus in Mixteco, one of the Mexican languages, *zuka* on a medium pitch means 'mountain' and on a low pitch means 'brush'. In Ewe, a language of Togoland in West Africa, *havi* with high level pitch means 'friend', but with a low rising pitch means 'a young pig'. In Pekingese, the word *fu* has four different lexical meanings according to the pitch: 'husband' (high level pitch), 'fortune' (high rising pitch) 'government office' (low rising pitch) and 'rich' (high falling pitch) (Pike, 1945; Westermann and Ward, 1933; Bodmer, 1943).

In English, on the other hand, pitch is essentially a function of the breath-group rather than of the word: a word (other than a monosyllable) may be said to have an inherent stress-pattern, but no inherent pitch. If a word is spoken in isolation it will, of course, have pitch (usually falling pitch), but this has no relation to the pitch that the word will carry in context. Thus the word *tea* may be spoken in English with level, rising or falling pitch in accordance with the overall pitch-pattern of the sentence in which it occurs.

The primary functions of pitch in English are:

(i) to mark the relative prominence of words and sequences;
(ii) to mark the divisions between different sequences in an utterance;
(iii) to signal attitudes.

The same feature of pitch may, of course, perform all three functions. For instance, in the question: ǀ*Would you* ǀ*like some* ⌐*tea*, the rising pitch at the end gives special prominence to *tea*, marks the end of the utterance, and signals a question.

In practice, then, the choice of pitch or intonation for a particular utterance has three aspects:

(i) Breaking up the utterance into units which we shall call 'tone groups':

ǁ ǀhow do you say ǁ ᴧ or ǀ is this good ǀFrench ǁ

90

(Boundaries between tone-groups are generally shown by double upright lines.)

(ii)   Selecting in each tone-group the foot that is to carry the principal change of pitch. We shall call the stressed syllable of such a foot the *tonic*.

‖ ‖HOW do you say ‖ ⌃ or ‖IS this good ‖French ‖

(The tonic syllables are shown in capitals.)

(iii)   Selection of a particular pitch-pattern for the group: the curving arrows below represent the pitches for each group.

‖ ↗ HOW do you   say ‖ ⌃ or ↗IS this good   ‖French ‖

In speech, of course, grouping, tonic and pitch-pattern are selected as a rule simultaneously, without conscious thought, and with incalculable speed. For analysis, however, it may be helpful to approach a feature of speech as if it were consciously chosen even if it is not. and, for the sake of clarity, to examine features that arise simultaneously as if they arose one by one.

Tone groups. Each of these contains *one* tonic syllable only, and each will normally coincide with a unit of grammar or of information: *Is this good French?* or *then then you're away*, – though strictly speaking the tone-group is a unit of sound rather than a grammatical or lexical item. But there is clearly an important difference of emphasis between the groupings—

‖ I saw him at dinner ‖

and   ‖ I saw him   ‖ at dinner ‖

– the second focuses on *dinner* as the first does not.

The tonic. The tonic, or principal movement of pitch, gives special prominence to a particular foot, for instance to the last foot of *then then you're aWAY*. It marks, as it were, the principal information-point within the group. Thus, in such a sentence as ‖*Ahmed* ‖*paid off the* ‖*whole* ‖*debt* the tonic will probably fall on *debt* if one is not stressing or asserting any particular point. In special contexts it may, on the other hand, fall on any one of the other three stressed syllables: e.g.

(1)   ‖ ‖AHmed   ‖ paid off the   ‖whole   ‖debt ‖
      (Ahmed paid it, not Hussain.)
(2)   ‖ ‖Ahmed   ‖PAID off the   ‖whole   ‖debt ‖
      (He's paid; you can't sue him.)
(3)   ‖ ‖Ahmed   ‖paid off the   ‖WHOLE   ‖debt ‖
      (He's paid it all; the account is closed.)

In many questions, there are similar possibilities for shifts of emphasis or focus: thus in ‖*Do* ‖*gentlemen* pre- ‖*fer* ‖*blondes?* the tonic may fall on any one of the four stressed syllables and in each position will focus the question on a different point.

91

Despite the key role of the tonic, it is important to realize that pitch is not a feature of the syllable or foot, still less a feature of the word. The significance of the pitch is spread over the tone-group as a whole: the upward or downward turn on a tonic syllable is significant only in relation to the pitch of the group as a whole.

Pitch-patterns. English has a considerable range of pitch-patterns. There are perhaps five main possibilities for the movement of pitch:

1.   Yes ⌄   Falling pitch
2.   Yes ⌃   Rising pitch
3.   Yes – ⌃   Low level pitch, followed by a rise
4.   Yes ⌄ ⌃   Fall-rise
5.   Yes ⌃ ⌄   Rise-fall

These cannot, however, be satisfactorily handled in writing. They must be studied not in abstraction but in context and in sound. Pitch-patterns are undoubtedly meaningful, but it is extremely difficult to say what they mean: 'the kinds of meaning that they express in English are so generalized that we cannot readily isolate them for analysis' (Strang, 1962). In the contexts of everyday speech, the native speaker can produce the appropriate patterns without conscious thought; but it is difficult in a written description to correlate the patterns with their 'meanings'. It is also very easy to set up false correlations. Thus it has been frequently suggested that a rising pitch is standard for questions that can be answered 'Yes' or 'No'. Fries (1964), however, reports that of over 2,500 'Yes-no' questions in unscripted speech, over 60 per cent were spoken with falling pitch: his study underlines the dangers of failing to check statements about English against an adequate array of the facts.

An excellent practical treatment of pitch for the teacher of English as a second language will be found in A. S. Hornby's *The Teaching of Structural Words and Sentence Patterns* (Oxford University Press, 1962). This uses a very simple and effective notation, and presents pitch not in isolation but in conjunction with sentence-patterns and concrete situations which are readily understood by the child.

4.8. Notation for stress and pitch

This chapter is only a rough sketch of the functions of stress and pitch in English. I have treated them briefly not because they are unimportant but because a full treatment would be too long for an introductory text and of little practical value without recordings.

For this reason I have suggested only the outlines of a notation for stress and pitch: the three most useful symbols being:

I	placed before a stressed syllable to mark the onset of stress
^	to mark a silent stress;
CAPitals	to mark a tonic syllable.

To these one may add the arrows ⌐ and ⌐, placed before the tonic syllable to indicate rising or falling pitch. It is sometimes also useful to mark the pitch on which a group begins or ends. For this purpose the line ⁻ marks a high pitch, the line – a mid or 'ordinary' pitch and the line ₋ a low pitch.

I have not touched upon some difficult or controversial points: the recognition, for instance, of divisions between tone-groups, and the question of the number of different levels of stress which it may be necessary to distinguish. My suggested notation, then, is only approximate: for fuller treatment of the topic the reader should consult Pike (1945), Jones (1962), or O'Connor and Arnold (1951).

Chapter Five

GRAMMATICAL PATTERNING

5.1. The independence of grammar

A good deal of the previous chapter was in fact an introduction to English grammar, if we agree that grammar is (amongst other things) the study of the patterning of sentences and words. I say '*of patterning*' rather than 'of patterns' because language is an activity; 'pattern' suggests something static, 'patterning' carries a reminder that living language is language in motion.

Patterns of pitch and stress are perhaps the most basic and fundamental of grammatical devices: it is significant that one of the basic contrasts of grammar, that of noun and verb, is so often signalled in English mainly by the position of the stress (/ˈkɒnflɪkt, kənˈflɪkt; ˈrekɔːd, rɪˈkɔːd/; see § 4.6): and that another, that of question and statement, can be signalled entirely by pitch:

ǁ _ Tea's ⟋ REAdy ⁻ ǁ   ǁ _ Tea's ⟋ ⟍ REAdy _ ǁ

In these examples we have the identical sequence of words with two different pitch-patterns. The first pitch-pattern makes the sequence a question, the second makes it a statement. Both pitch-patterns are in a sense 'independent' of the words in that they can be 'lifted off' and applied to other sequences, e.g. *That's easy*, or *No butter*. We can arrange the results as follows:

I	II
ǁ_Tea's ⟋ REAdy⁻⁻ǁ	ǁ_Tea's ⟋ ⟍ REAdy_ǁ
ǁ_That's ⟋ EASy⁻ ǁ	ǁ_That's ⟋ ⟍ EASy_ǁ
ǁ_No ⟋ BUTTer⁻ ǁ	ǁ_No ⟋ ⟍ BUTTer_ ǁ

In group I, we have three items with two points in common: the meaning of a question and the pitch-pattern ǁ _ ⟋ ⁻ ǁ. Similarly, the items in group II are alike in that they are all statements with the pitch-pattern ǁ _ ⟋ ⟍ _ ǁ. The arrangement demonstrates:

(a) The extent to which pattern and words are independent;

(b) The role of the pattern in establishing the meaning of the sequences. The pattern of Group I 'shapes' this meaning as a question, the pattern of Group II 'shapes' it as a statement.

Pitch, of course, is not the only 'shaping' device of English grammar. Another is *order*: the question *Do cats eat bats?* can be transformed to a statement, *Cats do eat bats*, by changing the order of the items,

94

just as *cats eat bats* can be changed from statement to question by changing the pitch-pattern. This last example can be represented in three different ways to show the 'independence' of the grammatical pattern.

Formula I   /kæts i:t bæts/
Formula II   N + V + N
Formula III   Members of the order *chiroptera* are sometimes devoured by members of the species *felis domesticus*

The formulae I, II and III represent *cats eat bats* at three different levels:

Formula I, the phonemic transcription, is a shorthand rendering of *sound-features*, limited to basic contrastive units; a phonetic transcription would of course give more detail.

Formula II represents the *grammatical pattern*, noun–verb–noun. (A more general formula can be written for this particular pattern, but N + V + N is enough for our present purposes.) Note that the formula N + V + N describes an infinite number of possible sentences which may share nothing except intonation with the sound-pattern of *cats eat bats*. *Children drive oxen*, for instance, or *larvae devour algae* are grammatically identical with *cats eat bats*, but constitute two quite different arrangements of phonemes. We shall write the more general formula in § 5.4.

Formula III is an attempt at rendering the *lexical* meaning of *cats eat bats*. It is quite distinct both from the sound-sequence represented by Formula I and from the grammatical pattern represented by Formula II; it does not share arrangements of phonemes with Formula I or arrangements of words with Formula II.

This demonstrates a point that was made in a preliminary way in Chapter One: that we can set up descriptions for three quite distinct levels of language: the level of sound-features, the level of grammatical patterns, and the level of lexical meanings. In practice, no doubt, each level depends on the level below it: we cannot make a grammatical sentence without using sounds, or their equivalents in script, and we do not as a rule signal lexical meanings without using grammatical patterns to 'carry' them, though pictures, of course, convey some kinds of meaning without having any fixed or particular equivalents in writing or speech.

There is another way of showing the independence of grammatical pattern and lexical meaning. If *scranlets oggle hoggards* is an English sentence, its grammatical pattern is the same as that of *cats eat bats*, and without knowing the meaning of *scranlet*, *oggle* or *hoggard*, we can draw certain conclusions purely from its grammatical pattern: e.g. that there was more than one scranlet and more than one hoggard, or that scranlets were capable of oggling and hoggards of being oggled. The pattern itself, in other words, is meaningful: we have returned at this point to the distinction between grammatical and lexical meanings which was introduced in Chapter One.

5.2.   Jabberwocky

This distinction can be shown in more detail from the first stanza of Lewis Carroll's *Jabberwocky*:

> 'Twas brillig, and the slithy toves
> Did gyre and gimble in the wabe;
> All mimsy were the borogoves,
> And the mome raths outgrabe.
> > (*Alice Through the Looking-Glass*,
> > Chapter One).

This remarkable passage consists of two clearly contrasted kinds of material.

On the one hand are the non-English items which had later to be explained to Alice by Humpty Dumpty: '*Brillig* means four o'clock in the afternoon – the time when you begin broiling things for dinner. . . . *Outgribing* is something between bellowing and whistling, with a kind of a sneeze in the middle.' Humpty Dumpty was clearly a phonologist as well as a lexicographer.

On the other hand, we have a familiar set of sentence-framework, which we can exhibit by striking out all the 'Looking-Glass' words:

> 'Twas – –   and the   – y   – s
> Did – and – – in the –;
> All – – were the – – – s,
> And the   – – s   out – .

The lexical items, then, are all those which have to be explained by Humpty Dumpty: the grammatical framework, one might say, is what is left when these are taken away. In point of fact, however, as I indicated in Chapter One, *every* item in a sentence contributes something to its grammatical structure, and the 'Looking-Glass' words in *Jabberwocky* all have grammatical functions.

In nearly all cases, we can describe these grammatical functions without having to look up Humpty Dumpty's explanations of the words. *Toves*, for instance, is clearly a plural noun: it is marked as such in several different ways. It has, in the first place, one of the characteristic plural suffixes, $/z/$; this suffix might also mark a verb, as in **he* *toves there*, but this possibility is ruled out by the position of *toves* in front of *did*: **he toves did* is most unlikely to be modern English. Thirdly, *toves* stands last in the sequence *the slithy toves*, which we can parallel with *the jolly boys* or *the smelly dogs*; such a position, as we shall see, is one characteristically held by nouns in English.

The lexical meaning of *toves* is explained later by Humpty Dumpty. 'Well, *toves* are something like badgers – they're something like lizards – and they're something like corkscrews.' Notice that we have not used any of this information in establishing that *toves* is a noun. We have used only clues of form and environment – the ending in /z/ and the relation of *toves* to *did* and to *the slithy*. You may care to work out the status of the remaining Looking-Glass words in the stanza, using clues of the same kind: answers are suggested in Appendix B.

Consider meanwhile *why* it is important to identify *toves* as a noun. Imagine it as a 'real' word: now a real word is of no value to you unless you know how to use it. In order to be able to use *toves* one would need to know whether the proper patterns for it were patterns like *he toves there*; *John toves on Sundays*, or patterns like *the jolly toves*; *we hope to see some toves*. (Both kinds of pattern might, of course, be possible: we can, for instance, say *he plays there* as well as *we hope to see some plays*.)

5.3. The subject

The grammatical status of an item is thus of great practical importance: it may not matter very much whether we can label it as noun or verb, or something else, but it matters a great deal that we should be able, as it were, to steer it through the complex patterns of speech.

If we lose the clue to the pattern, we shall lose the meaning too; this sometimes happens with a newspaper headline such as:

GENERAL MASTERS CHEATS

in which the signals that would establish the pattern for us have been cut out by the editor to save space, so that we have no means of telling whether the meaning is that a general has got the better of people who tried to defraud him, or whether it is that General Masters is himself a fraud.

The problem will fall away if we can decide what the basic components or 'constituent' parts of the headline are; whether it splits up as:

	(1) General	(2) masters cheats
or as:	(1) General Masters	(2) cheats

In either case, we shall have to divide the headline into two parts, which I have labelled (1) and (2). Two such parts are the principal components of a very large number of English sentences, though not, of course, of all the possible sentences of English.

The traditional names for these parts are *Subject* and *Predicate*. It is important to realize from the outset that subject and predicate are words or groups of words which are related by grammatical signals, and that their grammatical relationship does not necessarily parallel the relationship of their referents in the external or non-linguistic world.

Perhaps I can clarify this point with an example. Suppose that we have to report a particular set of facts: for example, that a visiting ambassador has given an apple to an ape in the zoo. In this situation we have about six different items: the visit, the ambassador, the giving, the apple, the zoo and the ape. In our sentence reporting the incident, any one of these may stand as subject: we have a choice between:

(1) The visiting ambassador gave an apple to the ape at the zoo.
(2) An ape at the zoo was given an apple by the visiting ambassador.
(3) An apple was given by the visiting ambassador to an ape at the zoo.
(4) The ambassador's visit was the occasion of the gift of an apple to an ape at the zoo.
(5) The zoo was the scene of the gift of an apple by the visiting ambassador to an ape.
(6) The gift of an apple to an ape by the visiting ambassador took place at the zoo.

Although each of our six sentences throws the emphasis on a different component of the real-life situation, all six describe the same set of events: their referential meanings, if not identical, are very similar. The six different arrangements of subject and predicate show again the independence of the patterns of grammar from the patterns of life.

It is important not to pretend that life and language are more closely parallel than they really are. It happens that, in a great many English sentences, the grammatical subject represents the actor or 'performer' in the external world, as in *John eats fish*, and the verb the action that he performs, so that we tend to equate grammatical subject with real-life 'actor', 'doer' or 'performer'. This equation, however, does not hold good: *subject* in grammar, is simply the name for a particular component of a sentence, which we recognize in English mainly by its position in the sentence and by certain formal marks that link it with the verb.

The subjects of our six sentences above range in length from two words (*the zoo*) to twelve (*the gift of an apple to an ape by the visiting ambassador*). The subjects of English sentences vary very considerably in length and complexity: a subject may be a single noun or pronoun, or a sequence longer and more complicated than any of those shown above. It will, however, contain a noun or nominal element of some kind: e.g. in 'Going overseas is exciting', the principal component of the subject, *going overseas*, is the verbal noun *going*.

5.4. Sentence-components

The structure of predicates is normally more complex than that of subjects. We can illustrate this by expanding the story of General Masters:

Subject	Predicate
1. General Masters	cheats
2. General Masters	cheats the butcher
3. General Masters	cheats the butcher regularly
4. General Masters	cheats regularly

In the first of our examples, we have the simplest type of predicate, consisting of a single verb. Just as the principal component of a subject is normally a noun, so the principal component of a predicate in English is normally a verb: for our purpose, indeed, it will be the presence of the verb that identifies the predicate. We shall call this verb-element the *predicator*; we shall need this term in addition to the customary *verb*. A verb is a word; a predicator is a sentence-component. Just as the subject may consist of a single word or of a relatively complex sequence, so may the predicator, as in:

Subject	Predicator
General Masters	cheats
General Masters	is cheating
General Masters	may have cheated
General Masters	may have been cheating.

Just as the Subject, as shown in § 5.3, may consist of a single noun or a relatively long and complex sequence, so may the Predicator consist of a single verb or of a relatively long and complex verb-cluster. We shall later (§ 6.13) consider how such verb-clusters are built up.

The nucleus of an English sentence is normally but not always (§ 7.1) a subject-predicator structure. A third basic sentence component appears in our second example:

Subject	Predicator	Complement
General Masters	cheats	the butcher

99

Here *the butcher* serves as a *complement* or 'completing element'. The role of a complement in sentence-structure may be clearer if we choose a predicator other than *cheats*, as in

Subject	Predicator	Complement
The general	masters	the cheats
The ambassador	is giving	an apple to the ape.

The importance of the complement in the structure becomes clear if we cut the first of these sentences to 'The general masters . . .' or the second to 'The ambassador is giving . . .'. Both are now incomplete, since *masters* and *gives* (in the sense of giving a gift) are both verbs which, in the dialect of English with which we are concerned, normally require complements if they are to form utterances which are grammatically complete. Other verbs, e.g. *sing* or *cheat*, may be used either with complements ('They sing songs'; 'He cheats the butcher') or without them ('They sing'; 'He cheats').

Complements, as we shall see in Chapter Seven, may take many different forms.

A fourth type of component appears in:

Subject	Predicator	Complement	Adjunct
General Masters	cheats	the butcher	regularly

Our fourth component, *regularly*, is called an *adjunct* because it is 'added' or 'tacked on' to the original structure: it does not have the 'completing' function of a complement. The distinction of adjunct and complement may be clearer if we change the order of the elements: 'Regularly, General Masters cheats the butcher' (shifting the adjunct) preserves the original meaning, but 'The butcher General Masters cheats regularly', though it might still be English, is part of an altogether different structure with a distinctly different meaning.

The special status of an adjunct appears again if we re-write our original sentence as:

Evidently General Masters cheats.

There are now three distinct parts: '(1) Evidently; (2) General Masters; (3) cheats.' In 'General Masters' we recognize the subject, as before, and in 'cheats' the predicator; *evidently*, however, does not seem to be a part of either. 'Evidently General Masters' does not make sense without a radical change of pitch-patterning, which would transform the utterance to 'Evidently, General Masters.' 'Evidently cheats' is also an unlikely combination. *Evidently*, then, does not relate solely to 'General Masters' or solely to 'cheats': its relationship is to the rest of the sentence as a whole. Such a component is sometimes called a *sentence modifier* (Roberts, 1962); this term shows its function very clearly, though *adjunct* is preferable as being shorter.

We have now established the four principal components of an English sentence: their normal order, as in *General Masters cheats the butcher regularly* is Subject, Predicator, Complement, Adjunct (SPCA) and the nucleus of the structure is evidently SP (he cheats). Sentences without a predicator (e.g. *Waiter!* or *Quickly!*) are possible in English, but the SP structure is undoubtedly our favourite sentence-form. Complement or Adjunct may or may not be present: we may thus have *He cheats the butcher* (SPC) or *He cheats regularly* (SPA); moreover, each position may be taken by a single word: *Masters cheats me regularly* (SPCA) or by a group of some complexity:

Subject:	The General experienced in the ways of the world
Predicator:	may have been cheating
Complement:	the presumptuous young butcher
Adjunct:	since 8 a.m. on the fifteenth of June, 1965.

5.5. Immediate constituents

The analysis of a sentence depends largely upon the notion of *cuts*: we picture the sentence divided or 'cut' into its constituent parts. Often, though of course not always, our first cut will divide the sentence into *two* basic components, as in:

(1) General Masters   (2) cheats the butcher.

(1) Evidently   (2) General Masters cheats the butcher.

Our initial problem with GENERAL MASTERS CHEATS was that the sentence (like COLONELS MAN PUMPS) does not readily fall apart into two components – or rather that it may fall apart in either of two different ways.

The two parts into which a great many sentences, groups or words can be cut are known as their *immediate constituents* (frequently abbreviated as I.C.s): roughly speaking, the immediate constituents of anything are the components into which it can most readily be split; thus, the immediate constituents of a can of tomato soup are the tomato soup and the can. Most people would probably agree that the immediate constituents of the word *pegs* are (1) *peg* and (2) -s, or in phonemic terms, /peg/ plus /z/. (See § 6.5.) Similarly, for:

> *The visiting ambassador is giving an apple to an ape,*

most native speakers of English are likely to agree that the 'natural' cutting point falls between 'ambassador' and 'is', i.e. between Subject and Predicator. Why this is so is not very easy to explain, though in the first place *the visiting ambassador* is likely to form a tone group; in most people's speech, a new tone group would probably begin at *is*. Secondly, the two units resulting from our cut: (1) *the visiting ambassador* and (2) *is giving an apple to an ape*, are both felt to be grammatically viable: in other words, *the visiting ambassador* can correlate with a large number of potential predicates: *is having dinner*; *has interviewed the Queen*; *is unfortunately drunk*. Similarly, a large number of different subjects: *The King*; *The bartender*; *Mr Jones*; can readily be fitted to 'is giving an apple to an ape'.

If we made the cut at any other point we should be less likely to fit in with the pitch-pattern of the sentence, and less likely to arrive at two equally viable components. If, for instance, we cut after *the*, we should be breaking a tone group, and we should also be left with one very viable component, namely *the*, and one, namely *visiting ambassador is giving an apple to an ape*, which would not correlate at all readily with components other than *the* or items like it.

Very often, our cut for the immediate constituents of a sentence will fall between Subject and Predicator, or between the Adjunct and the rest. Immediate Constituents, however, must not be confused with Subject, Predicator, Complement and Adjunct (SPCA). A cut for immediate constituents normally divides a structure into *two*: thus for (1) *General Masters* (2) *cheats the butcher* the immediate constituents are (1) S (2) PC. For (1) *Evidently* (2) *General Masters cheats the butcher* the immediate constituents were (1) A (2) SPC.

In special cases, which lie beyond the scope of this text, a particular structure might have three I.C.s instead of two: the notion of I.C.s, however, is most useful when one is able to make single cuts, the key question being 'Into which *two* parts, if any, does this structure most readily fall apart?'

An immediate constituent of a given structure may, of course, have immediate constituents of its own. Thus, having cut *Cats eat bats* as (1) *Cats* and (2) *eats bats* we can divide each of these I.C.s:

> *Cats* as (1) *cat* and (2) *-s*;
> *Eat bats* as (1) *eat* and (2) *bats*.

Bats could in turn be resolved into (1) *bat* and (2) *-s*. Having reached this point, one cannot readily break down the structures any further; *cat*, for instance, cannot be broken up into smaller meaningful components, and is thus sometimes called an 'ultimate' constituent. Notice that each cut in this sequence has yielded two constituents only:

Cats		eat		bats	
cats		eat		bats	
		eat		bats	
Cat	-s	eat	bat		-s

The classical statement of the principle of immediate constituents is in Bloomfield's *Language* (1933). Cutting for immediate constituents is probably an art rather than a scientific procedure: those intending to master it should consult Gleason (1961). We shall need the notion of immediate constituents only occasionally: wherever possible, we shall, of course, justify our cuts by means of an objective test.

5.6. Heads and modifiers

One such test will be to find out the grammatical correlations of which a given item is capable. For instance, in:

(S) *An ape at the zoo* (P) *was given* (C) *an apple,*

the immediate constituents of the subject, *an ape at the zoo*, are (1) *an ape* and (2) *at the zoo*; each of these will readily combine with other items, and no other cut will give us such viable constituents. *An ape*, the first of our two constituents, will also correlate with the predicator ('an ape was given . . .'); this is not true of our second constituent, *at the zoo*. We cannot say **at the zoo was given*, and we cannot cut at any other point in the subject to extract an item that will correlate with the rest of the sentence, unless we set up the rather improbable statement: *the zoo was given an apple.*

This illustrates two useful points:

(i)   In a subject consisting of several words, one word will normally (but not invariably) act as *head* and show concord (§ 5.9) with the verb, as does 'ape' in our sample sentence. The remaining component is called a modifier: the modifier in our example is 'at the zoo'. The chief grammatical property of a head is that it can function on its own; *an ape* in our sample sentence can stand alone as subject. In formal terms, the head is an item which can by itself carry out the grammatical functions of the group to which it belongs.

103   H

(ii) The second point is that there are usually formal signals that enable us to identify the head. We can illustrate these rather clearly by adjusting one of our sentences from § 5.3:

(S) The gift of an apple to an ape by the visiting ambassador
(P) is being made at the zoo.

Here the head of the subject is *The gift*: its status as head is signalled partly by the fact that all the other nouns in the subject are in *prepositional groups*: 'of an apple', 'to an ape', 'by the visiting ambassador'. We have learned from an early age that nouns in groups like these, which begin with a preposition, never function as subjects. Each group, however, can be regarded as a modifier of the head: it adds to the meaning but it is a subordinate rather than a principal component of the sentence, as is clear from the fact that it can be removed without destroying the structure. *At the zoo* functions in a rather similar way as a modifier of *is being made*.

A headed group can play the part of complement as well as that of subject, as happens in the sentence:

The weary soldier saluted the man in the grey jacket.

Here the subject is the group *the weary soldier*, with *soldier* as head; the complement is the group *the man in the grey jacket*, headed by *man*. We can reduce the sentence to the two heads on either side of the verb: '*The soldier saluted the man.*'

Modifiers can take many different forms. *Weary*, in 'the weary soldier' is a one-word modifier; *in the grey jacket* is a modifier consisting of a prepositional group. In the sequence *a large helping of Christmas pudding*, the headword is *helping*: this is preceded by a one-word modifier, *large*, and followed by a modifier consisting of the prepositional group *of Christmas pudding*. This illustrates how one-word modifiers tend to precede their heads, while groups acting as modifiers tend to follow them.

Nearly all the heads in our examples so far have been nouns. A verb, however, may act as head, as in *He runs fast*, in which the immediate constituents of the predicate are *runs* and *fast* with *runs* as head. In the commonest types of verbal groups, however – *is running*, *has run*, *will be running*, etc. – there is not as a rule a separable head which can be substituted for the group as a whole. Such verbal groups will be discussed in § 6.13.4.

Modification is one of the most important relationships of English grammar, and takes many different forms:

(i)   One word may modify another (as in *green ginger*, *telephone box*, *big fire*, or *Pete's place*);
(ii) A group may modify a word, as in *an ape at the zoo*; or

(iii) A group may modify another group, as in *stone cold coffee in filthy cups*, of which the immediate constituents are (1) *stone cold coffee* and (2) *in filthy cups*, the head of the entire structure being *coffee*.

It will be seen that the relationship of modifier and head is very similar to that of an adjunct and an SP or SPC grouping: a modifier, indeed, is an adjunct of a special type. The difference is that an adjunct functions in relation to an SP or SPC grouping, a modifier in relation to a head: thus, in 'Evidently it was an ape at the zoo', *evidently* is an adjunct in the sequence '(A) Evidently (S) it (P) was (C) an ape at the zoo', in which *an ape* is the head of the complement: its status as head is shown by our being able to cut the sentence to 'Evidently it was an ape.'

5.7. Order

The order of elements is one of the basic signals of English grammar.

Within the word, indeed, the order of elements is fixed: we cannot, for instance, transpose syllables to form *long-be from *belong*. Certain groupings also follow a fixed order: *a* and *the*, for instance, invariably precede their nouns, and we cannot re-arrange a prepositional group, so as to obtain, say, *zoo at the from *at the zoo*.

Again, the order of subject and predicator distinguishes questions from statements: 'They have', for instance, from 'Have they?' Order, again, is often one of the signals distinguishing a statement from a command: contrast ˡᴬ You   ˡeat up your   ˡDINner   (statement, with tonic on *dinner*) with   ˡEAT up your   ˡdinner (command, with tonic on *eat*).

In English, a subject normally precedes its predicator in a statement and follows it in a question (*John eats fish. Does Victor?*) In a number of statement-patterns, however, the subject follows the predicator: the commonest of these is the *there*-pattern: *There are four cats up the tree*: see § 7.6. Others are such constructions as: 'Great was their astonishment' (Jespersen, 1924); or: 'Up goes the rocket.' In these sentences we identify *their astonishment* and *the rocket* as subjects because the items in the normal subject-position, namely *great* and *up*, do not as a rule function as subjects, and because elsewhere in the sentence we have forms that normally do.

As shown in § 5.6, single-word modifiers normally precede their heads, group modifiers follow them. (For adverb positions, see § 6.12 and §7.3). For single-word modifiers, there are some rather complex conventions of precedence: we say, for instance, *a lazy old Siamese cat*, not **a Siamese old lazy cat*. Generally speaking, the modifier felt to be most intimately related to the head comes nearest to it: thus,

Siamese might here be regarded as the most specific modifier of *cat* and *lazy* as the most general one. Normally the modifier which one wishes to emphasize will stand first: thus, *a horrible old man* is a more probable sequence than *an old horrible man*, though both are possible.

5.8. Markers

Since word-order, though very important as a signal, is not rigidly fixed, we need special devices to mark the functions of items in a sentence. We can clear the ambiguity of GENERAL MASTERS CHEATS by inserting *the*: 'The General masters the cheats.' C. C. Fries (1957) illustrates a similar point with the telegram: *Ship sails today*. This has two quite different possible meanings: 'Ship the sails today' (i.e. bring them on board) or: 'The ship sails today.' *Ship* in the first case is a verb; in the second it is a noun, and the word *the*, which we have inserted to clear the ambiguity, does this because it marks the status of *ship* and *sails*. Marking the status, moreover, is not simply a matter of sticking a grammatical label on a word: status as noun or verb, subject or predicator, determines the work of the word in the sentence, and is thus an essential element of meaning.

Here, as elsewhere, *the* functions primarily as a *marker*: an item that shows the status or function of some other item. *The* and *a* are typical markers of nouns: they are often called *determiners* because they are members of a small class of words which help to 'determine' or mark off the status of other words. In telegrams and newspaper headlines the omission of markers frequently causes ambiguity, as in the headlines: *Builders Strike Leader*, *Showbusiness Swings Left* and *Lord Rakes Leaves*.

Affixes, i.e. elements 'affixed' or 'tacked on' to words, may also act as markers. The /z/ of *toves* and *sails* is an example: note, however, that this does not by itself determine the status of either word as noun or verb, though it reduces the probability of their being either adverbs or adjectives. In the same way /ɪd/ is a marker of such a word as *reported*, but the word in its marked form can nevertheless function in such radically different patterns as: *He reported the accident*, and: *The reported outbreak has not in fact taken place*.

This brings me to a difference of some practical importance between the grammar of English and that of certain other languages. Compare, for instance, the Latin word *navigabamus* and the English word *sailing*. Both words are 'marked', i.e. both consist of a 'radical' form plus a marker. The Latin word consists of *naviga-* plus the marker *-bamus* (this simplifies its actual structure, but the simplification does not matter at this stage). Similarly the English word consists of *sail-* plus *-ing*. At this point, the grammatical similarity ends. *Navigabamus* means *we were sailing*: its grammatical status is virtually fixed by the marker *-bamus*. In the English translation, the meaning of this marker has to be distributed over three separate elements: *we*, *were* and *-ing*. *Sailing* approximates to only part of the meaning of *navigabamus*, and can probably enter into a greater range of grammatical patterns: *We are sailing today*; *We saw them sailing past*; *A sailing ship*; *The sailing was cancelled*.

Hence the Latin marker *-bamus* and the English marker *-ing* work in very different ways, which typify a general difference between the languages. In classical Latin, a word tends to carry a rather specific set of labels, so that looking at a word like *navigabamus* we can recognize it as a verb from its form alone. In English, there are fewer markers and they are much less specific, so that a form like *sails*, although marked, may be noun or verb with about equal probability. In English, then, we have often to look beyond the word to its environment in the sentence or the group, to decide its grammatical status or function.

This does not alter the importance of the contrast between marked and unmarked forms. Among nouns, we have the contrast of 'marked' *dogs* with unmarked *dog*; among adjectives that of unmarked *great* with marked *greater* and *greatest*; among verbs that of unmarked *sail* with marked *sails, sailed, sailing*. Although several of these groupings, such as the one beginning with *sail*, consist of more than two items, it is often helpful to think of them as sets of two-way contrasts; e.g. *sail – sails*; *sail – sailed*, etc. A two-way contrast – e.g. that of the dot and dash in Morse, or that of zero and one in an electronic computer – is an exceptionally convenient signalling device. In oppositions like these, we often find one member regarded as more neutral or normal than the other (Quirk, 1959); thus, *sail* might be regarded as the 'base', 'neutral' or 'zero' form, *sails, sailed* and *sailing* as forms marked for special purposes. We shall consider this point again in Chapter Six.

5.9. Concord

A particularly important function of certain markers is to help to show *concord*, i.e. the relationship of subject and predicator – or, more precisely, of the head of the subject with the verb, as in: 'An *ape* at the zoo *was* given an apple.' One of the clues that enables us to recognize a subject is that of its concord with the verb, though this normally appears only when we are using the present tense or the verb *to be*.

Nearly all English verbs have two present-tense forms, e.g. *do* and *does, come* and *comes*; the verb *to be*, incidentally, has in addition two past-tense forms, *was* and *were*. Each of these two forms patterns with a different group of subjects. Forms like *comes*, which we shall call *third-singular* forms, pattern with the pronouns *he, she, it*, or their grammatical equivalents; forms like *come* pattern with all other types of subject. For the moment we can represent this pattern informally as follows:

TABLE OF CONCORDS

SUBJECTS	VERBS			
	Be		Other Verbs	
	Present	Past	Present	Past
I	am	was	do	did
He, she, it, Mr Brown, the cat, the car	is		does	
We, you, they, The Browns, the cats, the cars	are	were	do	

The marks of concord reinforce other signals to show the status of the subject. Thus in 'The apes at the Pretoria zoo are particularly well-behaved', the subject, *the apes at the Pretoria zoo*, contains three different nouns: *apes, Pretoria*, and *zoo*. The head of the subject, *apes*, is in concord with the verb *are*; the subordinate status of the nouns *Pretoria* and *zoo* is also shown by their position in the prepositional group introduced by *at*.

English concords present special difficulties to learners whose home languages lack concord or use concords of non-English kinds. Thus in Afrikaans the same form of the verb will pattern with *all* subjects: the verb *is*, for example, unlike English *is*, patterns with *ek, jy, hy, ons* (I, you, he, us), and *was*, unlike English *was*, with all personal-pronoun subjects in the same way. In teaching English to Afrikaans-speaking pupils, there is something to be said for establishing habits of concord with *is* and *are* before any other forms of the verb are taught. (See § 6.13.6.)

5.10. Frames

'The grammar of a language', writes C. C. Fries (1957), 'consists of the devices that signal structural meanings.' It is difficult to put the notion of a 'structural' or grammatical meaning into words, but it should at this point be clear that the contrasts in English of noun and verb, or of question and statement, are primarily matters of 'structural' meaning. The 'devices' that signal meanings of this kind in English are very varied; among them we have already noted rhythm, pitch-pattern, word-order, 'grammatical' words like *the* and *do,* and affixes like /z/. In a single pattern, such as *Do cats eat bats?* one may find devices of all five kinds working together.

Since a grammatical pattern in English is seldom established by a single device, such as a marker, it may be helpful to regard English grammar not so much as a collection of classified items – (so many pitch-patterns, so many affixes, so many function-words, arranged as follows . . .) – but as a system of 'bonds' or 'correlations' between items and patterns. For instance given the pattern

Do —— eat bats?

we have the choice, in English, of a large number of possible items to complete the question: *fish, people, cats, small Siamese cats,* etc. Any one of these will correlate with the rest of the pattern, and the pattern is incomplete without some item of this kind. On the other hand, a large number of items do not complete the question: *fishing, come here, can't,* etc., and do not accordingly correlate with the pattern. What establishes the pattern, one might say, is the capacity of different items for correlating within it.

This basic notion of correlation provides us with an extremely useful tool for grammatical analysis. One of the purposes of grammar is to provide a meaningful classification of grammatical features, and such a *frame* as *Do —— eat bats?* may be a useful classifying tool. All the items that fit the blank and therefore correlate with the pattern will have some grammatical property in common: they will in fact be items of the type which we have provisionally designated S.

Frames are remarkably useful to the grammarian, but they also have their limitations. Such a frame as *Do —— eat bats?* is no more than a sequence of words with a blank in it. Its usefulness will depend very considerably on the frequency in English of sequences of this kind, and on the range of possibilities for filling the blank. *Do cats eat ——?,* for instance, is in some ways a less useful test frame than *Do —— eat bats?* because in the first case there are two possible kinds of filler: on the one hand, items like *bats* or *fish,* and on the other, items like *greedily* or *under the table.*

Furthermore, with such a frame as *Do —— eat bats?* one may wonder whether such items as *motor-cars* or *algebraic formulae* can be counted among possible fillers or not. This is rather difficult to decide.

On one view of the matter, a verb like *eat* implies an animate subject, e.g. a noun denoting some living creature to do the eating: on the other hand, such sequences as *This month's bills have simply eaten up my salary* are common enough in speech, and such sequences as *this sorrow eats my heart* are common enough in poetry.

We shall return in Chapter Six to the uses of frames. For the moment, provided that the general contrast of grammatical consistency with lexical and 'everyday' probabilities is clear, we need not linger to decide whether such sequences as Noam Chomsky's now famous sentence:

> *'Colourless green ideas sleep furiously'*

are grammatical or not.

5.11. Grammar and the child

The process of learning to produce connected speech is obviously one of the most important of all our early experiences. For a long time, of course, a very small child can produce non-linguistic noises only, and his first 'linguistic' ventures are likely to be attempts at single words. The next stage is often that of putting words together in pairs, and it is interesting that even during this very early phase in the long process of becoming articulate, small children appear to use 'grammatical' frames of a simple kind.

Braine (1963) reports a study of the speech of three small children aged 19–20 months. Each child had a small vocabulary of single words, which he was just beginning to combine in pairs. At this stage, one might expect the child to have no grammar at all, so that his combinations would be made at random and without regular or recurrent sequences or patterns of words.

Braine, however, found that definite simple patterns were already emerging, though these patterns often did not match those of adult grammar. Counting only the 'spontaneous' utterances of the three children, i.e. those which were not imitations of something that had just been said by an adult, he found regular sets of combinations all beginning with the same words; such as *more car, more cookie, more fish*, or *want baby, want car, want jeep*, or *allgone lettuce, allgone vitamins, allgone egg*. These combinations show the earliest beginnings of grammar; each of them consists of what Braine described as a 'pivotal' word plus one other. The 'pivotal' words, such as *allgone, more* and *want*, are differentiated from the rest of the child's vocabulary by their capacity for correlating with other words and for taking fixed positions. Thus part of the child's linguistic equipment may consist of such a frame as

Allgone ——,

in which *allgone* is a fixed initial element, while the second position is open to any other item in his vocabulary. This shows the beginning of a system of grammatical correlations, and the beginning also of a differentiation of the child's vocabulary into 'structural' items like *allgone* versus 'content' items like *lettuce*. The actual items of vocabulary, of course, vary enormously between different children, but it seems very probable that an elementary grammar of position, based on such frames as *allgone*—— or *want*—— is worked by a good many English-speaking children around the age of two. For children growing up into languages in which position is less important than it is in English, the beginnings of grammar may possibly be rather different.

It is rather depressing to compare the remarkable development of the child's mastery of the grammar of his native language during the first six years of life with his much less spectacular progress later. Between the ages of eighteen months and six years he normally advances from such simple structures as *allgone lettuce* to control of quite long and complex utterances, but twelve years later when he enters the university, we commonly find his teachers complaining that in spite of more than a decade of formal instruction 'he still can't write English and speaks it very badly'.

We cannot explore this problem in any detail here, though it is one that calls for thought. One aspect of it is that of motivation or need: once the basic structures of English are under the child's control, once he is able to communicate fairly effectively in his own way, his motivation to master the subtler conventions of speech and writing is proportionately reduced. Many of his difficulties are likely to arise over writing, and the 'reasons', particularly in the modern world, for learning to write are much less powerful than the reasons for learning to speak. Further, grammar at school is all too often presented in terms of *Thou shalt not*: instead of studying the creative processes of language that make us human, we are confronted with long lists of prohibitions: thou shalt not end with a preposition, thou shalt not confuse *shall* and *will* (§ 6.13.5), thou shalt not write sentences without verbs. Since many of these prohibitions bear no relation to the facts of educated speech, it is not surprising that grammar is a discredited study.

5.12.   The meaning of grammar

Braine's investigation is a study of one of the most fundamental aspects of grammar: the evolution of the habits and skills which eventually give us control of connected speech. It is on this 'creative' or 'generative' aspect of grammar that recent grammatical studies have tended increasingly to focus.

The word *grammar*, like many others, has meanings which have varied very considerably with time and place. Like the word *anatomy*, it has had two main senses. 'Anatomy' can refer either to the actual structures of human and other bodies ('Frogs have a complex anatomy') or to textbook descriptions of these structures ('Please lend me your Gray's *Anatomy* tonight'). 'Grammar', in the same way, may mean the actual structure of a language, or a description of that structure such as the *Grammar of American English* of C. C. Fries. Recently a third meaning, that of grammar as habit or skill, has become increasingly common: in this sense of the word, 'grammar' might be called the 'sentence-producing capacity' of man. ('Everybody has a grammar': Whitehall, 1956.)

Since grammatical patterns quite obviously depend on grammatical skills, it is this third aspect of grammar that is the most fundamental, and if we rank the three aspects of 'grammar' according to their practical importance, the order will be:

    i   Grammar as habits or skills;
   ii   Grammar as patterns in a language;
  iii   Grammar as description.

The separation of aspects i and ii, however, is somewhat artificial. On a simple view of the matter, the child learns the patterns by hearing them in the speech of others. On a more considered view, he learns the patterns not only because he hears them, but because he has a capacity for speech: cats and dogs who hear the patterns all day are never able to use them as human children do. We learn grammar, accordingly, neither from without nor from within, but by a complex interaction between our capacity for language and the 'linguistic behaviour' of other people.

In schools, however, grammar tends to be regarded as a set of rules to which 'current' English must conform. This notion is based on a misunderstanding of the 'rules' of English; there are certainly rules, but the only valid ones are those which emerge from an adequate description of usage; there is no guarantee that rules formulated *a priori* by grammarians will fit the patterns of actual speech and writing. And, as was pointed out in Chapter One, where educated usage and the 'rules' are in conflict, the 'rules' must give way.

We must, accordingly, distinguish rather carefully between rules (such as the one which forbids us to end a sentence with a preposition) which are the inventions of grammarians, and rules (such as the one prohibiting such constructions as *he do*) which undoubtedly reflect the established patterns of English speech. It is also important to remember that spoken and written English are organized in rather different ways (see § 4.1).

It seems probable, however, that as we progress in the study of language, the 'rules' of grammar may appear less complicated than they do at present. Nearly all human beings manage to learn one language, and enormous numbers learn two languages or more; most of us, moreover, can handle many of the basic patterns of the grammar of our native language by the time that we are five or six. This suggests either that language is simpler, or that people are more intelligent, than one is generally led to believe: in either case there is hope for increasing clarity in our understanding of the languages by which we live.

Not long ago, it was customary to regard grammar as the general study of linguistic form, covering phonology as well as sentence-structure, together with a good deal of what would now be regarded as lexical or semantic material. Thus Grattan and Gurrey (1925) define the grammar of a language as 'a scientific record of the actual phenomena of that language, written and spoken'. More recent writers tend to separate the levels of phonology, grammar and lexis: as I have shown in § 5.1, it is often helpful to treat grammar as a level of language in some ways independent both of sound and of lexical meaning.

5.13. Grammar and the teacher

Sixty or seventy years ago it was fairly generally assumed that the first step in learning a language was to make a thorough study of its grammar; thus Nesfield (1897) quotes the London Matriculation Directory for that year on the scope of the English Language papers: 'The first essential of a sound and complete preparation will be a thorough grounding in the elements of English grammar.' If we define grammar as the complex of sentence-producing skills, this obviously still holds good: if, however, we regard it as consisting primarily of parsing and analysis, the proposition is more doubtful.

In the teaching of English as a *first* language, the study of formal grammar is increasingly giving way to work on composition and comprehension; in the teaching of English as a second language, 'formal grammar' is similarly giving way to exercises designed to build up the skills of reception and production: listening, speaking, reading and writing.

We cannot, however, design exercises that will establish the practical language skills, particularly those of speech, without ourselves understanding the patterns of English. The value to the pupil of

113

the study of descriptive grammar is at present rather uncertain: but there can be little doubt of its importance to the teacher. A simple illustration of this, which I owe to Professor L. W. Lanham, is the teaching of the pattern: *This is my* . . . In many African elementary schools, this pattern is taught quite mechanically: the child is able to say, *This is my head*, but though he has a further vocabulary of simple words like *pen*, *hand*, and *hat*, he is unable to use them in this pattern; i.e. he cannot say, *This is my hat.* All that he has been taught is to memorize a sentence: he has not learned to use *This is my* . . . as a pattern or frame for other items in his vocabulary, so that what he has been taught remains unproductive and of no practical value.

This is a very simple case of the neglect of the elementary principle of correlation: that one should teach not only pattern sentences, but also the range of items that fit the patterns, so that the pattern becomes not simply a memorized sentence but a creative element in the language of the child.

The most serious practical problems are those of countries in which the teaching of English in elementary schools has to be left to teachers who know very little English themselves and have very little opportunity of studying it. In this situation, theoretical accounts of English structure will be of no value at all: what the teacher is most likely to need is an extremely detailed programme which outlines for him *every lesson in full.* Elementary English courses of this kind are now being designed in fairly large numbers. As the teacher himself improves his command of English, he will be in a better position to introduce variations of his own, but this will take time. Meanwhile there is little doubt that English syllabuses for African primary schools are often far too sketchy and lacking in detail to be of much value either to the teacher or to his pupils.

In the teaching of English as a second language to pupils of any particular language group, one is likely to find, just as one does with the sound-systems, that the major points of difficulty are those at which there is a difference between the grammatical patterns of English and those of the home language of the pupils. Afrikaans and English, for instance, frequently differ on the position of the verb, so that an Afrikaans-speaking person may be inclined to say 'what best is', instead of 'what is best', because he carries over into English the pattern of his home language: 'wat (die) beste is.' English, again, has the distinction of 'I *come*' but 'he *comes*' where Afrikaans would use the same form of the verb in both frames (*ek kom, hy kom*); consequently Afrikaans-speaking children are apt to have difficulty with this particular pattern of English.

In the teaching of English grammar, then, as with the teaching of the English sound-system, it will be necessary for the teacher:

(a) to know what are the points of interference at which home-language patterns are causing difficulty for the pupil;
(b) to be equipped to deal with each point of interference systematically. To achieve this, as I have indicated, the teacher of English in African primary schools will require carefully programmed materials which he cannot as a rule be expected to design for himself.

The neglect of grammar in the teaching of English to English-speaking classes is mainly, no doubt, a reflection of the shortage of suitable grammars. There is a general feeling that practical grammar, i.e. the control of speech, is not taught in 'grammar' lessons: as I have indicated, the staple of language work in the senior school is not grammar, but composition and comprehension. Most pupils, as a result, are quite unable to discuss the basic patterns of their native language: this neglect of grammar closes, for many of them, a very interesting window on life.

Chapter Six

THE WORD: FORMS AND FUNCTIONS

6.1. The meaning of 'word'

Just as the term *grammar* has several meanings, so has the term *word*. Its commonest meaning – as in 'There are so many words that I can't spell' – is probably 'a group of letters between two spaces'; it will be convenient to call this an *orthographic word*.

As was shown, however, in Chapter One, a particular orthographic word, such as *fire*, may have several different manifestations at each of the principal levels of language. At the level of sound, for instance, we have [faɪə] and [faə]; at the level of grammar, *fire* (noun) and *fire* (verb); at the lexical level, the senses of 'conflagration', 'shoot', 'inspire', 'passion', and several others. Important distinctions of lexical or grammatical function may be reflected in spelling but not in sound (as with *fair* and *fare*) or in sound but not in spelling (as with /sʌm/ and /səm/, for which see § 6.10. Two distinct lexical items, as in 'I *took off* my coat' and 'the aircraft *took off*' may be identical both in sound and spelling; on the other hand, items otherwise identical are sometimes spelled in different ways, particularly on opposite sides of the Atlantic: compare British *axe, traveller, mould, colour* with American *ax, traveler, mold, color*.

The term *word*, then, is one in which many senses meet. Among other things, it may mean:
(i) a *range of sounds*, varying, in all probability, between different dialects, contexts, and individual speakers: e.g. /ænd, ənd, n̩d, n̩/;
(ii) an *orthographic unit*, varying in Modern English with typography and scripts and, unless it is a very recent invention, with a long history of variant spellings behind it;
(iii) a *range of grammatical items*: consider the roles of *round* in: a *round* of golf, a *round* table, he failed to *round* the cape, come *round* tomorrow, he walked *round* the house (Jespersen, 1924);
(iv) a *range of lexical items*: consider the changing referents of *head* in 'off with his *head*'; 'the *head* of the screw broke off'; 'we raised a considerable *head* of steam'; 'he is the *head* of the department'.

We cannot at any of these four levels establish criteria for a watertight definition of *word*. Perhaps the best working description of a word is Bloomfield's 'a minimum free form', i.e. the smallest form that can occur alone as a complete utterance. *Word* is too useful a

116

THE WORD: FORMS AND FUNCTIONS

word to be discarded altogether, and it may serve us well if we use it with full awareness of its many-sidedness. It is important, though, to remember that while *phoneme* is capable of precise definition and scientific treatment, *word* is probably not. In using the term, we must be careful to avoid slipping from one meaning to another, bearing in mind that *word* in different contexts may denote a sound-unit, a unit of spelling, a grammatical item or a lexical item.

A further point, already indicated in § 5.8, is that the scope and function of the word vary very considerably between languages. We have already seen that the word in Latin tends to be *marked* for a particular grammatical function (*navigabamus*) while in English the markers tend to be less restrictive (*sailing*). In modern Chinese, the typical word is likewise a rather short and simple form capable of a considerable range of combinations. Thus the word *shang*, with the general sense of 'above', may function as follows:

Shang: (i)   the 'above' one, i.e. the ruler or the lord;
Shang pien: (ii)   the 'above' side, i.e. the upper side of something;
Shang ma: (iii) to 'above' a horse, i.e. to mount him;
ma shang: (iv)   'horse above', i.e. on the horse.

These four roles of *shang* in Chinese correspond to those of noun, adjective, verb and preposition in English (Bodmer, 1943); the Western distinction of 'parts of speech' does not obtain in the grammar of Chinese. In Eskimo, at the other end of the scale, and in some of the languages of North American Indians, the typical word is much longer and more specific: Bloomfield (1933) cites a single Eskimo form meaning 'I am looking for something suitable for a fishline'; Sapir (1921) cites from the language of the Paiute Indians of south-western Utah a form which he regards as a single word, *wii-to-kuchum-punku-rugäni-yugwi-va-ntü-m(u)*, meaning 'they who are going to sit and cut up with a knife a black cow (or bull)'.

6.2.   Free and bound forms

We can now move on to consider the structure of words in English. At the outset, it is useful to distinguish 'free' forms from 'bound' ones. Consider the components of:

Sail, ride, fly; sailing, riding, flying; sailor, rider, flyer.

These components are of two principal types. /seɪl/, /raɪd/ and /flaɪ/ occur on their own and are therefore *free forms*: /ɪŋ/ as in *sailing*, and /ə/ as in *sailor*, occur only in combination with other forms and are therefore *bound* forms. Notice the two spellings of the marker /ə/ in *sailor* and *rider*. Our nine words contain five basic components: the free forms *sail, ride, fly*, and the bound forms /ɪŋ/ and /ə/. These combine to form the more complex free forms *sailing, riding, flying; sailor, rider, flyer*; each consisting of one free form in combination with one bound form (e.g. /seɪl/ + /ə/).

A free form is sometimes defined as one which is capable of occurring as an utterance on its own, and there is a fairly clear distinction in English between a large number of items, such as *sail*, which can do this, and a smaller but still substantial number, such as the prefixes *un-, im-*, or *non-*, or the suffixes *-s, -ive*, or *-al*, which normally occur only in such combinations as *sails, submissive*, or *rational*. Certain items, however, such as *the*, are not very likely to occur as utterances in isolation, but can nevertheless be regarded as *free* because of their relative mobility in relation to other items. Consider the changing positions of *the* in 'I saw the policeman', 'I saw the big policeman', and 'I saw, unfortunately, the big policeman'. A free form, then, is one which can 'jump about' in a sequence of speech (I owe this metaphor to Mr Paul Walters); contrast the fixed position of *-ing* in relation to *sail* in 'the sailing ship'; 'a later sailing'; or 'sailing is over for the winter'. A bound form, nevertheless, as in 'Did you say un- or im-?' or 'I'm feeling a bit anti- tonight', may occasionally be set free in the context of a question or a joke.

Bound forms often function as markers (§ 5.8), as in the case of /ə/ (*-or*) which marks *sailor* as a noun derived from *sail*. All markers, however, are not bound forms, as has just been shown for *the*, the commonest marker of nouns.

6.3. The morpheme

Sail, -ing, -or and *the* are all examples of the morpheme, the smallest unit of grammatical form; morphemes, as shown above, may be either bound or free. Gleason (1961) describes the morpheme as 'a unit which cannot be divided without destroying or radically altering the meaning'.

We can, of course, break down the morpheme *sail* into the phonemes /s-eɪ-l/, or *-ing* into the phonemes /ɪ-ŋ/, but these phonemes are units of sound, not units of grammar: considered as phonemes, they form only sound-combinations, not combinations of grammatical units. It is important to grasp this distinction: any sizeable segment of speech can be broken down or analysed in two ways:

(a) as a string of sound-units: e.g.

$$\text{cats} = /k/ + /æ/ + /t/ + /s/$$

(b) as a string of grammatical units: e.g.

$$\text{cats} = \{kæt\} + \{s\}$$

Equation (a) presents a sound-pattern; equation (b) a simple grammatical pattern; the curly brackets in (b) are to show that our units here are morphemes, minimum units of grammatical form, not phonemes, minimum contrastive units of sound.

Our two levels of analysis or description must be kept distinct. For instance, /s/, the initial phoneme of *sail*, enters also into the combinations /sʌn, ɑ:sk, pɑ:s/ but it functions in these as a sound-element without any particular grammatical significance. Elsewhere, of course, as in *rocks, cats, rabbits*, we find {s} with a very definite grammatical significance, that of a marker of plurals, but this function of {s} has no connection with its function as a phoneme in *sail*. The diphthong /aɪ/ (phoneme) and the word *I* (morpheme) can be contrasted in much the same way.

The independence of sound-feature and grammatical function can be shown more formally if we use such a frame as:

All —— are worthy animals.

Any one of a large number of words might occupy the blank and all items that fill the blank will have some grammatical feature in common. Among the possible fillers are *cats, dogs, foxes, oxen* and *sheep*. Each of these is 'plural' in meaning and 'correlates' with the plurals *all, are* and *animals*; in each, however, plural status is marked in a different way: in *cats* by /s/, in *dogs* by /z/, in *foxes* by /ɪz/, in *oxen* by /ən/ and in *sheep* by no formal marker at all.

The markers /s/, /z/, /ɪz/ and /ən/ are evidently variant forms (or allomorphs) of the *plural* morpheme, sometimes designated {Z_1}. The subscript $_1$ distinguishes this morpheme from phonetically similar markers with different grammatical functions, such as the /s/ of *cat's* in *the cat's tail*.

Sheep, however, lacks a marker; it is usual in such a case to say that the morpheme *plural* is present in its zero form. We can infer that the word is plural from its relationship with the other plurals in the sentence. A zero form of a morpheme is simply an accounting device: it enables us to write a general formula for all English plurals except for those, like *teeth* from *tooth* and *geese* from *goose*, which are formed by internal vowel-change.

This formula is {B} + {*plural*} in which {B} denotes the *base*, or radical form of the word, and {*plural*} the appropriate form of the plural morpheme – which in certain cases, e.g. *sheep, deer, Japanese*, may be zero. A base is a form which carries the principal component of meaning (as does *dog* in *dogs* or *sail* in *sails*): bases are distinguished from *affixes* or attached elements, such as /z/ in *dogs* or /ə/ in *sailor*. An affix that precedes the base is a *prefix*; one that follows it is a

119   ɪ

suffix. Thus in *overriding*, we have the base *ride*, the prefix *over-* and the suffix *-ing*.

Bases are often, but not invariably, free forms. Affixes are generally bound forms, but may be free ones; in *overriding* the prefix *over-* is a free form, the suffix *-ing* a bound one.

It has already been pointed out that markers which take the same phonetic form may fulfil different grammatical functions (§ 5.8). In such cases, they represent different morphemes. Thus, in:

    (i) He has three dogs
    (ii) That's the dog's dinner
    (iii) He dogs my footsteps

the phoneme /z/ marks the word *dog* (i) as plural noun, (ii) as a 'possessive' form, (iii) as a verb in concord with *he*. /z/ in these three contexts represents three different morphemes, *plural* in (i), *possessive* in (ii), *third-singular* in (iii). For *third-singular* see § 6.13.12. Some texts designate these morphemes (i) $\{Z_1\}$, (ii) $\{Z_2\}$, (iii) $\{Z_3\}$, We shall consider all three in later sections of this chapter.

Note that a morpheme is primarily a grammatical rather than a lexical unit. Morphemes, indeed, may be almost entirely without lexical meaning. The morphemes *a* and *the*, for instance, have been shown to have very definite grammatical functions in English (§ 5.8), but it might be difficult to state their lexical meaning except in obscure philosophical terms. To a lesser degree, this is true of many other function-words, such as *to* in the context *I'm going to sleep*. On the other hand, such morphemes as *dog* and *cat* correspond to lexical items with an obvious referential meaning.

Morphemes vary considerably: in size, in phonetic shape and in grammatical function. Morphemic analysis requires caution. A simple case is that of the bound morpheme /ə/ which we noted in *sailor, rider, flyer*. This is clearly distinct from the free form /ə/, normally spelled *a*, as in 'I'd like /ə/ cup of tea'. A more complex case is that of the status of the word *unit*. At first sight, one is inclined to regard *unit* as a single morpheme. We may be confirmed in this view if we try dividing the word into /ju:/ and /nɪt/: both of these happen to be meaningful items in English, but the meaning of *unit* is in no way a union or combination of theirs. If, on the other hand, we divide the word as /ju:n/ and /ɪt/, we recognize both components in a number of other settings: /j:un/ in *unity, unite, union*: /ɪt/ perhaps in *digit, limit, merit*. We need not here attempt to decide the status of *unit* as one morpheme or two, but we must be cautious in any statements about morpheme boundaries.

A fairly detailed account of analytic procedures is given in Gleason (1961). Here it will be worth noting that:

(i) A morpheme may consist of a single phoneme only, e.g. /s/ or /z/; it may on the other hand be quite extensive: *Honululu*, for instance, considered as an English word, is a single morpheme.

(ii) A morpheme may consist of part of a syllable, as does the /z/ of *dogs*, of a single syllable (as does *dog*) or of more than one syllable (as does *jaguar*). Morpheme and syllable boundaries, in other words, do not coincide.

(iii) It is a mistake to suppose that a morpheme *must* consist of phonemes and that morphemic change can invariably be stated in terms of simple addition of phonemes or groups of phonemes. We have already seen that this is not so in the case of contrasts like *tooth – teeth* and *mouse – mice*, in which the change from singular to plural is not a simple matter of adding a marker to a base. For such cases, it is more convenient to use a notation for a 'replacive' change:

$$\{maɪs\} = \{maʊs\} + \{aʊ \leftarrow aɪ\}$$

where the symbol $\leftarrow$ denotes 'is replaced by' (or 're-write x as y'). Here, of course, it is impossible to make a neat division of *mice* into two phonetic segments, one being the base form and one signalling its plural status.

(iv) In certain languages, a morpheme may be *discontinuous*; thus the Arabic words *Islam* (submission to God), *aslama* (a verb meaning *submit*) and *Muslim* (literally, one who submits) have a common element in the consonant sequence, $s - l - m$, a discontinuous morpheme which enters into a number of different combinations with groups of vowels. Such three-consonant radicals are typical of the Semitic languages: in Egyptian Arabic, for instance, we have *kitab* (book), *je-ktub* (he is writing) and *katab* (he wrote), all with the root $k - t - b$. Hebrew, similarly, has *zaakar* (he remembered), *yizkoor* (he was remembering) and *zikrii* (my remembrance) all with $z - k - r$.

6.4. The forms of markers

Our unconscious mastery of language is clearly shown in our control of the variant forms of markers, even in unfamiliar settings. We can illustrate this with the plurals of three imaginary 'English' words. One of Saki's short stories is about a breakfast food called Filboid Studge; let us suppose that there are several such products on the market, so that we need a plural form for *studge*, and for two other coinages resulting from the popularity of these products: *studgnik*, a studge-eater (on the model of *beatnik* and *sputnik*) and *stog*, a helping of studge.

Most English-speaking people are likely to agree that if these words have plurals, they will be as follows:

121

/stʌdʒ/   /stʌdʒɪz/
/stɒg/   /stɒgz/
/stʌdʒnɪk/   /stʌdʒnɪks/

in which we use the *plural* morpheme, in three different forms or *allomorphs*: /ɪz/, /z/ and /s/. These forms constitute the same morpheme primarily because they enable all three words to perform the same grammatical function; e.g. to take up the vacant position in *All —— are admirable.*

You will notice that the three forms of the marker are not interchangeable. We do not, for instance, have */stɒgs/ instead of /stɒgz/, just as we do not have */dɒgs/ instead of /dɒgz/.

These isolated cases are part of a highly important pattern, which will emerge if we study a small collection of English plural forms – for instance: *abbots, animals, beetles, breaths, cats, churches, dogs, foxes, horns, judges, machines, princes, puffs, steps, whizzes* (omitting for the moment unusual forms like *oxen* and *data*). If we group these according to the phonetic 'shape' of the plural marker, the arrangement will be:

/ɪz/   *churches, foxes, judges, princes, whizzes;*
/z/   *animals, beetles, dogs, horns, machines;*
/s/   *abbots, cats, breaths, puffs, steps.*

The next step is to consider whether we can explain this grouping. When we consider the phoneme which in each word precedes the plural marker, e.g. the /s/ of /fɒks/ or /fɒksɪz/, a very simple pattern emerges. In the words of the first group, this critical phoneme is a groove fricative: (/s, z, ʃ, ʒ/) or an affricate: /tʃ/ or /dʒ/ (§§ 2.13.2, 2.13.3). These all take the marker /ɪz/. In the second group, the corresponding phonemes are all voiced sounds and in the third group they are unvoiced sounds. This enables us to state the distribution of the three forms of the marker as follows:

/ɪz/   follows affricates and groove fricatives;
/z/   follows voiced phonemes other than these;
/s/   follows unvoiced phonemes other than these.

Although this does not cover the irregular plurals like *oxen*, it is a very economical description of the principles governing the forms of some thousands of English plurals. Notice that such a description of a distribution can sometimes be shortened by stating the less usual cases first.

The correlation in English between the three principal forms of this marker, /ɪz/, /z/ and /s/, and the final phoneme of the word it marks, establishes a particular type of complementary distribution. In § 3.4 a complementary distribution was defined in Gleason's terms as one in which each element 'occurs in a fixed set of contexts in which none of the others occur': the marker /z/, for instance, will not follow an unvoiced phoneme, nor the marker /s/ a voiced one, so that hypothetical forms like /dɒgs/, /pʌfz/, are un-English. The distribution of /ɪz/, /z/, /s/, is a special case in that the form of the marker is 'conditioned' by the nature of the phoneme which precedes it: i.e. if we know what this phoneme is, we can predict the form of the marker.

Our prediction, of course, will not be true in all cases: for *sheep* we might predict the marker /s/ and for *ox* the marker /ɪz/, and in both cases we should be wrong. But we should be wrong only because our account of English plurals was incomplete. A full account would include all the cases (e.g. *sheep, deer* and *Japanese*) in which the morpheme *plural* takes a zero form, and those (e.g. *oxen, data*) in which its forms are unusual; these, again, are in complementary distribution with plurals of the more usual type: the /ən/ marker, for instance, is limited in Modern English to the 'contexts' *oxen, children*, and the /ə/ marker occurs only in a limited number of words of Græco-Latin origin (*data, phenomena*, etc.).

One might ask why our three imaginary plurals have taken predictable forms, like /stʌdʒɪz/ instead of irregular forms like /stʌdʒən/, on the model of *oxen*, or /stʌdʒnɪkə/ on the model of *data*. There is, of course, nothing to prevent the creator of a new word from giving it any plural form he chooses. But whether unfamiliar forms will gain acceptance is another matter entirely. The cartoonist Al Capp, for instance, devised the word *schmoo* and announced that its plural would be *schmoon*. This form, however, has not passed into the language, though devotees of Al Capp refer freely to *schmoos*. We are now so habituated to forming plurals with /ɪz/, /z/ or /s/, that plurals that do not match this 'productive' pattern are unlikely, except in special cases, to gain acceptance.

The special cases nowadays are generally learned or scientific forms on Graeco-Latin models: having borrowed a Greek or Latin form (e.g. *datum, phenomenon, stimulus*), we tend to use a Latin or Latinized plural (*data, phenomena, stimuli*). On the other hand, as a word moves into colloquial speech, its plural tends to follow the prevailing English pattern. Thus, we go into the garden to look at our *japonicas* (Japanese quinces); we are perhaps unlikely to call them *japonicae* except at a meeting of the Botanical Society. Compare *petunias, chrysanthemums*. Some words, like *appendix*, have two plural forms: *appendices* follows a Latin model, *appendixes* has fallen into line with the prevailing English pattern.

Berko (1958) has shown that control of the formation of the

commonest plural forms is established at a very early age. In the course of a general study of children's learning of English morphology, she obtained the plurals of a number of nonsense words – like *wug* and *niz* – from children aged four to seven. Nonsense words were used to test whether the child could use his experience of English to form a plural on his own. This could not have been tested by using actual words, since the child might then simply have recalled the plural from memory. The experimental procedure was to show the child a picture first of one imaginary animal and then of two, and to tell him, for instance, 'Here is a wug: now there are two of them: there are two ——?', inviting him to complete the statement without telling him the plural form.

97 per cent of children in the first grade (aged about six) produced /wʌgz/ as the plural of *wug*, and 80 per cent gave /hiːfs/ as the plural of *heaf.* Only 38 per cent, on the other hand, offered /gʌtʃɪz/ as the plural of *gutch*, and only 33 per cent gave /nɪzɪz/ as the plural of *niz*. When asked (in the manner described above) for the plurals of these forms, most of the children responded with silence. Berko concludes that the majority of the children studied were able to apply the markers /s/ and /z/ to form the plurals of new words, but that they were at a loss with forms of a less familiar kind, requiring the marker /ɪz/. The more usual patterns are mastered first; having mastered these, the child is inclined for a time to produce such 'irregular' forms as *mouses* and *drived*, which are consistent with the dominant patterns of English, though not with the patterns which he will eventually learn as the established forms of these words.

6.5. The grammar of the word

The position of the *plural* marker which we have just been considering, is invariably at the end of the word it marks: such forms as /zdɒg/ are inconceivable in English, and the form /skæt/, though it has a meaning, is not the plural of *cats*.

The word in English consists of one or more morphemes *in a fixed order*. The order of elements in the sentence is relatively variable: we can, for instance, say *up the hill we went* as well as *we went up the hill.* Within the word, however, variation of this kind does not take place. The grammar of the word is thus more rigid than that of the sentence.

All English words consist of a free form either alone or in combination with other forms, bound or free. Thus *lady* is a free form which takes the bound affix /z/ to form the plural *ladies*; it may on the other hand combine with another free form, *bird*, to produce *ladybird*, or with both free form and affix for *ladybirds*.

Some such formations can be built up only by steps in a fixed order:

124

unladylike, for instance, consists of three morphemes, {un-} plus {-lady} plus {-like}, but the order of formation must be:

    (1) {lady-} + {-like} = *ladylike*
    (2) {ladylike} + {un-} = *unladylike*

The alternative would be to take as a first step {un} + {lady} = **unlady*; this is ruled out because **unlady*, useful as it might be, is not an English word. Our formation series in this case is accordingly *lady – ladylike – unladylike*: the order of steps in the series depends on the principle of 'immediate constituents' (§ 5.5), often abbreviated as I.C.s. The 'immediate constituents' of a word are its component parts which operate as wholes at the level of structure immediately below it: thus the I.C.s of *unladylike* are *un-* and *ladylike* because these are the 'wholes' which combine to form it.

By the same criterion of 'wholeness', the I.C.s of *developments* are {*development*} and {*-s,*} not {*develop-*} and *{*-ments*}, and those of *immediately* are {*immediate*} and {*-ly*}, not *{*im-*} and {*mediately*}. It is not always easy, however, to decide at what points the cut for immediate constituents should fall: for *dehumanization*, for instance, the formation series might run: *human, humanize, humanization, dehumanization*, or *human, humanize, dehumanize, dehumanization*, although the version given second is neater, on the grounds that *de-* is more intimately linked with the verb *humanize* than with the noun *humanization*.

For the techniques of immediate constituent analysis, the reader is referred to Gleason (1961) or Nelson Francis (1954): a much less detailed account of the components of words will suffice for the purposes of this text.

6.6. Affixes and paradigms

One basic distinction, however, must be made between two types of component, both of great importance in the formation of English words. Consider the groupings below:

    (i) person, persons;
    (ii) person, personal, personality, impersonal, impersonality, personalize, personalization, depersonalize, depersonalization, personable, impersonate, impersonation, interpersonal . . .

Each series consists of the same 'base' or radical form, *person*, in combination with one or more affixes. Here, however, the similarity ends.

Series (i) is limited and fixed, it consists of only two phonetic forms /pɜ:sn̩/ and /pɜ:sn̩z/. Both are nouns, though each can enter into a number of different grammatical combinations. The majority of

125

English nouns come in similar pairs (*dog, dogs*), generally consisting of a marked and an unmarked member: such a pair is an example of an *inflectional series* or *paradigm* ('paradigm' means 'pattern'). The type of marker used in it is an *inflectional affix.*

Series (ii) is variable and unlimited. It consists of a number of phonetic forms, including nouns, adjectives and verbs: a precisely similar series may not exist for any other base (e.g. the base *man* has quite a different set of derivatives). Many of the markers in this group have the effect of changing the grammatical status of the word (e.g. *person, personal, personalize*): we call such markers *derivational affixes* and the set of words that they form with a given base is a *derivational series.*

The marker of Series (i) can be added to several of the items of Series (ii) (*personalities, personalizations, impersonations*). In all cases it will stand last: derivational affixes, in other words, always precede inflectional affixes in English.

The *possessive* marker as in *dog's,* might also be treated as an inflectional affix. It can, however, be rather easily separated from its noun, as in *The Queen of England's racehorses, Mr Jones of Babraham's dogs*; its behaviour is thus very different from that of the plural marker, which cannot be moved about in this way. It will thus be more convenient not to regard the *possessive* marker as an inflectional affix.

Perhaps the basic distinction between the two series is that Series (i) is 'closed' and Series (ii) is 'open'. A number of new derivatives of *person* (*depersonalize, interpersonal*) have appeared during the past century and new formations of this kind are quite likely. It is improbable, on the other hand, that English will develop a new inflectional affix, so that a system like Series (i) can be described as 'closed'.

Inflection (the Latin radical means 'bending') does not, as we have seen, consist invariably of the addition of an affix to a base. It may be carried out by a 'replacive' change (§ 6.3, iii), as in the case of *mouse – mice* or *tooth – teeth.* Inflection can roughly be described as the change of form in a word that signals such grammatical distinctions in English as that of singular or plural in nouns, or that of past and present in verbs: the distinguishing mark of inflectional affixes is that they form closed systems, as shown below.

The four principal inflectional series (or paradigms) in English are:

(i)   the noun paradigm: e.g. *person – persons* (see also § 6.8);
(ii)   the verb paradigm: e.g. *drive, drives, drove, driving, driven* (see also § 6.13);
(iii) the adjective paradigm: e.g. *full, fuller, fullest* (see also § 6.11);

(iv) the personal pronoun paradigm: e.g. *I, me, my, mine* (see also 6.9).

Each of these systems is closed: for nouns in English we distinguish only singular and plural; for adjectives only three degrees of comparison; for verbs a maximum of five basic forms. The language is unlikely to develop an inflectional marker for a fourth degree of comparison or for a new distinction of grammatical number. There are, of course, variant forms for each paradigm, e.g. *datum – data* for certain nouns, *good – better – best* for the adjective *good*, and many 'irregular' paradigms – e.g. *bend, bends, bending, bent* – for verbs. Note that a paradigm consists normally of a base form which undergoes *inflectional* change: thus, *beautiful – more beautiful – most beautiful* is not an adjective paradigm, because *beautiful* remains uninflected; it has the same form in all three constructions.

6.7. The classification of words

Some general labels, such as 'noun' and 'verb', for classes of grammatically similar words, are indispensable in any discussion of language at work. Up to this point I have been using the traditional terms 'noun' and 'verb' without defining them. We must now consider how they might in practice be defined.

Using our four paradigms, we can tentatively classify a substantial number of words according to the patterns that they follow. But this classification will be tentative only. Thus *stronger* and *strongest* are adjectives at first sight until one remembers such forms as *the stronger shall prevail, the arm of the strongest*. Further, a great many forms fit two different paradigms: thus, *drive* might be part of the noun paradigm, *drive – drives*, or of the verb paradigm, *drive, drives, drove, driving, driven*.

This shows the limitations of classification by paradigm in English. Two of the noun forms, *drive* and *drives*, coincide with two of the forms of the verb: we only know that *drive* has two paradigms because we have recognized it in two different sets of grammatical frames (§ 5.10), such as:

(a) We went for a drive.   I like long drives.
(b) I shall drive us home.   Peter drives too fast.

The (a) frames define *drive* and *drives* as nouns, the (b) frames define them as verbs. Only because we know that *drive* and *drives* can enter both kinds of frame are we able to distinguish the two paradigms of *drive*. Classification on form cannot be undertaken without reference to environment.

127

This indicates that for the classification of grammatical items in English we should have to consider several factors. The primary factor would be the capacity of a given item for fitting particular types of environment – the capacity of a noun, for instance, for taking up the position of a subject. But we should also consider the roles of markers – e.g. determiners and derivational and inflectional affixes – and might occasionally also use the criterion of the kind of meaning associated with a particular class of word.

Advisedly, I put the criterion of meaning last. This is the traditional basis for the classification of the 'parts of speech': a noun, we are sometimes told, denotes a thing; an adjective, a quality; a verb, an action or state. Such a description may be a useful clue to the usual roles of words of these three kinds, but as a definition it is quite unworkable.

If adjectives (Kennedy, 1942) are words which 'define nouns by expressing their qualities', what are we to make of 'Mary has beauty, wit, charm and poise', in which *beauty*, *wit*, *charm* and *poise* all define the noun *Mary* by expressing the qualities of its referent, though no English grammarian would agree to call them 'adjectives'? Again, if verbs are words 'which express an action or state', what of: 'After the murder there was silence'? *Murder* undoubtedly expresses an action, *silence* a state, but in this context they are evidently not verbs: *murder* is marked as a noun by *the*, and *silence* by a position typical of nouns.

Before proceeding, I would like to stress again that recognition and classification of grammatical items is not, despite its difficulties, an abstract pursuit for grammarians. As soon as we fail to recognize grammatical function, communication breaks down: any ambiguous sentence, such as *COLONELS MAN PUMPS* (§ 4.2), is an illustration of this. We may manage without technical labels of any kind, but unless we know somehow how *MAN* functions in this sentence – i.e. unless we can recognize it as noun or verb (whether we know these particular labels or not) – the meaning will be lost to us.

On the other hand, word-classification is by no means the be-all and end-all of grammar. One can learn a language without being able to say whether a given word is a noun or a verb, though for control of English, one must, of course, be able to 'handle' nouns and verbs in speech, even if one is unable to name them. Technical terms are, of course, indispensable for a formal description of language, but the 'parts of speech' do not, perhaps, have the paramount importance which some old-fashioned grammars assign them, and in English they cannot be discussed out of relation to the pattern of the sentence as a whole. Jespersen (1924) concluded that only five classes of words 'are grammatically distinct enough for us to recognize them as separate "parts of speech" '; these five classes are nouns, adjectives, pronouns, verbs and particles, the particles comprising all words 'that cannot find a place in any of the first four classes'. (Jespersen prefers the term *substantives* for what I shall call nouns.) Particles are highly important elements of English grammar: unfortunately our sub-classification of the particles is at present by no means reliable or complete, though useful and suggestive outlines will be found in such texts as Fries (1957) and Strang (1962).

Jespersen's first four classes – nouns, adjectives, pronouns and verbs – are those which were shown in § 6.6 to form paradigms or in-flectional series in English, though of course not all nouns fit the typical noun paradigm. Without attempting to offer a complete scheme for the grammatical classification of English words, I shall briefly sketch the principal features of each of Jespersen's four classes. (Grammatical *class* seems preferable to the traditional and rather confusing 'part of speech': the word 'class' is itself a reminder that the same phonetic form may 'belong' to two or more different classes.) It will be convenient to consider adverbs along with adjectives (§§ 6.11 and 6.12) and to present certain 'particles' in relation to the classes of words with which they habitually pattern, e.g. determiners with nouns, qualifiers with adjectives and adverbs, and auxiliaries with verbs. Other particles are briefly considered in § 6.14, and more fully in § 7.9.

In the course of classification, it will be useful to bear in mind our initial rough distinction between lexical and grammatical functions and items (§§ 1.5 and 5.1). Most English words probably function simultaneously in a lexical and a grammatical role: *eat*, for instance, in *I eat my dinner* has both the grammatical function of a predicator in an SPC pattern, and a lexical function roughly equivalent to that of *edo* in Latin, *mange* in French or *eet* in Afrikaans. Other items may have a primarily lexical function in one context and a primarily grammatical function in another: Whitehall (1956) makes the illuminating contrast of 'grammatical' *is* in:

New York is ruined

with 'lexical' *is* in:

New York is no more

Notice that grammatical *is* is readily reduced to /s/ or /z/; lexical *is* tends to retain its full phonetic form: *New York's ruined; New York is no more.*

We could not, however, base a useful description of English grammar on the rough-and-ready contrast of 'full' and 'empty' words. What is needed is a precise account of the patterning of items in the sentence, which should be based, as far as possible, on objective criteria of position and of form.

I ought perhaps to point out that a dictionary is seldom a very reliable guide to the grammatical classification of words. Many dictionaries use an outmoded terminology: *the*, for instance, is listed as 'adjective and adverb' in the 1964 edition of one of the standard students' dictionaries, which does not list the word *determiner* at all. And having looked up *poor* in five different dictionaries, I found that only one (the largest) indicated that it could function not only as an adjective but also as a noun in the common construction: *the poor*.

On the other hand, the classificatory scheme that follows (§§ 6.8–6.14) is not offered as definitive or final. As Sapir pointed out in a different context, 'all grammars leak'. There are, however, degrees of leakiness, and a grammar based on close observation of English and the tradition of analysis which owes so much to Sapir is obviously preferable to one which arbitrarily describes English as if it were Latin.

6.8. Nouns

The typical function of a noun in an English sentence is that of subject or complement, though it can act in other roles as well; most nouns can be inflected for number: a noun in a sentence is often marked by a determiner. These features are illustrated by *cats* and *bats*, in such a sentence as 'The cats dislike the bats.'

Noun-Positions. A typical noun is a word that fits one or more of the following positions:

(a.1) The —— was good. (*dinner, furniture, experience*)
(a.2) The —— were good. (*dinners, people, experiences*)
(a.3) —— was good. (*Peter, Mary, Mr Brown*)
(b.1) I saw the ——. (*dinner, furniture, people*)
(b.2) I saw ——. (*Peter, Mary, Mr Brown*)

To avoid such incongruous constructions as: *The murder was good*, or: *I saw the atom*, we can write a general notation for these two kinds of frame:

(a) (D) + —— + *be* + Adj.
(b) PN + Vt + (D) + ——.

Here D denotes *determiner* and the brackets round it show that this item may or may not be present: *be* indicates an appropriate form of the verb *to be*, Adj an adjective, PN a personal pronoun and Vt a transitive verb. Note that certain pronouns could occupy the vacant slots in (a.3) (e.g. *he*) and (b.2) (e.g. *him*). Our two basic noun-positions, of course, are those of subject and complement (§§ 5.3 and 5.4), though forms other than nouns may act as complements (*The*

man was fat, §§ 7.4 and 7.6). The subject-position immediately before
a verb (i.e. in the frame —V) is very typical of nouns.

Our test-frames are of some value for establishing whether a given
item is capable of functioning as a noun: they do not, of course,
enable us to decide whether an item in a particular context is a noun or
not. In some cases (e.g. that of *'Twas brillig*; § 5.2 and Appendix B)
we cannot decide from any clues of form or position whether a given
item is a noun or not.

Determiners are usually the clearest signals of the presence of nouns.
The following invariably act as determiners; i.e. as markers preceding
a noun:

A, an, my, our, the, their, your.

The following frequently act as determiners:

*This, these; that, those; his, her, its; one, many a, more, several, no,
all, both.*

Any of these that will pattern with a plural form would fit the vacant
slot in: *Ship —— sails today*, thereby marking *sails* as a noun.

Inflection. Most English nouns, as shown above, are two-form
words in the spoken language: the normal paradigm contrasts an unmarked form with a marked one (*dog – dogs*). There are, of course,
many special and unusual formations. The marked forms show plural
number (see § 6.10). I have suggested in § 6.6 that the marker
possessive, as in *the dog's dinner*, ought probably not to be treated
as an inflectional affix, because it can fairly readily be separated from
the noun, as in *Lord Macpherson of Dundreary's spectacles*. Some
writers, however, prefer to regard this as a 'genitive' or 'possessive'
case-inflection (see § 6.10).

The marker *plural* seldom shows noun-status unambiguously
without other clues; in *the slithy toves* the primary signal of the
presence of a noun is not the /z/ of *toves* but the determiner *the*.
Several groups of English nouns are without number-contrast:

Equipment, gold, furniture (no plural forms);
Bellows, scissors (no singular forms);
Grahamstown, Ebenezer (no plural forms except in special cases).

Accordingly certain items, which operate as nouns in sentences,
may be without noun-inflection: we do not, for instance, have **the
poors* though we may say *The poor are hungry*. Some writers, e.g. Sledd
(1959), prefer to call such items 'nominals' rather than 'nouns'; I
would prefer, however, to keep the traditional name and where
necessary to distinguish inflected nouns (*dog – dogs*) from nouns incapable of inflection.

Strang (1962), pp. 86–90, lists plural formations in some detail.

Derivational Affixes. There are a large number of derivational
131

affixes which help to mark the status of nouns; four quite common ones are:

> /ə/ as in *director, liner, platelayer*;
> /mənt/ as in *shipment, payment*;
> /ʃən/ as in *construction, devotion*;
> /ɪst/ as in *communist, anarchist*.

6.9.　Personal pronouns

The eight personal pronouns are an important group of function-words. Each has a paradigm of three or four forms, each of which has a characteristic position:

Subject:	I like fish.
Object:	Fish like me.
Possessive (D):	Bring my fish.
Possessive (S/C):	That fish is mine. Mine is there.

I have here marked the two 'possessive' forms, one as D for 'Determiner' and one as S/C for 'Subject or Complement' to distinguish the usual functions of these two forms in the sentence. The 'Determiner' form (like *the* or *a*) characteristically precedes a noun: the 'subject or complement' form may function in either of the positions shown.

Inflections. The personal pronouns are inflected as follows:

Subject	Object	Possessive (D)	Possessive (S/C)
I	me	my	mine
we	us	our	ours
you	you	your	yours
he	him	his	his
she	her	her	hers
it	it	its	its
they	them	their	theirs
who	whom	whose	whose

The traditional role of a pronoun in an English sentence is that of a *substitute*: for instance, in: 'John has arrived, but he looks ill', *he* substitutes in the second part of the sentence for *John* in the first. On the other hand, in: 'It's raining', *it* does not appear to be a substitute for anything in particular; *it* is in fact a very common 'utterance initiator' as in 'It seems to me . . .' or 'It's time to go home'.

Pronouns resemble nouns in their capacity to stand as subjects and complements; on the other hand, they do not as a rule pattern with adjectives and determiners: we do not speak of **the us* or **a blue he*.

English pronouns do not show the contrast of polite and familiar forms that is given by Afrikaans *u* ('you', polite and formal) and *jou*, *jy* ('you', familiar and, according to circumstances, contemptuous or friendly). *You* and *thou* contrasted in this way in the English of Shakespeare's time. *Thou* signalled contempt in one type of context, friendly 'solidarity' in another. 'I thou thee, thou traitor' said the Attorney-General in his savage cross-examination of Sir Walter Ralegh (1603); on the other hand, the Society of Friends later adopted *thee* and *thou* for use to one another in the 'Plain Speech' which the Quakers deliberately adopted, and which, in a few Quaker communities, continues to this day. Some Oriental languages maintain complex social distinctions between pronouns; thus Malay (Schlauch, 1960) is said to distinguish ten levels of civility, using special pronoun forms, for instance, for peasants speaking to one another, for a subject addressing the sultan, or for superiors addressing inferiors 'ordinarily', 'pointedly', or 'with affected modesty'.

While English pronouns are relatively simple in this respect, their inflections are nevertheless more complex than are those of nouns. While nouns are inflected for number (*dog – dogs*) and possibly for case (*dog – dog's*) some pronouns are inflected for number, case and gender, three grammatical categories which we must now explore.

6.10. Number, gender and case

It is important to realize that certain distinctions which are built into the grammatical system of English are not inevitably reflected in other grammatical systems or, for that matter, in the real world.

One of these is the distinction of number. Most nouns in modern English are inflected for number, and whenever we use a noun in a sentence we are forced to mark its grammatical number. Consider:

> (1) The man proposes.
> (2) The men propose.
> (3) Man proposes.

Even in (3), where the notion of number is irrelevant, it is still grammatically marked by the inflections of *man* and of the verb. In the present tense, the verb (as in *the sheep grazes*) will frequently register number even where the noun does not. In Old English, number would have been marked even more elaborately: where Modern English inflects the noun for number and in some cases the verb, Old English inflected determiners and adjectives too, so that the plural of *se goda wer* (the good man) was *þa godan weras*; where Modern English marks number once, by the form of the noun, Old English marked it three times.

Chinese, on the other hand, does not inflect for number at all: number is only marked when it is needed. Thus, the Chinese:

/jin sɪŋ pen ʃen/
man nature root good

means both 'the nature of man is radically good' and 'the natures of men are radically good' (Sweet, 1900). Here number is relatively unimportant. When it has to be shown, Chinese uses a numeral or some other term for quantity. Both the English and the Chinese conventions have their advantages: the English is more specific, the Chinese more economical.

Some peculiar English number-forms were noted in the previous section. Others are *pants*, *shorts* and *clothes*: we wear clothes for a number of good reasons, but it is by an arbitrary grammatical convention that our *pants* are invariably plural.

A more important set of grammatical patterns is illustrated by the following:

(c) *a pencil, a man, a bean*

but not:

(uc) *a gold, *a hydrogen, *a rice.

(uc) / səm gould, səm haɪdrədʒən, səm raɪs/

but not:

(c) */səm pensl, səm mæn, səm biːn/.

The nouns marked (c) above are *countables*, which pattern in the singular with *a* but not with /səm/. (Distinguish the two forms of *some*: /səm/ in the sense of 'a quantity of'; /sʌm/, in colloquial style, meaning 'a fine, a remarkable' as in 'that was some dinner'. Formal style avoids this use of *some*.)

The nouns of the group marked (uc) are uncountables, patterning in the singular with /səm/ but not with *a*, except in very special contexts: e.g. 'The crown was made of a peculiar reddish gold.' Possibly *any* noun, e.g. *water*, as in *a drink of water* and *the waters of Babylon*, may be countable in some contexts and uncountable in others; this complicates the teaching of the distinction, though the change of status generally carries with it a change of meaning: compare '*a large rabbit*' (countable) with 'a large helping of *rabbit*' (uncountable).

The distinction of countables and uncountables is clearly an arbitrary matter of grammar: compare *penny* and *money* in the following:

Countable	*Uncountable*
These pennies *are* bright.	This money *is* bright.
A sum of *pennies*.	A sum of *money*.
This is *a* penny, but not:	*This is *a* money, except in very specialized contexts

Careful handling of the distinction is necessary if the foreign learner is to be steered away from such forms as *a luggage, *a police*. Hornby (1959–1962) outlines a method of introducing the contrast of countables and uncountables gradually.

While the number of a noun is almost invariably marked in an English sentence, its gender and case are not: the remnants in modern English of grammatical gender and case are virtually restricted to the pronoun system.

Grammatical *gender* should not be confused with biological sex. The contrast of grammatical gender is shown in the English pronouns *he, she, it*. In many languages, however, nouns, adjectives and determiners are also inflected for gender. Thus in Old English we had *se cyning* (masculine: the king) but *seo hlaefdige* (feminine: the lady), in which the gender was shown by the form of the determiner (*se* or *seo* in the nominative case); incidentally *þæt wif* (neuter: 'the woman') and *se wifmann* (masculine, 'the woman') show how grammatical gender fails to parallel biological sex. There are similar anomalies in German: thus *das Mädchen* (the girl) is neuter, but *die Rübe* (the turnip) feminine, so that 'the girl fetches the turnip', substituting pronouns for nouns, would become 'it fetches her'. In the Bantu languages, there are usually at least five genders and often many more; these are marked by prefixes which assign each noun to a 'class' or 'gender'; there is no correlation of these noun-classes 'with sex-reference or any other clearly defined idea' (Guthrie, 1948).

Gender, then, is a relatively arbitrary device for the grammatical classification of words. Its usefulness appears in such a sentence as: 'When the ape was given the apple, he rolled under the bench.' Here, unless the pronoun *he* was in some way marked so as to refer back to *ape*, we should be uncertain whether it was the ape or the apple that rolled: gender in English is thus primarily a convention for the patterning of pronouns with nouns and for marking their relationship. I have briefly sketched this convention below:

(1) *He* and *who* pattern with nouns like *boy, husband, king*.
(2) *She* and *who* pattern with nouns like *girl, wife, queen*.
(3) *He, she* and *who* may pattern with nouns like *person, spouse, doctor*.

(4) *It* and *which* pattern with nouns like *table, chair, pot.*
(5) *It, he, which* and *who* pattern with nouns like *bull, ram, stallion.*
(6) *It, she, which* and *who* pattern with nouns like *cow, ewe, mare.*
(7) *It, he, she, which, who* pattern with nouns like *child, cat, baby.*

He in this sketch, of course, represents the pronoun *he, him, his*; *she* represents the pronouns *she, her, hers*; *it* represents *it* and *its.*

Although a good many English nouns can be arranged in pairs denoting male and female – *boy* and *girl, king* and *queen, duke* and *duchess* – their 'gender' is grammatically important only when they pattern with pronouns. In teaching it is probably better to handle gender as an aspect of the pronoun system rather than as an inherent feature of nouns. Memorizing pairs like *lord* and *lady, Czarina* and *Czar*, is unlikely to improve one's practical control of English. There are, of course, a few derivational affixes, notably *-ess*, for marking feminines, as in *waiter – waitress, god – goddess*. The domination of males is reflected in the fact that in these cases the base form is almost always a word denoting a man, the principal exceptions being *bride – bridegroom* and *widow – widower*. For a fuller treatment of gender, see Jespersen (1933) and Strang (1962).

Grammatical *case* is marked in such a set of pronouns as those of '*I* hit *him* and then *he* hit *me*'. A typical case-contrast is that of the subject-form *I* with the object form *me*. In such languages as Latin and Finnish, case is much more elaborately marked than it is in English today: thus, in the Latin for 'The ambassador is giving an apple to the ape', *legatus simiae pomum dat, legatus* (ambassador) is recognizable as a nominative or subject form, *simiae* (ape) as a dative or indirect object, *pomum* (apple) as an accusative or direct object (though it might be the subject in another context). In Modern English, these functions are shown by position in the sentence and by grammatical words like *to*. Latin, however, would have used contrasting case-inflections to show the roles of words in sentence-patterns: thus *legatus* as object would be *legatum, simiae* as subject would become *simia*. Old English marked the cases of determiners and adjectives as well as those of nouns: thus, 'the good lady' as subject would be *seo gode hlaefdige* but as object *þa godan hlaefdigan*.

In Modern English, case is probably a feature of pronouns only, though as I noted in § 6.8, some writers regard the marker *possessive* as in *the dog's dinner* as a 'genitive' case-inflection.

6.11. Adjectives

The typical role of an adjective is that of a modifier of a noun (§ 5.6) as in *the green tree*, or *my blue jacket*; its typical position, as in these examples, is between determiner and noun. But it may also function as a complement (§ 5.4) as in *my jacket is blue* or *The tree seems green.* Thus the test for a typical adjective is whether it fits both of the vacant positions in such a frame as

The —— man is very ——.

i.e. (as modifier) between determiner and noun or (as complement) after the combination of such a verb as *is* or *seems* with a function-word like *very*.

Very is one of an important group of structural words which might be termed *adjective/adverb qualifiers*: these include:

Very, quite, more, most, less, least, too, so, rather, somewhat, indeed, and *enough.*

A bit and *a little* often function in rather the same way. In general, qualifiers show 'intensity' or 'degree'; contrast *quite big, very big* and *too big*. They also mark adjectives and adverbs in rather the same way as determiners mark nouns. Consider such a pair as:

This is a green box.   (Adj. + N)
This is a telephone box.   (N + N)

In the case of *green box*, the structure is adjective plus noun, and we can use a qualifier: a *very green box*. In the case of *telephone box* the structure is noun plus noun and we could not use a qualifier: **this is a very telephone box* is non-English. Some forms, e.g. *solid* in:

Jones is a solid physicist

may be either adjective or noun. If *solid* is an adjective (meaning 'reliable' or possibly 'stout') we can insert a qualifier. 'Jones was a very solid physicist.' If, however, *solid* is a noun, and *solid physicist* means 'a physicist who studies solids' we cannot use a qualifier: compare **Jones is a very geology physicist,* which is clearly non-English.

Another test to determine whether a modifier is adjective or noun is whether it can be inflected for comparison, as in 'Jones was a solider physicist than I'. But as some adjectives, e.g. *beautiful*, are not inflected for comparison, this test cannot always be applied. (Note that in 'Mary was a very beautiful physicist' the qualifier shows the adjective status of *beautiful*.)

Adverb/adjective qualifiers may also distinguish adjectives from participles (§ 6.13).

Mrs Jones was entertaining last night

may mean either that Mrs Jones gave a party (in which case *entertaining* is a participle) or that she amused her guests (in which case *entertaining* can be regarded as an adjective). The test is again to insert *very*.

Mrs Jones *was very entertaining* last night
(V + Q + Adj.)

leaves us in no doubt of the meaning, because it shows unambiguously what is the structure of the predicate. (Q in the notation above stands for Qualifier.)

Inflection is seldom an unambiguous mark of adjective-status. Inflections are found only in the relatively limited group of adjectives that follow the pattern:

cool, cooler, coolest; strange, stranger, strangest.

Note that the marker /ə/ of *cooler* and *stranger* is potentially ambiguous: 'The cooler was cooler than the refrigerator'; 'The stranger looked stranger after he had taken off his hat'. Derivational affixes, again, often fail to mark adjectives unambiguously: consider *capital, hopeful, chemical* and *deterrent*, all of which may be either adjective or noun, though only *hopeful* is inflected for comparison.

Position. Adjectives follow definite conventions of position: the fixed order in a headed group is that of *a very fat cat*, i.e. (1) Determiner (2) Qualifier (3) Adjective (4) Noun. **Very cat a fat* would be impossible in English. There are subtler conventions for the order of a series of adjectives, as in *a large black Japanese pot*: normally in such a series the more 'general' items, such as *large*, will precede the more specific, such as *Japanese*.

6.12. Adverbs

If an item cannot readily be assigned to one of the other parts of speech, there is a strong temptation to label it an *adverb*. The traditional category of adverbs is accordingly somewhat ill-assorted, and for this district of English there are at present no entirely reliable maps.

Typical adverbs fit the last position in such a frame as:

He told us his story ――― ,

but the items that enter this position, e.g. *here, quickly, yesterday, soberly, well*, are somewhat heterogeneous. Some, such as *quickly* and *soberly*, carry the marker *-ly*; others, such as *well* and *yesterday*, are unmarked. Most of them could be moved into other positions: '*Quickly* he told us his story', 'He *quickly* told us his story' but this is not true of *well* ('Well, he told us his story' involves a radical change of meaning from that of 'he told us his story well.')

Setting aside *well* as a special case, we can regard a great many traditional adverbs as *movable modifiers*. Compare the sequences *the fat cat* with *cats eat quickly*. The adjectival modifier *fat* occupies a relatively fixed position between the determiner and the noun: we shall not attest **fat the cat* or *cat fat the*. The adverbial modifier *quickly* can, however, be moved: *Quickly, cats eat; cats quickly eat (their dinner);* this greater mobility is one of the distinguishing features of the majority of adverbs. We have already noted this mobility in the adverbial adjunct *regularly* in our pattern sentence *General Masters cheats the butcher regularly* (§ 5.4).

Note that in structures like *cats eat quickly* the one-word modifier *quickly* follows its head *eat* instead of preceding it: this is the normal position for an adverb modifying a verb. For fuller analyses see Nelson Francis (1958) and Strang (1962).

A number of typical adverbs, e.g. *here, now, well*, etc. have no formal marks of adverb-status. Others are marked by fairly characteristic derivational affixes as in:

Hopefully, slowly, aloud, lengthwise, forwards.

A few in informal usage have comparative and superlative inflections like the corresponding adjectives:

You can buy it cheaper at Mac's.

Some adverbs pattern with qualifiers (§ 6.11) as in 'He did it *very badly*'; others, however, will not: we shall not attest *'He did it *very now*.' There is a small group of adverb-substitutes, functioning rather as do pronouns in relation to nouns, as in 'It happened yesterday but *then* we didn't know you'd be coming', where *then* substitutes in the second part of the sentence for *yesterday* in the first. The principal adverb-substitutes are *then, there, thus* and *so*, and according to their relationship with these, a number of adverbs can be classified into substitute-groups:

1. *There-group* (*Adverbs of place*)	2. *Then-group* (*Adverbs of time*)	3. *Thus/so-group* (*Adverbs of manner*)
Outside	Today	Easily
Here	Now	Quickly
There	Recently	Well

In a cluster of adverbs after the verb an adverb from the first group normally precedes one from the second: thus, we would say: *I went outside today* rather than: *I went today outside*. The conventions, if the sequence includes an adverb of manner, are not so clear: thus, 'We'll manage it easily today' (manner before time) and 'We'll manage it today easily' (time before manner) seem equally possible. Again, where adverbs occur on both sides of the verb the order may vary: 'Here we slept yesterday' and 'Yesterday we slept here' are both quite possible according to context.

6.13. Verbs

6.13.1. *Verbs and predication*

The typical function of a verb is that of a *predicator*, as in 'Cats *eat* bats' or 'General Masters *cheats*'. Its typical position in English

139

statements is after the subject with which, as in these examples, it shows concord (§ 5.9); this partnership of subject and 'finite' verb is the basic element in the structure of the majority of English sentences.

A finite verb is one which takes a subject, and our sketch of the verb will be limited, on the whole, to forms that pattern with subjects. Our principal test-frame for a verb, but not our only one, will be:

(D) + N + V + (D) + N
The colonel is an Indian.
The cats eat the bats.

However, were I attempting a description of the verb in ideal terms, I should be tempted to begin with the imperative singular (*Run! Eat!*) as the primary or nuclear form. Such forms as *Run!* or *Eat!* stand, in a sense, outside the normal patterns of predication; in most languages (Diamond, 1959) they consist of the *base* or simplest form of the verb, and if we regard it as probable that language began with signals of a very general kind, such as cries of alarm, such a form as *Run!* may be the modern representative of the primitive undifferentiated word, before language began to distinguish what are now 'the parts of speech'.

Even in modern English, *Run!* is a very much simpler utterance than *Peter runs*. Not only is *Peter runs* longer, but it is grammatically more complex, using, for instance, the device of position (contrast *Peter runs* with *Run, Peter*) and the affix /z/ which marks the grammatical concord of subject and predicator. It also differentiates two parts of speech, noun and verb, marked as different by the combined signals of their positions in relation to one another and the affix upon the verb.

Predication, then, even in this apparently simple case, is a fairly complex grammatical relationship: we shall spend most of Chapter Seven on a sketch of different patterns of predication. The pattern is further complicated by the fact that an English predicator is more often a cluster than a single word; i.e., forms like *Peter is running* are commoner than forms like *Peter runs*. English, moreover, normally separates subject and predicator: we do not have self-sufficient forms like the Latin *amat* (he loves) but we use, as in 'he loves', one item for the subject and another for the predicator or verb.

Two forms, however, that are traditionally regarded as parts of the English verb do not invariably act as predicators. These are what we shall call the *-ing* and *-en* forms, e.g. *driving* and *driven* as in 'He was convicted of dangerous *driving*', where *driving* is clearly a noun, or 'Pure as the *driven* snow', where *driven* patterns like an adjective. For these two uses we shall retain the traditional terms *gerund* (verbal noun) and *participle* (verbal adjective); my main concern, however, in the rest of this chapter will be with the verb in its traditional role of predicator.

We can illustrate this with the three test frames:

(1) D + N + V + Adj.   The dinner was good.
                               The cat seemed asleep.
(2) D + N + V + D + N   The colonel was an Indian.
                               The cat ate the dinner.
(3) D + N + V + Adv.   The birds sing sweetly.
                               The colonel ate fast.

The 'V' position in any of these can be taken up by a verb or verb-cluster: we could, for instance, substitute *were singing* or *was eating* for the one-word verbs of (3).

The cluster *was eating* shows a distinction of primary importance: that of the *auxiliary* 'was' and the *lexical verb* 'eating'. *Was* in this combination functions primarily as a grammatical or structural item, while *eating* has both full-word status (§ 1.5) and grammatical function.

6.13.2. *The verb: basic contrasts*

The verbal clusters which the native speaker controls quite un-thinkingly in conversation – 'The colonel *might conceivably have been eating his dinner* when I telephoned' – present formidable problems in analysis. It is possible, nevertheless, that the pattern of an English verb is rather simpler than it looks on paper: much of it, indeed, can be stated in terms of fairly simple contrasts of marked and unmarked forms.

(i)   Taking the base form *drive* as our unmarked or neutral term, we have in the first place the contrast of *person*:

    I/you/we/they: *drive* (neutral)
    He/she/it: *drives* (marked)

Here *drives*, the marked form, patterns only with 'third-person singular' subjects; all other subjects, singular or plural, pattern with the unmarked form *drive*. 'Person' in English verbs is primarily a signal of concord, linking subject with predicator as in 'Mr Jones, despite his illnesses, *is* a very safe driver'. Here the 'third-singular' form of *is* signals its concord with the subject, *Mr Jones*; *illnesses* is disqualified from the role of subject both by its plural number and by its position in a prepositional group.

(ii) A second basic contrast is that of *tense*. Historically, English is a two-tense language, the contrasted forms being:

    I drive (neutral) and
    I drove (marked)

141

The base or 'neutral' form may have no specific reference to time, as in 'the Beatles drive me crazy', or it may, according to context, refer to past, present or future time. These times, of course, will not be marked by the verb, but by other forms in the sentence. Consider:

(a) 'He disappears for weeks and weeks, and then, only last Friday, we drive home and there he is, sitting by the barn.' (The *dramatic* or 'historic' present; compare the Player's speech in *Hamlet* II, ii, beginning 'Anon he finds him . . .')

(b) 'I drive the car.'

Normally, this means 'I am in the habit of driving', or something of the kind (the 'habitual' present); it is unlikely to mean 'At this present moment I am the driver', for which we are more likely to say 'I am driving'.

(c) 'We drive down the coast next Monday if all goes well.' (Present with reference to the future: for the sake of *drive* I have given a slightly artificial example, but 'we start for Italy as soon as possible', which is more colloquial, shows exactly the same use of the neutral form.)

Drive, then, which is traditionally termed the *present* form, is not so much 'present' as non-specific in its reference to time; *drove*, on the other hand, traditionally the *preterit* or 'past' form, refers specifically to times other than the present. Joos (1964) suggests that the unmarked tense should be called the *actual* and the marked tense the *remote*: this terminology fits both the 'preterit' and the 'subjunctive' uses of the marked form, as in:

> We *drove* home   (preterit)
> If we *drove* home, we'd still be late (subjunctive)

It is important to distinguish grammatical *tense* from notional *time*. Time, as in 'At 5.15 p.m. on Thursday 19th September' can be shown very precisely by devices other than tense. Some languages, like English, have two basic tense-forms; others, like Latin, have more. (For 'future' forms see § 6.13.2 (iv) below.) The contrast in English of marked and unmarked tense-forms is only the nucleus of a complex system of signals, in the form of the verb or verb-cluster, about time, and I do not suggest that it is necessarily the one which we learn first. Both present and preterite (or 'actual' and 'remote') are somewhat bare and abstract forms. A child who has grown up among English-speaking people is likely to say *I'm running* much more often than *I run*: i.e., to use the 'present continuous' form of the verb rather than the simple present. 'In the strict sense as a point without any dimension, the present has little practical value' (Jespersen, 1933). When we describe an action, past or present, we are likely to want to put more into our description than a bare indication of time: to show, for instance, that we have finished it or that we are still doing it. Hence

142

the verb-cluster that we use is likely to carry signalling features in addition to those of tense and person.

(iii) One of these additional features is termed *Aspect*: roughly speaking, the 'manner' of action: its duration in time or its relevance to the present. The basic contrasts of Aspect are the following:

> (a) I *drive* (neutral)
> I am *driving* (marked)

The neutral form specifies no particular 'aspect'. The '*continuous*' forms are marked by the appropriate form of the verb *to be*: *I am driving, we were driving, he was driving*: they specify aspect by showing the action as it were 'extended' or 'spread out' in time. Within the set of 'continuous' forms, the tense and person are marked by the form of the verb *to be* (by *am* versus *was*, etc.) and not by that of the lexical verb *driving*: this is the first of many cases in which we find the formal marks of tense and person transferred from the lexical verb to the auxiliary.

Our second type of aspectual contrast is:

> (b) I *drove* (neutral)
> I *have driven* (marked)

In this pair, we can regard the 'remote' or 'preterite' *drove* as the neutral form: it is marked only for tense, and shows no relevance to the present moment. On the other hand the *perfective* form *I have driven*, marked primarily by *have*, has reference or relevance to the moment of speaking; this point may be clearer if we set each form in a context:

> (1) 'I drove the car for several hours'
> (2) 'I have driven the car for several hours (and now I am tired)'

Here sentence (1), with *drove*, shows no connection between past action and the moment of speaking: sentence (2), with *have*, links the past action with the present moment; as Gleason (1961) puts it, it has *current relevance*. The use of *had*, incidentally, establishes a similar connection between two events located in the past:

'I had driven for several hours when I began to feel tired' – here the first action, driving for several hours, is marked as relevant to the second, feeling tired afterwards.

Is and *have* are the principal markers of aspect in formal English. *Get* and *keep* often mark aspect in informal speech. In *I get going* the aspect has been termed *inchoative*, i.e. 'starting' or 'beginning' (Francis, 1958). In *I keep going* the aspect may be termed *durative*: the emphasis on 'carrying on' is stronger than in the 'continuous' forms: contrast *I am driving* with *I keep driving*; *I was driving* with *I kept driving*.

143

(iv) Our fourth basic contrast is that of *mood*: as in:

> I *drive*   (neutral) versus
> I *may drive* (modal).

The neutral form, *I drive*, is unmarked by any particular mood or feeling; we may, however, require a form coloured by doubt, resolution, or obligation to act. Such a 'mood' can be marked by an auxiliary verb: the nine 'modal' auxiliaries, each of which may carry certain overtones of feeling not signalled by the neutral verb, are:

> *can, could; may, might; shall, should; will, would; must.*

Each of these auxiliaries can be used to refer to the future (e.g. in *I can clean the car tomorrow*) and two of them, namely *shall* and *will*, are sometimes said to form the 'future tense'. Note, however, that English has no inflections for reference to the future: in the system of an English verb there is no form to parallel the Latin *amabo* (I shall love). Old English, like Modern English, had only two tenses, past and present; English has therefore had to develop a number of special devices for referring to *future* time:

(1) The simplest of these consists of the neutral form of the verb with an adverbial marker of time as in:

> *We drive back tomorrow.*

The continuous form, as in 'We are driving back tomorrow', may often, with suitable adverbs, refer to the future.

(2) Perhaps the commonest 'future' pattern in colloquial English is, however, that of '*be* plus *going*':

> *We are going to drive back tomorrow.*

This has the advantage, incidentally, of shifting the marks of tense and person to the auxiliary *be*; it also by-passes the difficulties that have grown up around *shall* and *will* (§ 6.13.5).

(3) Thirdly, we have the forms with *shall* and *will*, the typical modals of the future. Except in first-person questions ('Shall I?' 'Shall we?'), *will* is now the dominant form, and traditional accounts of the distinction between *shall* and *will* probably bear little relation to the facts of educated speech (see § 6.13.5.).

While all the modals are capable of referring to future time, each has a special function of its own. *Can*, for instance, may signal ability or capability: 'I can jump over the hedge but you can't.' *Must* denotes obligation or compulsion: 'I must go home now, but I'd rather not.' *May* (in some contexts) denotes possibility: 'we may (or may not) go home.' *Will* often denotes resolution: 'I will cross the river in spite of your threats.' These meanings, however, are generally too subtle, complex and overlapping to be summarized briefly: it is probably better to avoid labelling any modal too specifically (e.g. 'may' = 'possibility') but to study each according to context as one finds it.

Two further sets of contrasts are perhaps established by subject–predicate structure rather than within the verbal group as such. We may, however, note them briefly in this section.

(v) First come what some writers call contrasts of *Status*. There are four basic patterns:

I drive	(Neutral)
I did drive	(Emphatic)
I did not drive	(Negative)
Did I drive?	(Interrogative)

Do is a typical marker of status, but not the only one. A negative, for instance, may take the forms *I am not driving*, *I have not driven*, an interrogative the forms *Am I driving? Have I driven?* (see also § 7.2).

(vi) Lastly we have contrasts of *voice*:

I *drive*   (neutral or 'active') versus
I *am driven*   (marked or 'passive')

In English, this contrast is shown primarily by the use of the auxiliary verb *to be*; in Latin it could be shown by inflection only: *amo*, I love; *amor*, I am loved. A passive construction signals, as a rule, that the grammatical subject does not act but is acted upon: it is therefore particularly useful when it is impossible, or inconvenient, or impolite, to indicate the performer of the action: 'He was driven crazy'; 'I am driven to the conclusion that you are incompetent'. If an active construction is changed into a passive, the 'doer' becomes, as a rule, the undergoer: *I drive*, *I am driven*. More will be said about passive constructions in Chapter Seven.

6.13.3. *Verb-inflection*

This section and the next provide a short catalogue of verb-forms: typical inflections in § 6.13.3 and typical patterns for verb-clusters in § 6.13.4.

The inflectional patterns of English verbs vary very considerably. Perhaps the most important is that of the verb *to be*, with eight different inflectional forms:

be, am, is, are, was, were, being, been,

not counting the archaic form which appears in *thou art*. The complexity of *be* reflects its derivation from four distinct Indo-European verbs:

(1) Aryan -ES, to be: compare Latin *est*, Sanskrit *asti*, Modern English *is*.

(2) Germanic ?WES-, to remain: compare Old English *wæs*, Modern English *was*.

(3) Sanskrit BHU-, to become: compare Latin *fuit*, was; Modern English *be, been*.

(4) Germanic ?AR-: compare Old English *eart*, Modern English *are*.

Most English verbs, however, have simpler paradigms:

Base	Third-Singular	Preterit or Remote	-ing	-en	
drive	drives	drove	driving	driven	(5 forms)
report	reports	reported	reporting	reported	(4 forms)
burst	bursts	burst	bursting	burst	(3 forms)
can	can	could	–	–	(2 forms)
must	must				(1 form)

Among these, the commonest is the four-form paradigm, in which the -*en* form and the 'preterit' are the same.

The preterit or 'past' is formed in a number of ways. *Drive* is one of the surviving verbs in which the preterit is formed by vowel change; the more normal form is now that of *report*, in which the preterite is formed by an 'alveolar suffix'. After alveolar stops this suffix takes the form /ɪd/ (*reported*); after other voiced sounds /d/, (*called*); after other voiceless sounds /t/, (*hopped*, /hɒpt/. There are, of course, a great many exceptions, but this is the productive pattern; a new verb like *jive* will follow the pattern, taking /d/, though there would be much to be said for the 'strong' preterite **jove*. However, only about 66 Modern English verbs form their preterites by vowel-change; in Old English, this was a much commoner pattern.

What I have labelled the -*ing* form is traditionally called the *present participle* if it acts 'adjectivally', or the *gerund* if it acts as a noun; the -*en* form, similarly, is called the *past participle* in traditional grammars. Note that the -*en* form frequently ends in -*ed* (*reported, defeated, abolished*) and is then identical with the preterite; we call it the -*en* form simply for brevity and to distinguish certain verb-clusters from one another.

With the exception of *be*, no Modern English verb has more than four or five inflected forms. The Old English verb had about sixteen; a complete verb in classical Latin had approximately 143, a Greek verb 268 and a Sanskrit verb 743.

Though an English verb has relatively few inflected forms, it does not follow that English verbs are particularly simple. Where the typical Latin verb is a complex word like *navigabamus,* the typical English verb forms complex clusters like *we were sailing;* for any given verb, the total number of possible clusters of this kind is likely to run to several hundreds.

6.13.4. *Auxiliaries and clusters (See also page 154)*

The verb-cluster in English has four basic patterns:

   (I)   Clusters ending in the *-ing* form:
         He (A) driving;
   (II)   Clusters ending in the *-en* form:
         He (A) driven;
   (III) Clusters ending in the base without *to*:
         He (A) drive;
   (IV) Clusters ending in the base after *to*:
         He (A) to drive.

In each of my examples the bracketed (A) represents an auxiliary: e.g. *is* for clusters of types (I), (II) and (IV) or *may* for clusters of type (III). Auxiliaries pattern with verbs rather as do determiners with nouns, and qualifiers with adjectives and adverbs; they have many different functions, such as that of marking tense, mood, or continuity of action, but they also very frequently act as verb-markers; an auxiliary, in other words, such as *may,* is very often a signal that a full verb is coming.

Several of the verbs which in some contexts function as auxiliaries (*I get going*) function in other contexts as 'full' or lexical verbs (*I get my dinner*). In 'Yes, we have fish today', *have* is a lexical verb, denoting possession; in 'Yes, we have to go home' it is an auxiliary with a 'modal' meaning. For full-verb *be,* see § 7.6.

Each of the four types of cluster ends in a lexical verb; this can be regarded as the nucleus of the cluster though it is probably better not to call it the 'head' in the technical sense of § 5.6.

Auxiliaries are not easy to classify. We can, however, set up a rough overlapping grouping according to our four basic types of cluster:

   (I)   With clusters ending in an *-ing* form:
         am, is, was, were;
      also in colloquial and frequently in American English:
         get, gets, got.
      ('He is driving.' 'I get going.')
   (II) With clusters ending in an *-en* form:
         am, is, was, were; get, gets, got;
         have, has, had.
      ('I am driven'; 'We all got driven home';
      'Mary has driven me to distraction.')

147

(III) With clusters ending in the base without *to*:
    (a) The nine modal auxiliaries:
        can, could; may, might; shall, should; will, would; must;
    (b) *Do, does, did;*
        ('I can drive'; 'He may drive'; 'We did drive.')
(IV) With clusters ending in the base form after *to*:
    Have, has, had; ought; used; am, is, are, was, were;
('I have to drive'; 'I used to drive'; 'They were to drive me home.')

The more complex clusters can be regarded as combinations of simpler clusters of the four basic types: thus *he is going to drive* is a cluster of type (IV) – 'He (A) to drive' with a cluster of type (I) – 'He (is) going' in the position of (A). Similarly *he might have been driving* can be built up as follows:
    He might have (Type III) enters position (A) in *He (A) been* (Type II) to form *He might have been*; this cluster then enters position (A) in *He (A) driving* to form *He might have been driving*.

6.13.5. *Shall* and *Will*

The auxiliaries *shall* and *will* have a long and instructive history. In Modern English, their primary use is as modal auxiliaries in statements about the future: 'I shall have my hair cut this afternoon'. In Old English both were originally 'full' or lexical verbs, *sceal* (shall) with the meaning of 'ought' or 'owe', e.g. in *agief þæt þu me scealt* ('repay that which thou owest me'); *willan* (will) with the meaning roughly of 'wish'. Both wishes and obligations frequently refer to the future: it is not surprising, then, that *shall* and *will* gradually lost much of their lexical meaning and became function-words for use in statements about future time. For the past three hundred years, grammarians have struggled to establish distinctions between *shall* and *will* and between 'modal' and 'non-modal' references to the future: we are, for instance, frequently told that the correct patterns are the following:

Simple Future	Modal or 'Coloured' Future
(without feeling or 'modality')	(with feeling)
I shall	I will
You will	You shall
He will	He shall

This distinction was first laid down in the *Grammatica Linguae Anglicanae* of John Wallis (1653); it is unlikely, however, that it really fits the language. It is relatively easy to find contexts in which *I shall* has clearly a modal colouring, e.g. 'I shall take up the matter with my wife at once'; 'I shall settle this account as soon as possible' (Fries, 1940). Most if not all statements about the future are likely to carry an element of mood: mood, moreover, as in this example, is conveyed not merely by the form of the auxiliary but (as a rule much more clearly) by the context. *Will*, as I indicated in § 6.13.2, is now the prevailing form except in first-person questions (*Shall I? Shall we?*); in these it is probably avoided because of its association with determination or actual 'will'.

6.13.6. *Priorities in teaching the verb*

In teaching children the English verb, particularly when English is their 'second' language, one would be unlikely to begin with a survey of inflectional forms or a list of auxiliaries. A successful approach would be more likely to begin with potentially productive combinations like *This is my hat* or *I'm putting my hat on my head*. Verbs, in short, must be taught in concrete situations, and linked, as far as possible, with activity and movement: *I'm laying the table*; *I'm drawing a horse*.

This puts a premium on continuous forms and in particular on mastering, at a fairly early stage, the important uses of the verb *to be*. We have noted that the base, and indeed the preterite forms of the verb have a somewhat bare and abstract quality: compare *I drive* with *I'm driving*, *I drove home* with *I was driving home*. If we begin our teaching with the formal paradigm, it will take us much longer to reach the forms common in colloquial speech: thus, where analytical grammar tends to begin with regular verbs like *drive*, practical grammar is much more likely to begin with the verb *to be*.

If we check the frequencies of various forms of the verb in colloquial English an instructive pattern emerges. According to a recent estimate (McNally and Murry, 1962), among the twelve most frequent words the only verbs are *is* and *was*; among the twenty words next in order of frequency the verb-forms that appear are *be*, *are*, *had*, *have* and *said*. *Said*, the seventh verb to appear, is the first that is purely lexical in function, though *have* is a lexical verb in some contexts and an auxiliary in others. The frequency count establishes the overwhelming importance of the auxiliaries for the first stages of work on the language.

This importance will be reflected in any practical outline for teaching the verb. In Hornby's *The Teaching of Structural Words and Sentence Patterns* (Oxford, 1959), the first few lessons are spent on elementary patterns with *is* and *are*: *This is . . . Is this a . . .? He is . . .* and *Is he . . .?* These drills establish not only the basic contrast of word-order between question and statement, but also the elements of concord: *I am* versus *He is*, *He is* versus *You are*. Concord, moreover, is practised for some time with the verb *to be* (probably the commonest single marker of concord in English) before the introduction of lexical verbs: and lexical verbs, when they first appear, are presented in the present continuous form – 'I'm touching my desk', 'I'm shutting the door' which enables the pupil to continue practising his concords with the verb *to be* for a number of lessons before he begins to meet elements from the 'normal' paradigm, e.g. the contrast of *touch* and *touches*. The supreme problem for the teacher of English is to devise a rational order of presentation: a means of presenting one element or contrast at a time. Hornby's scheme for the verb represents a remarkable advance in this direction.

6.14. Particles

A number of highly important English words do not fall into any of the classes – nouns, pronouns, adjectives, adverbs, and verbs – outlined in §§ 6.8. – 6.13. Such words are *and*, *of*, *to* and *how*: it is convenient to group them under the heading of *particles* ('little parts'), provided that we remember that their habits of patterning in sentences vary very considerably. 'John and Mary are here', for instance, is a possible English sentence; *'John but Mary are here' is not. *And* enters into one range of sentence patterns, *but* into quite another.

Any particle, moreover, is likely to enter into sentence-patterns of several different kinds: compare, for instance, the roles of *when* in 'When did you see them?' 'He asked when I had seen them' and 'He told us when to come'. This diversity of patterning makes it impossible to present an orderly and brief account of the English particles. Grammarians have grouped and described them in a number of different and sometimes conflicting ways, and there is at present no generally accepted classification or description of their functions.

All particles are uninflected, though, as was shown in the case of *some* (§ 6.10), they may take significant variations of phonetic form: compare *up* in *He galloped up*, /ʌp/, with *up* in *He galloped up the hill*, in which it may take the reduced form /əp/ (see also § 2.18). This, however, is not an inflectional change.

According to function, the particles appear to form two fairly distinguishable groups:

(a) *Structural particles*, such as *and* or *to*, which establish sentence-patterns and mark grammatical relationships;

(b) *Attitude-particles*, such as *yes* and *no*, which may stand outside ordinary sentence-structure and signal attitudes or responses.

The contrast, however, is not absolute. In 'Why did he do it?', for instance, *why* signals an attitude, and at the same time helps to establish a sentence-pattern. Contrast *yes* in 'Yes, I did it' or *well* in

'Well, I shan't'. Here the 'attitude-particles' are relatively independent of the SP structures which they introduce.

Structural particles. Traditional grammar distinguishes two major groups of what are here called structural particles: *prepositions* and *conjunctions.* The prepositions form a fairly well-defined class, for which a convenient test is that a personal pronoun immediately after a preposition will be in object or possessive (S/C) form ('eaten by *him*', 'a book of *his*'; see § 6.9). 'Conjunctions' do not 'govern' pronouns in this way, and different conjunctions pattern so variously that the blanket-term 'conjunction' is perhaps rather misleading. *And*, for instance, connects single words ('John and Mary'), groups ('roast beef and baked potatoes') or SP structures ('Mary knitted and John slept'). *If*, on the other hand, links SP structures only ('Mary knitted if John slept'): Such sequences as **'John if Mary' or **'roast beef if baked potatoes' are clearly incomplete. Both *and* and *if*, however, are traditionally labelled 'conjunctions'.

English has a relatively large number of prepositions, but the nucleus of the English preposition system consists of nine one-syllable items:

at, by, for, from, in, of, on, to, and *with.*

Of these the commonest are probably *of, to* and *in*, in that order (Fries, 1940). Each of these seems originally to have denoted a simple relationship in space:

Position: *At* home; *by* the tree; *in* the pot; *on* the stove
Direction: *To* the lighthouse; *from* London
Association: Men *of* Suffolk
               Cargo *for* Port Elizabeth
               Monkeys *with* tails

Of appears to originate in the spatial notion *off* (Men *of* Suffolk = men *off* Suffolk), *for* in that of *fore*, in front of; *with* in that of *mid* ('amidst'/'against'). These simple spatial senses, however, are now overlaid by a profusion of others: the *New English Dictionary* has forty separately numbered entries for *with* and sixty-three for *of*. These, perhaps, do not reflect a range of separable 'meanings' so much as a range of distinguishable relationships between the items that these prepositions connect. This range of usage reflects the frequency with which the basic prepositions occur in speech and writing: it is clear from vocabulary studies that *of, to* and *in* are among the twelve commonest words in English. The high frequency of *to* arises partly from its role in such verb-clusters as those of 'We *have to hurry*; we *are going to dine* with the Smiths' (§ 6.13.4), in which it acts as a marker of the 'infinitives' *hurry* and *dine*.

151

The English preposition system has been built up in a number of different ways to express the diversity of relationships which it can now convey. For instance, by transference of meaning we can frequently use an originally 'spatial' word to express a time-relationship: '*in* those days'; '*at* ten o'clock'. Again, a number of compound prepositions – *into, onto, within, throughout,* have been formed by combining simpler items. This list shades off into that of 'group prepositions': 'in front of', 'on behalf of', 'in connection with', 'in place of', etc., which, although they contain items (like *place* or *connection*) which are not prepositions, tend to function as do single-preposition units.

Many of the particles that function as prepositions in some contexts function rather like adverbs (§ 6.12) in others. Compare:

(a) He rode over the hill;
(b) He rode over.

In sentence (a), *over* functions as a preposition, i.e. as a connective: it 'preposes' (stands before) another item, and were this item a personal pronoun it would be in object form ('He rode over me'). In sentence (b), *over* 'preposes' nothing: it is clearly no longer a connective, and our preposition has become a 'postposition' which acts on its own as a modifier of *rode*. We might call it an adverb, though *over* by itself does not pattern very readily with adjective-adverb qualifiers (§§ 6.11, 6.12): one might hear 'he rode straight over' but not **very over* or **rather over*, just as one might say 'right in' but not **very in* or **rather in*.

In the case of *rode over* and *rode in* it is probably more important to recognize the roles of *over* and *in* as modifiers in their own right than to devise special terminology ('adverb'? 'verbal particle'? 'postposition'?) for describing them. Notice, however, their close association with the verb: an association which is not affected by separating the verb and the particle as in 'He rode the stallion over', of which the immediate constituents are clearly *not* (1) *He rode* (2) *the stallion over*.

A particle frequently joins a verb to form a unit whose meaning cannot be deduced from that of either verb or particle on its own. Contrast the well-known pair:

He ran up a big hill;
He ran up a big bill.

The substitution of pronouns for *hill* and *bill* will show up the difference in structure: *He ran up it* (the hill) versus *He ran it up* (the bill). In the second case, *ran up* is a separable verb of the kind already briefly noticed in § 4.6.

A rough grouping of structural particles according to function might distinguish:

Connectives, including the *prepositions* in one group, *co-ordinators* such as *and* and *or* in a second, and *subordinators* such as *that* and *who* (in certain patterns) in a third (see § 7.9);
  Interrogators such as *why, how, when* and *where* (in certain patterns);
  Determiners, such as *a* and *the*;
  Modifiers, such as *over* in 'he rode over' or *up* in 'he rode up';
  Negators, such as *not, neither* and *nor*;
  Qualifiers, such as *rather, very, somewhat*;
  Substitutes such as *then* in 'We arrived at tea-time and then it started to rain'.

This, however, is a very rough classification, which makes no attempt at grouping the particles according to the sentence-patterns which they form. Several groups of structural particles pattern characteristically with certain classes of lexical words: determiners, for instance, with nouns (§ 6.8) and qualifiers with adjectives and adverbs (§§ 6.11, 6.12). Others have functions which will be discussed in the course of a further analysis of sentence-patterns in Chapter Seven: it is much easier to consider structural particles in relation to the sentence as a whole than as words in isolation.

Attitude-particles, unlike structural particles, tend to detach themselves from sentence-structure, as in '*Yes*, I'd like some' or '*No*, I don't want to do it'. If an attitude-particle does not stand alone, its normal position (as in these examples) is before the sentence which it introduces, though other positions are possible. Notice that certain positions, e.g. that of *yes* in **I yes did it*' are impossible in normal English.
Attitude-particles include the following:
Attention-signals: Yes, uh-huh, and in American usage *sure.* Listeners use these to assure speakers that they are listening.
Exclamations, ranging from *hey, oh,* and *ow* to the more complicated oaths.
Hesitators: er, um and *well.*
Responses: Yes, no, maybe, perhaps, etc.
With these, of course, we are approaching the point at which language shades off into non-linguistic sound: it is not easy to decide whether *ow!* is really an English word or just a noise. But even our most 'spontaneous' exclamations are liable to bear the stamp of our linguistic culture, as one of Kipling's characters points out: 'That man is no Afghan, for they weep "Ai! Ai!" Nor is he of Hindostan,

for they weep "Oh! Ho!" He weeps after the fashion of the white men. who say "Ow! Ow!" ' (Jespersen, 1922).

Auxiliaries: an additional note

Palmer (1965) gives a systematic account of English auxiliary verbs. Our twelve auxiliaries are:

(i) BE, HAVE and DO;

(ii) WILL, SHALL, CAN, MAY, MUST, OUGHT, DARE, NEED and possibly USED. (We count *would*, *should* and *might* as preterits – 'past-tense forms' – of WILL, SHALL and MAY).

Auxiliaries contrast in a number of ways with lexical verbs such as EAT, RUN, SMOKE. For instance:

(a) They can precede the subject in certain types of sentence, notably questions. (*Are you smoking?*; contrast **Smoke you?*).

(b) They pattern with NOT (*I do not smoke*; contrast **I smoke not*) and unlike lexical verbs have special negative forms (*don't* but not **smokn't*).

(c) Like pronouns, they function as *substitutes*. Consider the exchange:

'Do cats eat bats?' 'Yes, they do.'

They and *do* in the second sentence are both 'substitute' or 'deputising' words. *They* refers back to *cats*; *do*, similarly, refers back to *eat bats*. *Do*, one might say, is acting here as a pro-predicate or pro-verb: it 'picks up' the meaning of *eat bats* from the previous sentence. If the previous sentence were 'Do pigs fly?' *do* in 'Yes, they do' would refer back to *fly*. This function of an auxiliary has been called 'code': without the 'key' to the code (*eat bats* or *fly*) one cannot perceive its full meaning.

Note to Chapter Six

Most grammars offer schemes of word-classification. For useful discussions of the problems of classification see Fries (1957), Sledd (1959) and Strang (1962).

Chapter Seven

A SKETCH OF THE SENTENCE

7.1. What is a sentence?

We have as yet no very satisfactory definition of *sentence*. The school definition: 'A sentence is the expression of a complete thought' is very nearly meaningless, since it is impossible to tell whether thoughts are complete or not. Perhaps the best available formula, despite its roundabout wording, is that of Bloomfield (1933):

'When a linguistic form appears as part of a larger form, it is said to be in *included position*; otherwise it is said to be in *absolute position* and to constitute a sentence.'

Thus, *ate the rat* does not normally stand in absolute position, though in special circumstances perhaps it might; such a form occurs normally in 'included position' in such a sequence as 'Bonzo ate the rat', which is a sentence because of its capacity to stand alone. The basic criterion for a sentence is thus probably that of being grammatically self-contained. We can describe it provisionally, as a *minimum complete utterance*.

On this view of the matter such fragments as *the rat* or *did he?* have a rather doubtful status as sentences; in Bloomfield's terms, they are likely to function as 'completive' elements as in: 'He ate the rat.' 'Did he?' or 'What did he eat?' 'The rat.' There might, however, be occasions on which either 'The rat' or even 'Did he?' was uttered on its own, and even the monosyllable *rat* might on occasion be a sentence, since in certain circumstances it requires no *linguistic* context: spoken between enemies, for instance, it would make its point without the assistance of other words. The minimum sentence is thus a single word consisting of a single morpheme: this morpheme, in turn, may consist of a single phoneme, as does the word *I*, /aɪ/, though the phoneme, of course, is a unit of sound and not of grammar.

Rat!, however, represents a 'minor' rather than a 'favourite' sentence form (Bloomfield, 1933). Minor English sentence-forms include exclamations – *Waiter!*; *You there!* and certain proverbial forms – *the more, the merrier*; *Old saint, young sinner*; which are usually in some way balanced or antithetical. They also include 'completive' forms, such as *Yes*, *No*, and *Thank you*, which supplement or complete a previous sequence of speech or behaviour or both: as does the response *No, thank you*, to the offer of a cigarette. Minor sentences are of great importance in daily living: it is, however, with favourite

155

sentence-forms that English grammarians have, until quite recently, been mainly concerned.

In § 5.4, I presented one of the favourite English sentence-patterns – SPCA – 'General Masters cheats the butcher regularly' with a warning that all sentences do not fit this pattern, important as it may be. In §4.1, we glimpsed the organization of the sentence in spoken colloquial English, which evidently differs from that of the sentence on the written page. In this chapter, I shall present some important variants on the SPCA pattern, but before moving on to these, a note on the basic *uses* of the sentence may be in order.

7.2. Statement, negation, question and command

If we consider the purposes of speech, for the moment without reference to grammatical form, the three basic types of utterance appear to be *statements* ('He's eating'), *questions* ('Is he eating?') and commands ('Eat!') Of these, as I suggested in § 6.13.1, the command as a rule is grammatically the simplest and historically *perhaps* the most primitive, though this last point is incapable of proof.

Statement, question and command, of course, represent different types of intention rather than different grammatical forms, though each, in a given language, is likely to be represented by a distinct set of grammatical patterns.

> You eat your fish.
> Did you eat your fish?
> Eat up your fish!

For commands in English the simplest pattern is the isolated verb, ↗ *Eat!* unmarked except for stress and (frequently) rising pitch. The verb, however, as in *Eat your fish!* may precede a complement of some kind; to this again may be added a 'vocative' as in *Penny, eat up your fish!* or *Stop the cab, will you!*

For statements the normal pattern is SP(CA), the brackets indicating that complement and adjunct may or may not appear: *Penny eats* (SP); *Penny eats her fish* (SPC); *Penny eats her fish reluctantly* (SPCA). We shall explore these patterns later.

For questions we may have the order SP, with rising final pitch: ↘ She ˈdrives the ↗ CAR   ? or an inversion of this order: *John is here* (SPC), becoming *Is John here?* (PSC). This inversion of the normal order of subject and predicator to form a question has been standard practice in English for a thousand years or more; but the question in Old English depended far less on auxiliaries than is the case today. In Old English a question with a lexical verb would take a form on the lines of *Lives John here?* In Modern English, such a question would now be signalled with an auxiliary: *Does John live here?*

Does John live here? repays study. Writing v for the auxiliary and V for the lexical verb, the formula is v + N + V + Adv.; the lexical verb retains its normal position immediately after the subject: the auxiliary is moved to precede the subject and thereby signal the question. The marks of tense and person are transferred from the lexical verb to the auxiliary. There is a parallel order of elements in *Is John living here?*, but with a different auxiliary (*be*) and a different form of the lexical verb.

Negations (*John doesn't live here*) use auxiliaries in a rather similar way. The affirmative or neutral pattern, *John lives here*, is not converted to a negation in Modern English by the simple insertion of *not*: 'John lives not here' accords, perhaps, with the formal archaic English of the Authorized Version of the Bible (1611), but it is hardly a modern construction. One way of transforming an affirmative into a negative sentence, if its pattern, like that of *John lives here*, is SPC, is to insert the appropriate form of *do* after the subject, followed by *not* and the base of the lexical verb: *John does not live here*. Alternatively, we may substitute for the original predicator such a combination as *is not living*: in either case the negative particle *not* stands between the auxiliary and the lexical verb.

Patterns with 'Do'. Do as an auxiliary plays many parts. In contexts such as *I do my work*, it is, of course, not an auxiliary but a 'full' or lexical verb. As an auxiliary, however, it may signal emphasis: *I did do my work*; negation: *I did not do my work*, or question; as in *Did I do my work?* Each of these examples contrasts the lexical and the auxiliary uses of *do*; in each it is the auxiliary that carries the marks of person and tense.

7.3. Transitive and intransitive patterns

The main complexities of an English sentence are usually to be found in the predicate; i.e. in the elements P(CA), Predicator, Complement, Adjunct, of our basic formula. We shall conclude our survey of the elements of English grammar with a short study of predicates. The key to this lies in Bloomfield's conception of the sentence as a self-contained grammatical unit.

Our simplest SP structures consist simply of noun (as S) and verb (as P) as in *Dogs fight, Children shout, Cats sleep*. Each of these structures can be expanded in two ways:

	SP	SPC
(a)	Dogs fight noisily.	Dogs fight wolves.
(b)	Children shout loudly.	Children shout remarks.
(c)	Cats sleep sweetly.	Cat sleep the sleep of the just.

In the SP sentences above, the expansion was by means of a modifier (in all cases an adverb) in the SPC sentences, the expansion was by means of a complement (in all three cases a noun or nominal group). Removing the modifier from a sentence of the SP group changes the meaning much less drastically than does removing the complement from the parallel sentence in the SPC group. For this reason we retain the notation SP for the sentences of the left-hand column. Compare the reduced form, e.g. *Dogs fight*, with the originals, 'Dogs fight noisily' and 'Dogs fight wolves'. Further, it is possible to move the modifiers but not the complements. We shall attest *Noisily, dogs fight*, and *Dogs noisily fight* as well as *Dogs fight noisily*, but not **Wolves dogs fight* as well as *dogs fight wolves*. *Wolves fight dogs* is acceptable, but reversing the pattern involves a potential change of meaning, which would be quite important if the verb were *eat*.

We can call a pattern like that of 'Dogs fight wolves' a *transitive* pattern and that of 'Dogs fight noisily' an intransitive pattern. Transitive, from the Latin *transeo*, 'I go across', means 'crossing' or 'passing over'; hence in a transitive construction we may picture something passing from subject to complement, as is illustrated if we substitute a pronoun for the complement noun (*Dogs fight them*): the pronoun will take an objective form (*them, him, me*), if it has one.

I have deliberately used the same verb in each pair of sentences, though it is clear that each verb acts in two radically different ways. Transitivity, then, is a feature of sentence patterns rather than of individual verbs: nearly all English verbs are transitive in some contexts and intransitive in others. (A few verbs, as will be shown in § 7.4, cannot be regarded as either transitive or intransitive.)

The principal test for a transitive pattern is that it can be converted into a passive: our three SPC structures can all be converted in this way. 'Dogs fight wolves' becomes *Wolves are fought by dogs*; 'Children shout remarks' becomes *Remarks are shouted by children*, 'Cats sleep the sleep of the just' becomes *The sleep of the just is slept by cats*. This transformation, however, cannot be carried out for a sentence that has no complement: 'Dogs fight noisily' does not become *Noisily is fought by dogs*. Nor can we convert an SPC structure to a passive if the predicator is *be*: there is no 'passive transformation' for 'John is fat' or 'John is here'.

A second test, already mentioned, is that of pronoun substitution. The following sentences are all transitive because a pronoun in the position of the complement noun will take the objective case:

She addressed *Mrs Jones*.	She addressed *her*.
We met *the harvesters*.	We met *them*.
I telephoned *the doctor*.	I telephoned *him*.

The complement in such a pattern is accordingly known as the Direct Object, though its status as object will be marked only if it is one of the personal pronouns with an objective form. Further, the test of pronoun substitution cannot be carried out for all transitive sentences – it cannot, for instance, be used for *Cats sleep the sleep of the just*.

The principal *intransitive* patterns are SP (*Children shout*) and ASP (*Unfortunately, children shout*). Note that *shout*, as in *Children shout remarks*, can also enter a transitive pattern.

Since the adjunct or modifier can in all cases be cut without radically changing the structure, the verb of an intransitive sentence is sometimes described as a verb of *complete predication*. An intransitive sentence has no complement and cannot take a passive transformation: if it includes an adjunct, the adjunct (as in the example above) can usually be regarded as a modifier of the rest of the structure. I have shown already (§ 5.4), that each of our principal components, S, P, C and A may be represented by a single word or by a group of words. Some expansions of certain components will be considered in § 7.7 – 7.9.

7.4. Linking or equational patterns

We can now compare the transitive pattern with another:

Transitive	*?*
Dogs get bones.	Dogs get fat.
He grew cabbages.	He grew old.
Cats eat bats.	Cats seem intelligent creatures.
S (affects) O	S (is) C

Here the transitive sentences represent situations in which Subject and Object, S and O, are distinct; and in which the referent of S (e.g. dogs) can be regarded as 'doing' something to the referent of O (e.g. bones). In the other sentences, the situation is different: C represents an aspect or quality of S (Mittins, 1962). To illustrate one of the transitive sentences we should need a picture of two different things, for instance a dog and a bone; for each of the others, however, the illustration might show one thing only: a fat dog, an old man, an intelligent-looking cat. We can call these *equational* or *linking* sentences because the verb sets up a kind of equation or link between subject and complement. (I shall suggest in a moment why it is reasonable to regard 'fat' and 'old' and 'intelligent creatures' as complements in these patterns.)

The three transitive sentences will all take passive transformations, even though the results are not always elegant: *bones are got by dogs*.

But the linking pattern cannot be turned into the passive: *fat is got by dogs* is a just-possible sentence, but it has lost the meaning of 'dogs get fat'; **old was grown by him* and **intelligent creatures are seemed by cats* are both non-English. The linking pattern, however, is quite distinct from the intransitive: from the intransitive *dogs fight noisily* we can cut the modifier *noisily* without radically changing the meaning; we cannot, however, remove *fat* in the same way from 'dogs get fat' to leave **dogs get*. If we remove *old* from 'he grew old' we are left with *he grew*: this is a sentence, but we have radically changed the meaning of the original. **Cats seem*, except in a rather remote philosophical context, is again an improbable sentence: it requires completion by some such items as *intelligent creatures*. It seems reasonable, then, to regard 'fat', 'old', and 'intelligent creatures' as the *complements* of our linking sentences, though their function does not match that of an object-complement in a transitive pattern (such as *wolves* in 'dogs fight wolves'). The complement of an equational sentence is sometimes for this reason called a *subject complement*.

The complement of an equational sentence, as our examples show, may take either of two principal forms: an adjective, as in 'Dogs get *fat*', or a noun or nominal group, as in 'Cats seem *intelligent creatures*'. The same 'linking' or equational verb may often take a complement of either kind, as in:

The kitten became *larger* (Adjective complement).
The kitten became *a cat* (Noun complement).

He seemed *enormously fat* (Adjective as head of complement).
He seemed a *gross creature* (Noun as head of complement).

In either case a passive transformation is impossible (we cannot, for instance, have ***'a kitten was become by the cat'). In all equational patterns the item to the right of the verb is essential to complete the structure; neither *seemed* nor *became* is a verb of complete predication.

Only a limited number of verbs form linking patterns. *Seem* is one of the principal linking verbs: *become* is another. The verb *to be* is traditionally classed as a linking verb, but there are certain advantages in keeping the verb *to be* in a class by itself: its inflections and certain features of its patterning with function-words tend to set it apart from all other verbs in Modern English. (*To be*, for instance, patterns much more readily with *there* than does any other Modern English verb: for this see § 7.6.)

Other verbs that occur typically in linking or equational patterns are *look* and *appear*: *feel* occurs in equational patterns ('he felt a fool') but also in transitive patterns ('he felt the rock under his hand'). *Taste*, *smell* and *sound* function both in equational and in transitive patterns ('it smelt good', 'he smelt a rat'). A few verbs can function in patterns of all three kinds, intransitive, linking and transitive: such a verb is *turn*.

   (i) 'The wheel turns' (SP) or
         'The wheel turns slowly' (SP with modifier);
   show *turn* in intransitive patterns;
   (ii) 'The helmsman turns the wheel' (SPC)
shows *turn* in a transitive pattern; transitive because it takes a passive transformation: 'The wheel is turned by the helmsman.'

   (iii) 'The weather turns cold' (SPC)
shows 'turn' in a *linking* pattern; a passive transformation is impossible (*'Cold is turned by the weather'), but *cold* is recognizably a complement because it completes the sense and cannot be cut without radical change of meaning: *'The weather turns', indeed, is an improbable sentence.

   Very occasionally, as in *Helen made an excellent model* (Mittins, 1962), the pattern of a sentence may be either equational ('Helen was a good model') or transitive ('Helen constructed a good model'). Such a sentence is potentially ambiguous, though the meaning will generally be clear from the context.

7.5. Transitive patterns

Transitive patterns are of several different kinds. Compare in the first place:

(A)	(B)
We sent a telegram.	We sent him a telegram.
The waiter brought dinner.	The waiter brought us dinner.
Mary made a hat.	Mary made me a hat.

   Group (A) are transitive sentences on the model of *dogs fight wolves*; the complement is a Direct Object (§ 7.3) consisting of a single item: *a telegram, dinner, a hat*. In Group (B), the complements are *double*, each consisting of two items: an 'inner complement', sometimes called an *indirect object* (*him, us, me*), and an outer complement, matching the direct object in the corresponding sentence of Group (A): *a telegram, dinner, a hat*. For these sentences, we can write the formula S + P + IO + DO.

   The position of the Indirect Object is normally between the verb and the direct object, as in 'We sent *him* a telegram'. If we alter the construction by introducing this element with a preposition, as in 'We sent a telegram *to him*' what was previously the Indirect Object will now stand last, but it has now changed its function. It is no longer an Indirect Object – no longer part of the complement, as we can show by

161

cutting the sentence to 'We sent a telegram'. Grammatically, this requires no completion: *to him* functions as an adjunct or sentence modifier, the immediate constituents being (1) 'We sent a telegram' (2) 'to him'.

Quite a number of English verbs form indirect-object patterns: *keep* as in 'They kept him some dinner', *write* as in 'I wrote him a letter', *show* as in 'I'll show you the door'. For all these sentences we can write the formula S + P + IO + DO (Subject, Predicator, Indirect and Direct Objects). The same verbs, of course, may pattern with complements consisting of a single item: *keep cats, write letters, show your passes.* One of the commonest verbs occurring in indirect-object patterns is *give*, as in *The cat gave her kitten a mouse*; notice that in this, as in all indirect-object patterns, the nouns in the complement have two separate referents, in this instance 'kitten' and 'mouse'.

In another type of transitive pattern, both items in the complement have the same referent, as in:

> *They called him a liar* or
> *The class thought him foolish.*

For a pattern with a verb like *give*, we have a choice of two passive transformations: 'The cat gave her kitten a mouse' can take either of two passive forms: 'The kitten was given a mouse by the cat' or 'A mouse was given by the cat to the kitten'. *They called him a liar*, however, has one passive transformation only: 'He was called a liar by them'; we cannot move *a liar* into the position of subject. An element like *liar* in such a structure is sometimes called an *Object Complement*: we can write the formula for *They called him a liar* as S + P + DO + OC (Subject, Predicator, Direct Object, Object Complement). As our examples show, an object complement may be either noun (*liar*) or adjective (*foolish*).

A few verbs pattern both with indirect objects and object complements; this is the basis of such ancient jokes as 'Call me a porter'; 'O.K., you're a porter.'

A rather limited number of verbs form object-complement patterns. One group consists of verbs like *consider, think, believe*; another of verbs like *vote, appoint* and *elect*. For the first group the object complement may be either adjective or noun:

> They considered him brilliant.
> They considered him a genius.

– in the second group it can only be a noun or noun-headed group:

> They elected her president.

(but not 'They elected her beautiful'.) A few verbs function in patterns of both kinds: 'We made her president'; 'We made her beautiful'.

At this point, it may be helpful to set out our four basic transitive patterns in series: in the list below, S marks Subject, P Predicator, SC Subject Complement, IO Indirect Object, DO Direct Object and OC Object Complement.

	S	P	SC	IO	DO	OC
1.	The room	got	colder.			
2.	Penny	got			a cough.	
3.	Mother	got		us	tea.	
4.	The tea	got			us	talking.

Not many verbs, of course, are sufficiently versatile to fit all four patterns; I have chosen *got*, not because I regard it as an elegant verb, but to show that the sentence-pattern is to a certain extent independent of the particular verb that we happen to choose.

7.6. The patterns with 'be'

For several reasons, it is convenient to regard the verb *to be* as forming patterns of its own. It has, for instance, eight inflectional forms instead of the usual four or five. It does not pattern in formal English with pronouns in the objective form (*It's me!*, common enough in the spoken language, is still discouraged in formal writing). Further, the verb *to be* has in English a special relationship with the sentence-initiator *there*.

Our three principal patterns with *be* are:

> (a) The lorry was here.
> (b) The lorry was old.
> (c) The lorry was a Ford.

None of these can be reduced to **The lorry was*; we can thus regard *here*, *old*, and *a Ford* as complements of three different kinds: adverbial, adjectival and nominal. Each could, of course, be very considerably expanded:

> (a) The lorry was here under the trees a few minutes ago.
> (b) The lorry was old, green, battered and disreputable.
> (c) The lorry was an old green battered disreputable Ford.

Notice that pattern (a) is restricted to adverbs or adverbial sequences of place or time: we cannot have **The lorry was quickly*, with an adverb of manner. None of our three *be*-patterns takes a passive transformation.

Patterns of type (a) can be readily converted to begin with *there*:

'The lorry was here under the trees' becomes *There was a lorry here under the trees*. This transformation involves:

(i)   Moving *was* to precede the subject.
(ii)   Substituting *a* for *the*.
(iii) Beginning the sentence with *There*.

The particle *there* in this position cannot be assigned to any particular word-class: 'It is just the word that gets this peculiar English construction started' (Roberts, 1962). In this position as a sentence-initiator, it is often phonetically distinct from the adverb of place *there*; contrast:

/ðɛə/ goes the lorry.
/ðə/ was a lorry here yesterday.

Both forms would be written *there*, but the first has implications of place or pointing and can be regarded as an adverb; compare 'Over the hill goes the lorry': the reduced form /ðə/ marks a change of grammatical function: *there* has become a purely structural word, a kind of dummy subject preceding the verb. Possibly, as Jespersen has suggested, we are reluctant to begin a sentence with *a*: instead of 'A lorry is under the trees' we tend to say: 'There's a lorry under the trees', hiding the 'indefinite' subject behind the verb.

7.7.   A table of sentence-patterns

We can now gather our basic sentence-patterns into a table, numbering them for reference and beginning with the patterns of *be*.

Group A: Patterns with 'be':
S + *be* + C

Number:

1   The lorry was here   (*Be* + Adverbial Complement)
2   The lorry was old   (*Be* + Adjective Complement)
3   The lorry was a Ford   (*Be* + Noun Complement)

Group B: Intransitive Patterns:
S + P

4   Children shout   (Verb)
5   Children shout noisily   (Verb plus modifier)

Group C: Linking or Equational Patterns:
S + P + SC   (Subject Complement)

6   The kitten became larger (Adjective Complement)
7   The kitten became a cat   (Noun Complement)

Group D: Transitive Patterns:
         S + P + C   (Various patterns of Complement)
8 We sent a telegram   S + P + DO
9 We sent him a telegram   S + P + IO + DO
10 They called him a liar   S + P + DO + OC
11 They elected her president   S + P + DO + OC

Our table reflects, of course, only a selection of the sentence-patterns that are possible in English, and is limited to basic sentences in the simplest possible form. Each of the principal components of our basic sentences consists of a single word, or at most of a noun preceded by a determiner, but each component could be considerably expanded: for the subject of Sentence 1, for example (*The lorry*) we could substitute 'The battered old green lorry belonging to the Naicker brothers', without altering the basic sentence-pattern. Similarly for the predicator of Sentence 11 (*elected*) one could substitute such a verb-cluster as 'ought to have been electing', again without changing the basic pattern of the sentence as a whole.

7.8. Headed and non-headed groups

Between the items that make up a particular sentence or sentence-component, there are two possible kinds of relationship. One of these, as it happens, is exemplified in:
   (a) *The battered old green lorry belonging to the Naicker brothers*;
the other in:
   (b) *have been electing.*
The first of these groups is *headed* (§ 5.6) in that it contains a single item, *lorry* (perhaps more strictly *the lorry*), which can deputize for the group as a whole, e.g. by standing as subject in sentence-patterns 1, 2 and 3 in § 7.7. But the second group contains no such item: we cannot extract from it any word or combination of words to stand as predicator in sentence-pattern 11.

Headed groups were introduced in § 5.6, and simple relationships of modifier and head have been repeatedly presented in the intervening sections. Our basic sentence-patterns, on the other hand, with the exception of pattern 5, are all non-headed. Consider pattern 4, *Children shout*. This can enter into larger patterns: 'I hear children shout' or 'Children shout all day'. But in none of these larger patterns of which *children shout* is a component can its place be taken, without radical change of meaning, by either *children* or *shout*. (In pattern 5, *children shout noisily*, the head is 'children shout' and the modifier 'noisily'.)

SP or SPC structures, then, are non-headed in that no single

165

component can take the place of the structure as a whole. Other non-headed structures are prepositional groups ('to an ape'; 'at the zoo') and SP sequences introduced by *if, because* and similar connectives: *if we had a cat, because it's raining*, etc.

7.9. Co-ordination and subordination

Headed structures follow two principal patterns, those of co-ordination or subordination.

Co-ordination is the relationship of elements that are grammatically equivalent, as in 'We ate and drank' (in which *ate* and *drank* are co-ordinate elements of the predicate) or 'we ate apples and pears' (in which *apples* and *pears* are co-ordinate elements of the complement). The typical co-ordinator is *and*. The co-ordinated items may be words ('John *and* Sylvia'); groups ('Over the hills *and* far away'); or SP (C) structures ('Mother talks *and* Father reads the paper'). The test for a co-ordinate structure is whether it can be replaced by *either* of its two principal components: thus, 'We ate and drank' can be reduced either to 'We ate' or to 'We drank'. In this sense a co-ordinate structure may be said to have two heads, or in some cases more than two, as in 'We bought butter, eggs, bacon and bread', in which *butter, eggs, bacon* and *bread* are co-ordinate elements of the complement.

Subordination, on the other hand, is a relationship in which one element becomes subsidiary to another. Thus, in: 'An ape at the zoo has eaten the apple', *at the zoo* modifies *an ape* and is an element subordinate to the SPC pattern of: 'An ape has eaten the apple'. English has a number of devices for signalling subordination.

The first of these, as shown in § 5.7, is *word-order*: an English adjective normally precedes the noun that it modifies, as in *white wine*. This convention enables us to recognize the head in groups in which one noun modifies another: *government office, quality control.* Here the relative positions signal that the heads are *office* and *control*. Other languages may follow different conventions of order: compare *white wine* with the French *vin blanc*, in which the modifier follows the head.

A second set of patterns of subordination is established by *prepositions*. A prepositional group such as 'at the farm' or 'on the table' can function in various ways: it may, for instance, be the complement of *is* in: 'John is *at the farm*' or: 'The mouse is *on the table*'. It may also occasionally take the position of subject, as in: '*On the table* is a mouse', though the concord of subject and verb in: 'On the table are nine mice' shows that *on the table* is still complement rather than subject in this structure. The complement in all these patterns is the entire group 'on the table': the noun *table* is subordinated by the

166

preposition *on*, and cannot be regarded as the head of the complement.

Though prepositional groups occur as complements, they are more commonly found as modifiers, as in:

> The cat *at the farm* has ginger kittens;
> The mouse *on the table* is eating cheese.

Notice that in both these sentences the removal of the modifier does not affect the SPC structure ('The cat has ginger kittens'; 'The mouse is eating cheese'); it is helpful in such cases to regard the preposition as a sort of shunting device that directs the modifiers into sidings off the main line of SPC traffic, thus

> The cat ————————→ has ginger kittens.
>   at
>   the farm
> The mouse ————→ is eating cheese.
>   on
>   the table

In both sentences the prepositional groups are subordinate elements (in this case modifiers) in the headed groups *the cat at the farm* and *the mouse on the table*.

A rather similar pattern of subordination is established by means of the connectives *who, which* and *that*. Here one SP(C) structure becomes a subordinate element in another; *who* in 'The man who did it has gone away' subordinates the verb *did* by backing it out of the line of SP traffic which flows from the subject *man* to the predicator *has gone*:

> The man————————→ has gone away.
>   who
>   did it

Here the clause *who did it* becomes a modifier of the subject *the man*. *Who* in such a position is sometimes termed a 'relative pronoun', and as subject of 'did it' certainly has something like pronoun status. I prefer, however, to regard it as a connective (§ 6.14) because this does not raise awkward questions about case. The complement of *asked* is the entire structure *who had done it*: if one emphasizes the pronominal function of *who* one is apt to wonder why its form, after the verb *asked*, is not *whom*, though *'He asked whom had done it' would be rejected by most educated speakers of English.

Yet another pattern of subordination is established by a special group of connective particles termed *subordinators*. These include:

> *As, because, how, if, since, when, where, whether, while.*

The typical role of a subordinator is to connect two SP structures, converting one into a complement or modifier of the other. Thus in:

167

He asked if we had done it, the subordinator *if* converts the SPC structure: 'We had done it' into the complement of 'he asked'; the sentence patterns as:

S	P	C
He ⟶	asked ⟶	if *we had done it.*

$$(S \longrightarrow P \longrightarrow C)$$

Notice that *if we had done it* is a sentence-fragment that normally could not stand alone.

Again, in: 'If John did this, we shall all have to resign', the particle *if* subordinates *John did this* to *we shall all have to resign.* 'John did this' might stand alone; *If John did this,* however, is incomplete and functions as adjunct or sentence-modifier (§ 5.4) to: 'We shall all have to resign'. In patterns like these, the subordinated structures are those that could not stand independently. The sentences *I like fish* and *It's cheap* are both complete as they stand, but in the combination *I like fish because it's cheap* the second has been subordinated to the first; *because it's cheap* is a sentence-fragment or at best a 'completive' form. The subordinators, unlike certain other connectives, may stand either between the two structures that they link, or in front of the first:

> I'll come *if* you call me
> *If* you call me, I'll come.

Another group of connective particles are termed *co-ordinators* because they join elements of equal or 'co-ordinated' grammatical status: the principal English co-ordinators are:

(a) *And, not, or, but;*
(b) *Both—and; either—or; neither—nor; not (only)— but (also).*

For the one-word co-ordinators of group (a) the normal position is between the items which they connect ('I liked John *but* I disliked Mary'); the co-ordinators of group (b) function in pairs, one before each of the items which are linked: 'I liked *both* John *and* Mary'; 'I liked *not only* John *but also* Mary'.

Fries (1952) describes the co-ordinators as 'signals of levelling' and this is a useful clue to their mode of operation. Thus in *The man and his dog are looking for rats,* the plural form of *are* shows that *and* has co-ordinated or 'levelled' *man* and *dog* into a plural subject; contrast: 'The man, with his dog, is looking for rats' or: 'The man is looking for rats with his dog'. Here the singular form of *is* shows that the subject is *man*: the preposition *with* subordinates the group *with his dog* to the status of a modifier. Some people, of course, would say: 'The man with his dog are looking for rats', using *with* as a co-ordinator, but many others express disapproval of this pattern, though Shakespeare sometimes uses it.

Chapter Eight

A NOTE ON LEXICON

8.1. Word and lexical item

Thinking of a language, one is apt to think first of words, but of the three systems of which all languages consist, phonology, grammar and lexicon, the lexicon or vocabulary is in some ways the most difficult to describe or explore.

It is possible, of course, to draw up an alphabetical list of words, to explain their meanings and to call the result a dictionary. Enormously useful, however, as many dictionaries are, no dictionary gives an *organized* account of lexical meanings. It would be a remarkable coincidence if the patterns of meaning in a language coincided with the alphabetical arrangement of words in a dictionary.

Further, as I have already suggested in § 6.1, the orthographic word is not the basic unit of lexical meaning. Consider the word *King* in the following settings:

(a) The King is opening Parliament tomorrow.
(b) 'King to Queen's Knight's second.'
(c) 'If you trump that King, you're no friend of mine.'

In all three sentences we have the identical orthographic word, *King*, but with three different referents (§ 1.4): in (a) the head of the State; in (b) a chessman; and in (c) a playing card. In each of these cases, moreover, the word is a member of a different 'set'; the three sets being:

(a) King, Queen, Prince, Duke, Baron, Knight . . .
(b) King, Queen, Rook, Bishop, Knight, Pawn;
(c) Ace, King, Queen, Knave, ten, nine, eight . . .

Each of these sets is a group of words with referents in a particular field: the nobility in (a); chess in (b); playing cards in (c). Such a group is a *lexical set*: in each the word *king* gets its meaning, or some of it, by its relation to the other members of the set. I shall show how this happens in § 8.2; my point for the moment is simply that the word *king* has three quite different referents according to context, and thus represents at least three different lexical items.

Parallel cases could easily be multiplied. *Figure,* for instance, has several fields of reference: for example, mathematics and corsetry;

letter represents one lexical item in 'I've a letter for the post' and another in 'What's the second letter in *psychology*?'

Further, a lexical item may consist of more words than one. In 'He *fell out* with his mother-in-law but now he has learnt to *put up with* her', the meaning of *fell out* is distinct from that of the words *fall* and *out* in other contexts, nor could we arrive at the meaning of *put up with* by adding together those of the words *put*, *up* and *with*. This is generally true of phrasal or 'separable' verbs (§ 4.6): consider 'He turned down my offer' or 'They ran up an enormous bill'. In 'The aircraft *took off*' and 'After the *take-off* it circled the airfield' we have two distinct grammatical forms: *took off*, a phrasal verb, and *take-off*, a noun. Both, however, represent the same lexical item.

Lexical item can perhaps be very roughly defined as 'unit of lexical meaning; i.e. of non-grammatical meaning' (§§ 1.5; 5.1); thus the two forms of *run* in 'I run' and 'He goes for a run' are grammatically different but lexically the same, whereas the two forms in 'They are back from their run' and 'The chickens are in their run' are grammatically the same but different in lexical meaning.

8.2. Meaning and the child

For the child, the development of meaning and of vocabulary is a process primarily of *differentiation*. We begin to communicate with others by means of a small repertoire of expressive sounds; from these we develop a small vocabulary of all-purpose or multi-purpose words, which is gradually expanded into a large vocabulary consisting of much more specific items.

A child who knew one word only would have to use this one word for all purposes of communication. This, of course, is a hypothetical case: by the time that babbling has begun to approximate to words, the child has already a modest range of 'differentiated' expressive noises (§ 3.1): howling, cooing, laughing, gurgling, according to circumstances. Differentiation, then, has begun before the emergence of words.

When, however, babbling begins to take form in more or less recognizable words, it is much easier to trace the process of differentiation. Lewis (1936) gives an instructive account of the development of a small child's animal-vocabulary over a three-month period beginning at the age of one year nine months.

At the beginning of this period the child was using the form /tiː/, at first apparently with reference to the cat, and later also for a small dog, a horse and a cow. About six weeks later he started to use the form /gɒgɪ/, at first for a toy dog and later for a small, real dog. About three weeks later the form /hɒʃ/ appeared: this designated a horse, for which the child still occasionally said /tiː/; /hɒʃ/ was also used for a large dog. About ten days after this the form /mʊka/ was used for a cow, and /gɒgɪ/ for a large dog; meanwhile the cat was redesignated /pʊʃɪ/. At the end of the three-month period, the child's animal-vocabulary had sorted itself out as: /pʊʃɪ/, cat; /mʊka/, cow; /hɒʃ/, horse; and /gɒgɪ/ for all three kinds of dog: the large dog, the small dog and the toy dog. It was perhaps a pity that three of his four items had been learned in 'baby-talk' forms that would have to be un-learned later: small boys are sometimes highly intolerant of forms like *moo-cow* and *doggie*. But this matters less for our present purposes than the establishment, admittedly in rudimentary form, of a lexical set.

Three distinct processes are apparent here.

(i) In the first place, there is differentiation: at the beginning of the period the child uses the 'all-animal' form /tiː/; at the end of it he has a set of four differentiated items.

(ii) Secondly, the forms are getting closer to those of adult English: the unrecognizable /tiː/ has become /pʊʃɪ/, a tolerable approximation to *pussy*; /gɒgɪ/ no doubt will in time become *doggie*, and the adult forms *cat* and *dog* will appear later.

(iii) Meanings are also beginning to approximate to those of adult English: the referents of /hɒʃ/ and /gɒgɪ/ have become more or less aligned with those of *horse* and *dog*.

Words are a means of organizing our experience into categories: one of the primary uses of the word is as a *classifying tool*. The child's set of four animal words enables him to sort out four kinds of animals and to classify them more or less as adults do: one of the most interesting steps in the process is the development of the use of /gɒgɪ/ for three different kinds of dog.

In the process of this development, which is, of course, only a small element in the relationship of parent and child, one imagines two key types of incident or exchange. One might represent these as:

(i) Parent: That's a doggie.
    Child: /gɒgɪ/.
(ii) Parent: That's not a doggie, it's a horse.
    Child: /hɒʃ/.

These two kinds of exchange are perhaps fundamental to the establishment of meaning, which probably involves: (i) Recognition: the realization that this is X; (ii) Definition: the recognition that X is not Y. Definition is the setting of limits to the meaning of a term: the drawing of boundaries between one item and another. The boundaries established, in a preliminary way, during the process which Lewis has recorded for us, are those of a child's approximations to the adult terms *horse, dog, cat* and *cow*; later, of course, as his vocabulary develops together with his experience, he will extend the set, for instance with *mouse, rat, goat* and *monkey*, and he will continue to extend it as long as there are creatures for him to discover and words with which to name them.

8.3. Lexical sets

A lexical set is thus a rather loose group of 'mutually defining items'; notice that such a set is capable of being extended indefinitely: it does not have the *limitation* that is characteristic of grammatical contrasts (e.g. singular versus plural, past versus present) in which we have a limited choice within a 'closed system' rather than a wider choice over an 'open set'.

A lexical set may, of course, include words belonging to different grammatical classes: thus *soaring, fly, glider, swooped* and *dive* have a lexical theme in common and may be regarded as members of the same lexical set, though it would be difficult, if not impossible, to devise a grammatical frame (§ 5.10) in which all five could be accommodated in the same position. (All would fit the vacant slot in '*I said* "——"!' but such a frame is not an instrument for grammatical definition.)

It is important to remember that lexical sets consist of words and not of things or 'ideas'. A typical lexical set is the colour-vocabulary. The physical spectrum represents an unbroken continuum or range of colour; most of us distinguish different colours at different points in the range, but two different languages will not necessarily divide the range in the same way. Thus everyday English has six basic terms for the colours of the spectrum, *red, orange, yellow, green, blue, purple*; Navaho has three, which for the sake of simplicity we can here call X, Y and Z. The sets compare as follows:

English	R	O	Y	G	B	P
Navaho	X		Y		Z	

This illustrates rather neatly how our vocabulary (more strictly, our repertoire of lexical items) resembles a sort of 'grid' (Catford, 1959 and 1965) or fencing system laid out over our experience of the world. Different languages put up the fences along different lines; this obviously has an important bearing on problems of translation.

Thus, in English the word *uncle* denotes 'father's brother' as well as 'mother's brother' for which Xhosa has two separate terms: *ubawokazi* and *umalume*. Here, and in the field of family relationships generally, the Xhosa lexicon makes distinctions that the English lexicon does not. Further, the meaning of *ubawokazi* is only partially reflected in the translation 'father's brother'. For a Xhosa, the distinction between the mother's family and the father's is often of great social and practical importance: this has no exact parallel in any Western community.

Probably no two words from different languages are ever exactly equivalent. Consider English *uncle*, Afrikaans *oom* and Xhosa *ubawokazi*. I may use any word of the three to refer to my father's brother. This, however, is as far as their similarity will take me. For my mother's brother I may use *oom* or *uncle* again, but in Xhosa I shall need an entirely different word: *umalume*. If I refer to your uncle and not to mine, the Xhosa prefixes are changed and the words become *unyokalume* (your mother's brother) and *uyihlokazi* (your father's brother). There is a difference of another kind between Afrikaans *oom* and English *uncle*. Afrikaans children will address any grown-up man as *oom*, regardless of whether he is a blood-relation or not: as a term of address, it is at once friendly and respectful. English children, however, do not use *uncle* in the same way. Though it is sometimes used of a friend of the family, particularly in South Africa, an English-speaking child would not address a stranger as *uncle* where it would be quite normal for a polite Afrikaans-speaking child to say *oom*.

These differences are not simply matters of isolated words. The full meanings of *oom*, *uncle*, *umalume* and *ubawokazi* reflect the different patterns of family and personal relationships in Afrikaner, English and Xhosa societies, and a full exploration of these meanings would involve some analysis of the three cultures behind them.

8.4. Collocation

This brings us to the other lexical aspect of a word, namely its *collocation*. Roughly speaking, the collocation of a word is its propensity for particular neighbours or environments: thus *pen* tends to 'collocate' with *ink*, *ham* with *eggs* and *pepper* with *salt*. Each of these pairs may be regarded as a *collocation*: i.e. a group of words that tend to occur together.

There is obviously a certain overlapping between the notion of a collocation and that of a lexical set. The terms, however, are distinguishable. Thus *horse*, *cow*, and *stable* may be expected to collocate, but *stable* is not an item in the lexical set to which *horse* and *cow* belong. Similarly, the words *car* and *petrol* will collocate fairly frequently, but are members of different lexical sets.

Collocation is also distinguishable from *context* (§ 1.3). The context of an item is its general setting or environment; a collocation, on the other hand, is a specific grouping of items, e.g. the item *fish* and the item *chips* tend to occur in collocation. It follows that it is easier to describe the collocations of a word than to describe its contexts. A context must be described in impressionistic terms; for a collocation we can lay down fairly specific criteria: e.g. if we wish to survey the collocations of a given word in a Shakespeare play – say, those of the word *gods* in *King Lear* – we can agree that any words in the text within a specified distance of *gods* – say, within five words of it on either side – can be counted as being in collocation with it. We may then find that certain words, or kinds of words, collocate with *gods* much more readily than do others: one would, for instance, expect to find a rather frequent collocation of *gods* with words denoting authority and power.

Our habits of collocation show up neatly in word association tests, in which the subject is given one word, e.g. *chair*, as a stimulus, and responds with another, e.g. *table*. Miller (1951) reports on the responses to various words of a thousand men and women tested in 1910. To the word *lamp*, for instance, 650 of the thousand subjects responded with *light* and 49 with *oil*; at the other end of the scale were such responses to *lamp* as *student, tall* and *wisdom*, each given by one person only. Similarly to the word *chair*, 191 responded with *table* and only one with *beauty*. Thus, for any given word we tend to recall the items that normally collocate with it; the normal collocations, on the other hand, are by no means inevitable.

Unusual collocations are often exploited in poetry. Thus *Christ* and *lamb* are a fairly common collocation but in T. S. Eliot's *Gerontion* we have 'Christ the tiger'; *April* is apt to collocate with words denoting the beauty of springtime, but in the first line of *The Waste Land* 'April is the cruellest month'. In Dylan Thomas's line, 'The force that through the green fuse drives the flower' we have two contrasted collocations: *force, fuse*, and perhaps *drives* on the one hand, *green* and *flower* on the other. One of the great social functions of poetry is that of adjusting and rejuvenating the language: this is reflected in the poet's relative freedom from normal and established habits of collocation.

Since the same grammatical item may belong to different lexical sets, meanings are often uncertain without clues of collocation. Consider the sentence: 'The captain is unfortunately drunk.' *Captain* here may be drawn from the set: 'Admiral, captain, commander, lieutenant-commander, lieutenant', or from the set: 'General, brigadier, colonel, major, captain, lieutenant'. (Notice that *captain* is near the top of the naval set and near the bottom of the military one.) Given a collocation: 'The captain conferred with the admiral' or 'The captain saluted the general', we are in a better position to decide what kind of captain is meant, though we cannot, of course, be quite certain without further evidence. (*Captain*, of course, has other possible collocations than these: e.g. in the fields of football and of mining.)

The value of the concept of collocation for the study of vocabulary lies in its specificity. In studying collocations, we examine the relationships of particular *words* to one another in particular texts or sequences of speech, and in particular their 'tendency to co-occurrence' (Halliday, McIntosh and Strevens, 1964). We do not have to fall back upon impressionistic descriptions of contexts or 'associations'.

Nevertheless, the concepts of collocation and lexical set provide only limited information about the central problems of meaning, 'the relation of language to the rest of the world' (Robins, 1964), i.e. its engagement with phenomena. Wittgenstein's statement that 'For a large class of cases . . . the meaning of a word is its use in the language' (Strang, 1962), is an exceedingly useful pointer, but should not be allowed to turn us away from considering the all-important relationships of words and things.

8.5. Dictionary and thesaurus

With this, we reach a basic principle for the construction of dictionaries, already stated in § 1.3: that meaning depends on context. The business of the lexicographer, the maker of dictionaries, is not to say what words ought to mean, but to report their meanings as he finds them in the language. A good dictionary is thus essentially a report rather than a piece of legislation.

This is evident from the editorial methods of the staff of the great *New English Dictionary*, a project which originated at a meeting of the Philological Society in London in 1857, and was completed in 1928 with the issue of the tenth and final volume by Oxford University Press. (A supplement appeared in 1933.) 'The aim of this dictionary', to quote the Preface, 'is to furnish an adequate account of the meaning, origin and history of English words now in use, or known to have been in use at any time over the past seven hundred years.' During the seventy years which it took to compile the dictionary, several hundred volunteer readers in the United States and in Britain sent in a total of over six million slips, quoting words in context from an enormous range of texts. These quotation slips – not preconceived definitions – formed the raw material of the Dictionary. To quote the Preface again: 'To a great extent the explanations of the meanings have been framed anew upon a study of all the quotations for each word collected for this work.'

While other dictionaries may not aspire to the scope and magnitude of this one, the basic principle of the *New English Dictionary*, that of reporting usage, is one which all dictionaries ought to follow. It is a principle, of course, which leads to difficulties when a usage that is strongly disapproved of by influential people (such as 'disinterested' for 'uninterested') is nevertheless extremely common. Here the lexicographer should report both the usage and the disapproval, as Webster's *New Collegiate Dictionary* of 1963 does in the case of *ain't* cited in § 1.9. One of the lexicographer's most important decisions will thus be on the marking of the status of an item: e.g. *obs.* for 'obsolete', '*coll.*' for 'colloquial', '*dial.*' for 'dialect'.

Another difficult decision will be on the listing of words for inclusion. Is *apartheid*, for instance, an English word or not? Its inclusion in several recent dictionaries suggests that it is now regarded as being English as well as Afrikaans: its collocations in the two languages will naturally be rather different.

In modern English, new words (*sputnik*, *beatle*) and new meanings (*with it*, *jet*, etc.) appear with such rapidity that no dictionary can hope to provide a report that is completely up to date. All dictionaries, moreover, gradually become obsolete as the language changes. A dictionary more than twenty years old may be an adequate guide to the language of the past, but there will be rather serious gaps in its treatment of the present. Further, since no dictionary is entirely reliable, the serious teacher of English ought probably to make a habit of using at least two, one as a check on the other.

For the foreign learner, as many teachers of English as a second language have found to their cost, an English dictionary, or for that matter a bilingual dictionary, is a very dangerous tool. The reason for this is the 'untranslatability' of words, to which I referred in § 8.3.

A further almost indispensable book for the exploration of vocabulary is *Roget's Thesaurus of English Words and Phrases*, first published in 1852 and from time to time brought up to date in later editions. A dictionary enables one to find a signification, given a word; the *Thesaurus* enables one to find words, given a signification. Thus, if one requires a word for a particular brand of villainy one turns to *villainy* in Roget's index, which refers one to section 940; section 940 list about 150 items in this general field of meaning, ranging from 'improbity' to 'mouth-honour'. with numerous cross-references to other sections. *Roget's Thesaurus* in short, is a treasury of lexical sets, of considerable value both to writers and teachers of English.

8.6. Teaching vocabularies

'Words' vary enormously in their usefulness and relative frequency. A few, such as *and, the* and *to*, are probably used many times a day by nearly every speaker of English. Others, for instance *bed, book, box, begin,* are rather less common but still almost indispensable for the ordinary purposes of life. Others, such as *contributor, convolution, copious, copyright,* are rarer still.

The statistical study of vocabulary has an obvious relevance to teaching problems, and the twentieth century has seen a great many investigations in this field. A number of these are described and criticized by Fries and Traver (1963).

Godfrey Dewey, for instance, reported in 1923 on a study of vocabulary and speech sounds for students of shorthand. Dewey made a selection of texts, including passages from the Bible, newspapers, scientific works and personal correspondence, amounting in all to a hundred thousand orthographic words. In this body of material he found 10,161 different words (presumably spelling-forms) of which only nine formed 25 per cent of the corpus of 100,000. These nine words were *the, of, and, to, a, in, that, it* and *is.* The next two were *I* and *for.* Dewey found that 69 different words made up over 50 per cent of the 100,000, and that 1,027 words, occurring more than ten times each, made up 78·6 per cent.

Dewey's study was by no means the first attempt at a statistical chart of our vocabulary, and there have been many since on a much larger scale. The famous *Teacher's Word Book* of E. L. Thorndike, first published in 1921 and later expanded and reissued, reports frequencies based on a count of nearly four million running words.

However, the initial findings of all such studies have been the same. A very small number of words accounts for a very high proportion of the total in every count. The commonest words are grammatical items like Dewey's leading nine; *of, and* and *the* are commonly placed in the top ten. The less frequent items are generally lexical, as shown above. Once the first few hundred words have been listed, the assessment of frequencies will depend rather heavily on the type of material surveyed.

These findings have important consequences for language teaching. The commonest and most useful items ought obviously to be presented first, both in the teaching of English as a second language, and in training English-speaking children to read and write. In both fields, the findings of statistical studies of vocabulary have already been applied with considerable success. There remain, however, some rather intractable problems for constructors of teaching vocabularies.

The earlier studies of vocabulary were based exclusively on written texts; and only quite recently have materials based on recordings of unscripted speech become available. Again, the unit of most studies to date has, in effect, been the orthographic word: thus *bear* (carry) is

177

not as a rule distinguished from *bear* (animal) or *copy* (noun) from *copy* (verb). Many 'teaching vocabularies' are thus in effect only graded lists of spelling-forms. On the other hand, it is much more difficult to count lexical and grammatical items rather than orthographic words.

Further, as has been shown in recent studies of spoken French, the relative usefulness of words cannot be assessed simply from their frequency of occurrence in speech. For instance, in recordings of 163 conversations in which 175 different people took part, two of the names of days of the week, *mercredi* and *vendredi*, failed to appear. Yet these are essential items for almost any teaching vocabulary. In this study, 1,063 words each occurred twenty times or more in the recorded conversations, but these included a number of synonyms or near-synonyms, and other items unnecessary or unsuitable for inclusion in a basic vocabulary for the foreign learner. On the other hand, these 1,063 most frequent words did not include many items, particularly concrete nouns, of obvious practical value.

Statistical criteria, in short, though useful, cannot be taken as final. One of the most useful teaching vocabularies, the Basic English list of C. K. Ogden, was not built up statistically: it consists of 200 names of 'picturable objects', 400 'general' names, 150 'qualities' and 100 'operators', all carefully selected to avoid overlap and to cover the widest possible range of meaning. The 850 Basic English words include only 499 placed in the first (i.e. 'most frequent') thousand by Thorndike: 'the "logical" method of Ogden and the "counting" method of Thorndike produced fundamentally different results' (Fries and Traver, 1963).

Both Basic English and the Thorndike list represent remarkable pioneering studies. All existing teaching vocabularies, however, are capable of improvement; it is much to be hoped that studies now in progress, such as the Survey of Educated English Usage at University College, London, and the Survey of Child Language at the University of Leeds, will produce more reliable criteria for the construction of teaching vocabularies than has any previous work in English.

There can, of course, be no such thing as a single all-purpose English-teaching vocabulary: different people need English for different purposes. A student who learns English primarily for the pleasure of reading Shakespeare needs one sort of vocabulary; a student who learns English primarily in order to fly aeroplanes efficiently needs another. Our vocabulary, moreover, changes from year to year: lists adequate for the foreign learner in 1966 may require considerable adjustment in ten years' time. There are no panaceas in the teaching of English; only prescriptions for the individual case, though prescriptions in this field as in others will be more effective if they are based not on folklore but on scientific study. This book will have served its purpose if it has brought home to a few readers not only the practical importance of the scientific study of English, but some of its intrinsic fascination.

Appendix A

A TEST IN PHONEMICS

I do not offer the following quiz as a comprehensive examination on the material of Chapters Two and Three. I include it simply to illustrate various kinds of questions that can be set on elementary phonemics; I have found these particular questions quite useful in my own teaching. For most of the questions you will:

(a) write a phonemic symbol or transcription between slashes; or
(b) write an X in the brackets after the correct alternative; or
(c) complete a description by writing in the appropriate word or a short note; or
(d) complete a diagram.

Example:
(a) The first phoneme in *bet* is /b/.
(b) This is a vowel ( ), consonant (X).
(c) The mode of articulation is: *plosive.*
In your description of vowels, mention lip-rounding only when you are specifically asked to do so. Answers are given in Appendix D.

———

1. The first phoneme in *slogs* is / /.
2. This sound is voiced ( ), unvoiced ( ).
3. This sound is nasal ( ), oral ( ).
4. The point of articulation is ....
5. The mode of articulation is ....
6. The second phoneme in *slogs* is / /.
7. Its mode of articulation is ....
8. The vowel in *slogs* is / /.
9. For this vowel the vocal cords are vibrating ( ), not vibrating ( ).
   This vowel can be further described as: (a) ....
                                                (b) ....
                                                (c) ....

(Fill in items (a), (b), and (c) to complete the description of the vowel.)
10. The last phoneme in *slogs* is / /.
11. This differs from the first phoneme in *slogs* because it is ....
12. The initial phoneme of *unite* is a ....

13. Write *measure* in I.P.A. symbols /   /.
14. The point of articulation of the second consonantal phoneme of *measure* is ....
15. The last vowel of *measure* is known as ....
16. The vowel of *hurt* is /   /.
17. What has the vowel of *hurt* in common with the second vowel of *measure*? Both are: (a) .... (b) ....
18. How is the vowel of *hurt* distinguished from the second vowel of *measure*?
    /   / is normally: (a) .... (b) ....
    /   / is normally: (a) .... (b) ....
19. The point of closure for the first phoneme of *pot* is ....
20. If this closure were alveolar, the phoneme would be /   /.
21. If the closure were velar, the phoneme would be /   /.
22. In the formation of these three sounds, the velum is ....
23. The vowel of *good* is /   /.
24. The first vowel of *absolute* is /   /.
25. The first vowel of *streaming* is /   /.
26. The vowel of *swoop* is /   /.
27 – 30. Enter these four vowels on the chart.

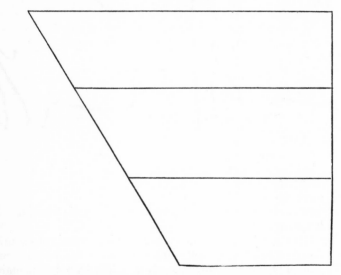

31. For which of these four vowels are the lips most rounded? /   /.
    Answer by giving one vowel only.
32 – 34. Write down in I.P.A. symbols: 32. *Unite* /   /
          33. *Care* /   /   34. *Flow* /   /

35. Enter all *glides* in these three words as arrows on the chart below. Label each glide clearly.

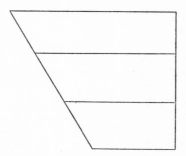

36. Complete the outlines of the vocal organs below to show the formation of /p/ and /n/.

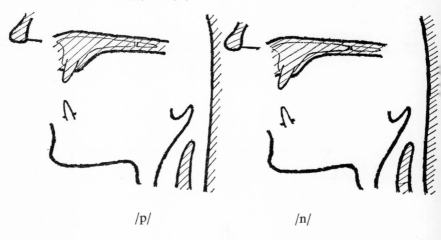

/p/   /n/

37. The final phoneme of *ridge* is /   /.
38. The mode of articulation for this phoneme is that of the class of sounds known as ....
39. List the principal actions of the vocal organs in forming this sound.
40. The words in each of the following pairs differ by one phoneme only. The phonemes by which they differ, differ by only one major feature. Write after each word:
(a) The symbol for the phoneme that is not in the other word.
(b) The feature by which it differs from the corresponding phoneme in the other word.

Example: *pin* (a) /p/   (b) absence of voice.
          bin (a) /b/   (b) voice.

(a) *tin*   (a) /   /   (b) ....
    din   (a) /   /   (b) ....
(b) *slam* (a) /   /   (b) ....
    slang (a) /   /   (b) ....
(c) *ten*   (a) /   /   (b) ....
    tan   (a) /   /   (b) ....

41. Group the following consonants into three classes according to mode of articulation, and state the mode of articulation for each class:

$$/f, p, g, j, v, w, t, s/$$

	Consonants	Mode of Articulation
Class I : /	/	....
Class II : /	/	....
Class III: /	/	....

42. Group the following consonants into classes according to point of articulation, and state the point of articulation for each class:

$$/t, k, n, p, b, g, s, l, m/$$

	Consonants	Point of Articulation
Class I : /	/	....
Class II : /	/	....
Class III: /	/	....

43. If the following were words, ten of them, considered simply as sound-combinations, would probably not be English words. Underline these ten words:

/trɪd, tlɪd, klʌd, leŋ, goʊm, ŋɑːtɪ, ndriːn, nɔɪl, nɒstrɒg, ziː, zlɒnk, zɒŋk, kraʊs, kgɒl, kreɪm, stɒd, tsɒd, zbɒd, smuː, msuː, snuː, vɒt, vrɒt, swɪt, ʃoʊm, lwem, hɒʃ, tʃɒmp, dɒmp/

Appendix B

THE PARTS OF SPEECH IN *JABBERWOCKY*
(See § 5.2)

For *brillig* there are unfortunately several possibilities. The possible parallel patterns for *'twas brillig* are *'twas morning* (*'twas* plus noun), *'twas blue* (*'twas* plus adjective) and *'twas here* (*'twas* plus adverb), so that *brillig* might be adverb, adjective or noun. *'Twas eat*, however, is not a possible parallel: * *'twas eat and the slithy toves* is definitely non-English, so that *brillig* cannot be a finite verb.

Toves has already been identified as a plural noun.

Slithy is marked as an adjective by the affix -y (compare *slimy, greasy, smelly*) and its position between determiner and noun.

Gyre and *gimble* are verbs immediately following the auxiliary *did* and preceding the prepositional phrase *in the wabe*; compare: 'did eat and drink in the hotel'.

Mimsy, like *slithy*, is marked as an adjective by the affix -y and by its characteristic position between the qualifier *all* and the verb *were*; compare: 'all red were the roses.'

Borogoves is a plural noun, marked by the determiner *the* and the affix -s.

The mome raths parallels 'the slithy toves' as a sequence of determiner plus adjective plus noun: with the same clue of the -s affix marking a plural noun, which stands in the position of subject to *outgrabe*.

Outgrabe is an irregular past-tense verb; past because *were* is past. We learn from Humpty Dumpty that the corresponding verbal noun is *outgribing*; hence the past is formed by changing the vowel, as with *run – ran*. This clue, plus that of its position, shows it to be a verb, though without Humpty Dumpty's hint it might possibly be taken as an adjective parallel to *mimsy*: 'all mimsy were the borogoves, and the mome raths were outgrabe.'

Appendix C

PERIODICALS AND RECORDINGS

PERIODICALS

English Language Teaching: a quarterly published by the Oxford
University Press (London) for the British Council.
English Teaching Abstracts: The English Teaching Information
Centre, State House, 63 High Holborn, London w.c.1.
Language: the quarterly Journal of the Linguistic Society of America.
Language Learning: a quarterly journal of applied linguistics, 1522
Rackham Building, Ann Arbor, Michigan, U.S.A.
The Linguistic Reporter: Newsletter of the Center for Applied
Linguistics, 1755 Massachusetts Avenue, N.W., Washington, D.C.,
United States of America.
Word: journal of the Linguistic Circle of New York.

Of these *Language Learning*, *English Teaching Abstracts*, *The
Linguistic Reporter* and *English Language Teaching* are inexpensive
and of considerable interest both to the newcomer to language studies
and to the practising teacher.

RECORDINGS

A great deal of recorded material, both on tape and on discs, and of
widely varying quality, is available for the teaching of English. Useful
records of pitch or intonation patterns, for instance, have been made
to accompany O'Connor and Arnold's book on *The Intonation of
Colloquial English* (Longmans, 1951), and the Macmillan Company of
New York (60 Fifth Avenue, New York, U.S.A.) supply useful tapes
to accompany their *English 900* textbooks. The safest course for the
teacher seeking advice on tapes and recordings is to consult the
British Council's English-Teaching Information Centre, State House,
High Holborn, London w.c.1.

Appendix D

ANSWERS TO PHONEMICS TEST

1. /s/
2. Unvoiced
3. Oral
4. Alveolar
5. Fricative
6. /l/
7. Lateral and Resonant
8. /ɒ/
9. Vibrating
  (a) Low
  (b) Back
  (c) Short
10. /z/
11. Voiced
12. Semivowel
13. /meʒə/
14. Palato-alveolar
15. Schwa
16. /ɜ:/
17. (a) Mid
  (b) Central
18. /ɜ:/ is normally
  (a) Long (b) Stressed;
  /ə/ is normally
  (a) Short (b) Unstressed
19. Bilabial
20. /t/
21. /k/
22. Raised
23. /ʊ/
24. /æ/

25. /i:/
26. /u:/
27–30. See chart in section 2.14.
  (Score 1 for each vowel correctly placed.)
31. /u:/
32. /ju:naɪt/
33. /kɛə/
34. /floʊ/ or /fləʊ/
  (Score up to 6 for questions 32–34, deducting one mark for each error.)
35. The four glides are /ju, ɛə, aɪ, oʊ/: see section 2.16.
  (Score 2 for each glide correctly shown.)
36. For /p/ show:
  (i) Bilabial closure
  (ii) Velum raised
  (iii) Tongue relatively flat
  For /n/ show
  (i) Lips open
  (ii) Tongue touching alveolar ridge
  (iii) Velum lowered
37. /dʒ/
38. Affricates 39. See § 2.13.3.
40. *tin:* /t/, absence of voice
  din: /d/, voice
  slam: /m/, bilabial closure
  slang /ŋ/, velar closure
  ten /e/, mid vowel
  tan /æ/, low vowel

41.

Consonants	Mode of Articulation
Class I : /f, v, s/	Fricative
Class II : /p, g, t/	Plosive
Class III: /j, w/	Semivowel glide

42.   Consonants   Point of Articulation

  Class I : /p, b, m/   Bilabial

             ....

  Class II : /n, s, l, t/   Alveolar

             ....

  Class III: /g, k/   Velar

             ....

43. /tlɪd, ŋɑːtɪ, ndriːn, zlɒnk, kgɒl, tsɒd, zbɒd, msuː, vrɒt, lwem/
 See § 3.3.

Appendix E

FURTHER READING AND REFERENCES

This appendix gives a short list of basic works recommended for further reading, and a complete list of references cited in the text.

FURTHER READING

The following can be strongly recommended:

Brown, Roger (1958): *Words and Things*, Macmillan.
A full and very readable survey of psychological studies of language.
Fries, C. C. (1957): *The Structure of English: An introduction to the construction of English sentences*, Longmans.
Gimson, A. C. (1962): *An Introduction to the Pronunciation of English*, Arnold.
A basic text for phonology.
Gleason, H. A. (revised edition, 1961): *An Introduction to Descriptive Linguistics*, Holt, Rinehart and Winston, New York.
Lado, R. (1957): *Linguistics Across Cultures*, University of Michigan Press.
Applied linguistics for language teachers.
Mittins, W. H. (1962): *A Grammar of Modern English*, Methuen.
Lively and amusing exercises systematically arranged as an excellent practical introduction to modern grammar.
Quirk, R. and Smith, A. H. (1964): *The Teaching of English*, Oxford University Press.
A lively and scholarly introduction by several hands.

REFERENCES

Abercrombie, David (1965): *Studies in Phonetics and Linguistics*, Oxford University Press.
Barber, Charles (1964): *Linguistic Change in Present-Day English*, Oliver and Boyd, Edinburgh.
Baugh, A. C. (1957): *A History of the English Language*, Routledge and Kegan Paul (first published 1952).
Berko, Jean (1958): The Child's Learning of English Morphology, *Word*, *XIV*, pp. 150–177.
Bloomfield, L. (1933): *Language*, Holt, Rinehart and Winston, New York.

Bodmer, F. (1943): *The Loom of Language*, George Allen and Unwin.

Braine, M. D. (1963): The ontogeny of English phrase structure, *Language*, vol. 39.

Brooks, C. and Warren, R. P. (1946): *Understanding Poetry*, Henry Holt, New York.

Brown, Roger (1958): *Words and Things*, The Free Press of Glencoe, New York.

Catford, J. C. (1959): 'The Teaching of English as a Foreign Language', Chapter 7 of Quirk and Smith's *The Teaching of English*.

Catford, J. C. (1965): *A Linguistic Theory of Translation*, Oxford University Press.

Chomsky, N. (1962): *Syntactic Structures*, Mouton, 's-Gravenhage, Holland (first published, 1957).

De Villiers, Meyer (1962): *Afrikaanse Klankleer*, Balkema, Cape Town and Amsterdam.

De Saussure (1959): *Course in General Linguistics*, Wade Baskin's translation, Peter Owen, London (original first published 1915).

Diamond, A. S. (1959): *The History and Origin of Language*, Methuen.

Drever, James (1955): *A Dictionary of Psychology*, Penguin Books.

Downing, John A. (1964): *The Initial Teaching Alphabet explained and illustrated*, Cassell.

Francis, W. Nelson (1958): *The Structure of American English*, The Ronald Press Company, New York.

Fries, C. C. (1940): *American English Grammar*, Appleton-Century-Crofts, New York.

Fries, C. C. (1957): *The Structure of English*, Longmans (first published by Harcourt and Brace, 1952).

Fries, C. C. (1964): 'On the Intonation of Yes-No Questions in English', pp. 242–254 of *In Honour of Daniel Jones*, Longmans.

Fries, C. C. and Traver, A. A. (1963): *English Word Lists: a Study of their Adaptability for Instruction*, George Wahr Publishing Co., Ann Arbor, Michigan.

Fry, D. B. (1960): 'Linguistic Theory and Experimental Research', *Transactions of the Philological Society*.

Fry, D. B. (1964): 'Experimental evidence for the phoneme', pp. 59–72 of *In Honour of Daniel Jones*.

Gimson, A. C. (1962): *An Introduction to the Pronunciation of English*, Edward Arnold.

Gleason, H. A. (1961): *An Introduction to Descriptive Linguistics*, Holt, Rinehart and Winston, New York.

Gleason, H. A. (1965): *Linguistics and English Grammar*, Holt, Rinehart, and Winston, New York.

Gowers, Sir Ernest (1958): *The Complete Plain Words*, Her Majesty's Stationery Office.

Grattan, J. H. G. and Gurrey, P. (1925): *Our Living Language*, Thomas Nelson and Sons.

Gray, William S. (1956): *The Teaching of Reading and Writing*, Unesco and Evans Brothers Ltd., Paris and London.

Guthrie, M. (1948): *The Classification of Bantu Languages*, Oxford University Press.

Halliday, M. A. K., McIntosh, A. and Strevens, P. (1964): *The Linguistic Sciences and Language Teaching*, Longmans.

Hornby, A. S. (1959–1962): *The Teaching of Structural Words and Sentence Patterns*, three volumes: Stage One (1959), Stage Two (1961), Stage Three (1962), Oxford University Press.

Hundleby, C. E. (1965): *Xhosa-English Pronunciation in the South-East Cape* (Ph.D. thesis, Rhodes University).

Irwin, O. C. (1957): 'Phonetical Description of Speech Development in Childhood', Chapter 26 of the *Manual of Phonetics* edited by L. Kaiser, North-Holland Publishing Company, Amsterdam.

Jespersen, O. (1922): *Language*, George Allen and Unwin.

Jespersen, O. (1924): *The Philosophy of Grammar*, George Allen and Unwin.

Jespersen, O. (1933): *Essentials of English Grammar*, George Allen and Unwin.

Jones, Daniel (1962): *An Outline of English Phonetics*, ninth edition, Heffer, Cambridge (first published 1918).

Jones, Daniel (1963): *Everyman's English Pronouncing Dictionary* twelfth edition, J. M. Dent. (Note: The system of transcription in this Dictionary differs at certain points from that of the present text.)

Joos, M. (1964): *The English Verb*, University of Wisconsin Press.

Kaiser, L. (1957): *Manual of Phonetics*, North-Holland Publishing Co., Amsterdam.

Kennedy, B. H. (1942): *The Revised Latin Primer*, edited by J. F. Mountford, Longmans (first published 1843).

Lado, R. (1957): *Linguistics Across Cultures*, University of Michigan Press, Ann Arbor, Michigan.

Lanham, L. (1963): 'Teaching English Pronunciation in Southern Africa', *Language Learning*, XIII. 3 and 4.

Lanham, L. and Traill, A. (1962): 'South African English Pronunciation', *English Studies in Africa*, V. 2.

Lanham, L. and Traill, A. (1965): *Pronounce English Correctly*, Longmans, Cape Town.

Lewis, M. M. (1936): *Infant Speech*, Kegan Paul, Trench, Trubner & Co.

Lewis, M. M. (1963): *Language, Thought and Personality in Infancy and Childhood*, George G. Harrap & Co.

Malick, Alice (1956): 'A Comparative Study of American English and Iraqi Arabic Consonant Clusters.' *Language Learning*, VII. 3 and 4.

McNally, J. and Murray, W. (1962): *Key Words to Literacy*, The Schoolmaster Publishing Co.

Miller, George A. (1951): *Language and Communication*, McGraw-Hill Book Company, New York.

Mittins, W. H. (1962): *A Grammar of Modern English*, Methuen.

Nesfield, J. C. (1897): *English Grammar, Past and Present*, Macmillan.

O'Connor and Arnold (1951): *The Intonation of Colloquial English*, Longmans.

Palmer, F. R. (1965): *A Linguistic Study of the English Verb*, Longmans.

Pike, Kenneth L. (1945): *The Intonation of American English*, University of Michigan Press, Ann Arbor, Michigan.

Pitman, Sir James (1961): 'Learning to Read' (*Journal of the Royal Society of Arts*, February 1961: obtainable from the ITA foundation, 9 Southampton Place, London w.c.1.)

Quirk, R. (1959): 'English Language and the Structural Approach' (article in Quirk and Smith, *The Teaching of English*).

Quirk, R. (1962): *The Use of English*, Longmans.

Quirk, R. and Smith, A. H. (1959): *The Teaching of English*, Secker and Warburg; reissued, 1964, by the Oxford University Press.

Roberts, Paul (1956): *Patterns of English*, Harcourt Brace and World, New York.

Roberts, Paul (1962): *English Sentences*, Harcourt Brace and World, New York.

Robins, R. H. (1964): *General Linguistics: An Introductory Survey*, Longmans.

Sapir, E. (1921): *Language*, Harcourt Brace and World, New York.

Saunders, W. A. (1962): 'The Teaching of English Pronunciation to speakers of Hokkien', *Language Learning*, XII, 2, 1962.

Schlauch, Margaret (1960): *The Gift of Tongues,* George Allen and Unwin.

Sledd, James (1959): *A Short Introduction to English Grammar,* Scott, Foresman and Company, Chicago.

Stetson, R. H. (1951): *Motor Phonetics,* North-Holland Publishing Company, Amsterdam.

Strang, Barbara M. H. (1962): *Modern English Structure,* Arnold.

Sweet, Henry (1900): *The History of Language,* The Temple Primers, Dent.

Ward, Ida (1962): *The Phonetics of English,* Heffer, Cambridge (first published 1929).

Westermann, D. and Ward, I. (1933): *Practical Phonetics for Students of African Languages,* Oxford University Press.

Whitehall, Harold (1956): *Structural Essentials of English,* Harcourt, Brace and World, New York.

Yao Shen (1961): 'Sound-Arrangements and Sound-Sequences', *Language Learning*, XI. 1 and 2.

References in this Index are to the section numbers which will be found at the top outer corner of every page.

The principal references to major topics are given in heavy type: thus sections **2.5** and **3.6** are shown as being of key importance for the concept of the phoneme.

The Index gives a fairly complete listing of the technical terms in the book. I have not attempted to index most of the words cited as examples, but references are given for certain frequently cited words, such as *dog, the* and *sail(-ing)*.

Close vowels, 2.14.
Closed system, 6.6; 8.3.
Closure, point of, 2.5; 2.13.1; 3.4.
Clusters, consonant, 3.3.
  „   verb, 6.13.4.
Collocation, **8.4.**
Colour-vocabulary, 8.3.
Command, 7.2.
Complement, **5.4;** 5.5; 6.8; 7.2;
  7.3; 7.4; 7.5; with *be*, 7.6.
Complementary distribution, **3.4;**
  3.5; 6.4.
Components of sentences, 5.4.
Concord, **5.9;** 5.8; 5.6; 6.13;
  6.13.6.
Consonant clusters, 3.3.
Consonants, 2.11; 2.12; 2.13; and
  spelling, 3.7.
Consonants, English, 2.13.
Consonants, short descriptions,
  2.17.4.
Content words, 1.5.
Context, **1.3;** 1.4; 3.3; 4.4; 7.1;
  8.4.
Continuant, 2.13.6.
Continuous aspect of verbs, 6.13.2
  (iii); 6.13.6.
Contrast, **2.4;** 2.8; 2.14; 2.17.4;
  4.4; 5.8; 6.13.2.
Conversation, 4.1.
Co-ordination, 7.7.
Correlation, grammatical, 5.5;
  5.10; 5.13.
Countable nouns, 6.10.
Definition, 8.2.
Dental fricatives, 2.13.2.
Derivational affixes, **6.6;** 6.8;
  6.10; 6.11; 6.12.
De Saussure, E., 1.4.
Description, 1.8; of vowels and
  consonants, 2.17.4; of language,
  5.1; 5.12.
Determiners, 5.8; 6.8; 6.9.
De Villiers, Meyer, 3.2.
Dialect, 1.9; 2.3.
Diamond, A. S., 6.13.
Diaphragm, 2.8; 4.3.
Dictation, 4.1.

Dictionary, 8.5; 6.8; 8.1.
Differentiation, of vocabulary,
  8.2.
Diphthongs, **2.16;** 2.15.
Direct object, 7.3; 7.5.
'Displacement', 3.1.
Distinctive features, of phonemes,
  3.5; *see also* contrast; 2.8; 2.13;
  2.14 and 2.17.4.
Distribution, **3.2;** 3.3; 3.4; 3.5;
  6.4.
Do, 5.9; **7.2.**
Dog, 1.4; 1.9; 5.5; 5.8; 6.3; 6.6;
  7.3; 8.2.
Drever, J., 1.3.
Education, 1.1; 1.8; 3.2; 5.13;
  6.13.6; 8.6.
Eliot, T. S., 8.4.
Empty words, 1.5.
Epiglottis, 2.8 (diagram vii).
Equational sentence-patterns, 7.4.
Ewe, 4.7.
Eye movements in reading, 3.8.
Favourite sentence-forms, 7.1.
Final position, 2.11.
Finite verb, 6.13.1.
Fire, 1.2; 1.4; 1.6; 6.1.
Foot, 4.5; 4.6.
Football, 1.7.
Foreign learners, 1.1; 2.3; 3.2;
  5.13; 6.13.6; 8.3.
Fortis consonants, **2.13.1;** 2.13.2.
Frames, **5.10;** 5.6; 6.3; 6.7; noun,
  6.8; adjective, 6.11; adverb,
  6.12; verb, 6.13.1.
Francis, Nelson, 6.5; 6.8; 6.13.
Free forms, **6.2.**
Free variation, 3.5.
French, 2.8; 2.15; 3.2; 3.3; 4.5.
Fricative, velar, 3.2.
Fricatives, 2.13.2.
Fries, C. C., 4.7; 5.8; 5.10; 5.12;
  6.13.5.
Front vowels, 2.14; 2.15; 3.4.
Fry, D. B., 3.5; 4.4.
Full and empty words, 1.5.
Future, forms for expressing,
  6.13.2 (iv), *shall* and *will*, 6.13.5.